PRAISE FOR MY STE

"My Steam Engine is Broken *provides a map for executives seeking to lead their organizations through the challenges of today and tomorrow. The key, as the authors assert, is with people. Most organizations don't just compete on products or services—they compete on culture. Nothing is more pertinent, and nothing is more challenging to grow and nurture. This book argues that we need to radically reassess many of the organizational behaviours that we have taken for granted for so long in order to create a culture that is appropriate for 'The Age of Ideas'. The book is full of passion and offers important messages on organizational change through building an extraordinary culture that will drive long-term success.*"

Johan C. Aurik, Managing Partner and Chairman
of the Board, A.T. Kearney

"*We talk of a knowledge economy but in 2014, knowledge only gets you to the starting post. It is the ability to learn and to relearn that keeps organisations relevant now. Organisations are simply groups of people. However, many large organisational structures are founded on the fantasy that, at best, they are well oiled machines. The job of leadership is to hire great people, to tease out a shared purpose from them and to allow, to encourage, to forgive their talents, hopes and mistakes in the service of this purpose. This is not idealistic hogwash – it is the only efficient and sustainable path to the future.*

Instead, sitting astride the machine, like a great sit-on lawn mower, leaders curtail, smother and silence those talents. This is not deliberate – it is because the tyranny of the idea of the hero-leader persists and the fear of mess, the difficulty of measuring curves over straight lines, the fear of not seeming certain – lead leaders back to the safety of the machine, reaching for levers.

But this idea is not safe. Quietly, the mavericks first, then the creatives, the young talented, disillusioned, the entrepreneurial, the round pegs, the senior women, the future leaders, the explorers

*and navigators are jumping ship and leaving the very institutions
that need them most. Already they are heading for the door,
leaving behind the grids and the grisly metrics, the fallen language
and the powerpoint, the KPI's and mandated behaviours to pursue
different, more human, ideas of what success looks like. None of
this is new.*

*This is a book, however, that calls on leaders to put on their
overalls, roll up their sleeves and start loosening the bolts of their
organisations. It's a book that invites bravery and imagination to
rethink organisations in a way that will make them fit for the future
and fit, crucially, for the most talented young people to join and
thrive in."*

Tracey Camilleri, Associate Fellow, programme director,
The Oxford Strategic Leadership Programme,
Saïd Business School, University of Oxford

*"As the steam-engine age progressed, the tendency grew to
analyse business as a blend of mechanical and measurable
factors. Reality is not so simple. As individuals we are biological
and we behave both rationally and with predictable irrationality.
Since organisations run on people power, this applies equally
to organisations. Most leaders recognise that it is their people
that make their organisations great. Few, however, recognise
how easily undesirable human behaviour, including their own,
causes catastrophic failure. The unwillingness to find, visualise
and fix these unmeasurable, and predictable, behavioural and
organisational risks leaves organisations - and their leaders -
unnecessarily vulnerable. Thus we see patterns of failure that are
repeated again and again."*

Anthony Fitzsimmons, founder and chairman, Reputability LLP

*"Creativity flourishes at the edges of things. It needs boundaries
and it needs constraints. The world of business has been described
to me as "amoral," as if our behavior there need not concern itself
too much with ethics. There is an affinity with the idea of self-
as-scientist rather than self-as-artist; that what is necessary for*

good business leadership is clarity, precision, measurability and emotional detachment. These qualities are not necessarily wrong, but they are not always appropriate to the business of getting good ideas out of people and implementing them. And they exclude consideration of the deeper values that people express through the work they do and the choices they make."

Piers Ibbotson, founder, Directing Creativity

"An oft-quoted phrase, misattributed to Einstein, is "The definition of insanity is doing the same thing over and over and expecting different results." While used mainly to denounce political rivals, it does accurately describe the business management practices of the last two decades. In recent surveys of CEOs about their biggest concerns, they ranked innovation, engagement, and talent development among the top. These are the same problems that ranked among the top over a decade ago. The biggest difference between then and now is the number of consultancies, initiatives, methods and media devoted to solving these problems. Why aren't they working?

Because lack of innovation, talent, and engagement are not problems, but symptoms – symptoms of command and control management practices that arose in the industrial age. The industrial age needed warm bodies to follow standard procedures quickly and efficiently. Because the work was mind numbing, monetary incentives were needed to keep people working hard. However, today we are firmly entrenched in the information age where we need intelligence, creativity, curiosity, collaboration and a sense of purpose to succeed. While companies understand this in the abstract, they still rely on the tried and true practices developed centuries ago.

In order to create the workplaces and the work forces that make the most of the human capacity to learn and create, we have to abandon command and control management. This change will require a leap of faith, jumping from the familiar practices that we know don't work to a world of uncertainty and experimentation. Leaping into uncertainty is never easy, but if enough people jump, more will follow."

Karen Phelan, business author; consultant;
co-founder Operating Principals

"This little book is not for the faint-hearted. It is no less than a Luddite charter, promoting the complete destruction of traditional command and control structures as a necessary precursor to embedding the creativity, innovation and connectivity required in organisations suited to the new age of ideas. Bracing stuff!"

Peter Rawlins, founder, Rawlins Strategy Consulting; former Chief Executive, London Stock Exchange

"You would have thought that with everybody going on about the 'pace of change', the rise of the digital economy, endless leadership initiatives and billions of pounds spent on consultants, today's organisations would all be thoroughly evolved entities - agile, adaptive and zen-like in their ability to make things happen at will. But not a bit of it. As the authors point out - and to borrow a phrase from Philip Larkin - we are still witnessing a long sigh out of the nineteenth century. Leaders continue to talk about 'levers' to pull as if they're running a machine, 'delivering' as if they were in charge of a post office, and 'execution' as if they managed a military phalanx. So there's a mismatch between the rhetoric and the reality. It's about time the gap was closed, and one way is indeed to change the language. No more steam trains and 'efficiencies': the machine metaphor has served us well but it doesn't work anymore."

Robert Roland Smith, philosopher, author and business advisor

"There is no one answer, is there? The way to change the way we work together is to consider just what a complex, interconnected organism we generally find ourselves in, and then think about the array of little nudges and tweaks that might start to effect some changes somewhere else. Telling an organisation what to do won't do it. You might as well try and tame a murmuration of starlings."

John Willshire, founder, Smithery Ltd

MY STEAM ENGINE IS BROKEN

MY STEAM ENGINE IS BROKEN

TAKING THE ORGANIZATION FROM THE INDUSTRIAL ERA TO THE AGE OF IDEAS

DR MARK POWELL + JONATHAN GIFFORD

LONDON   NEW YORK   SHANGHAI
MADRID   BARCELONA   BOGOTA
MEXICO CITY   MONTERREY   BUENOS AIRES

LID Publishing Ltd

Garden Studios

71-75 Shelton Street

Covent Garden

London

WC2H 9JQ

info@lidpublishing.com

www.lidpublishing.com

A member of:

Business Publishers Roundtable

www.businesspublishersroundtable.com

Printed in Great Britain by TJ International

ISBN: 978-1-907794-59-9

Cover and page design: Laura Hawkins
Cover illustration: Cameron Law

THIS BOOK IS DEDICATED TO ALL THOSE WHO DECIDED
TO MAKE AN EFFORT TO CHANGE SOMETHING
IN THEIR OWN ORGANIZATIONS.

TO THOSE WHO STOOD UP FOR CHANGE,
OFTEN AT GREAT RISK TO THEIR OWN CAREERS.

TO THOSE WHO SET OUT TO DO WHAT THEY THOUGHT
MADE SENSE; NOT WHAT THE ORGANIZATION TOLD THEM
TO DO OR WHAT HAD ALWAYS BEEN DONE IN THE PAST.

TO THE PATHFINDERS OUT THERE;
THE PEOPLE WHO ARE UNAFRAID TO CHALLENGE
CONVENTIONAL WISDOM.

THE WAR TO CHANGE OUR ORGANISATIONS FOR THE BETTER IS NOT LOST, IT HAS ONLY JUST BEGUN.

CONTENTS

ACKNOWLEDGEMENTS

Special thanks are due to all of the contributors to this book. Their insight and their comments on the subject matter of the book inspired us and reassured us that we were not alone in thinking that the organisation is in desperate need of change and that we were not entirely wrong in our thinking as to the ways in which that change might be brought about.

As a result, the process of writing the book became an enjoyable illustration of one of the key arguments in this book: that any enterprise needs to tap into the diverse ideas of as many people as possible and that the road to success lies via a process of collaboration and consultation.

These conversations fuelled our thoughts and started an ongoing dialogue that we very much hope you will join.

CONTRIBUTORS
Kathryn Bishop, Associate Fellow, Saïd Business School, University of Oxford

Tracey Camilleri, Associate Fellow, programme director, The Oxford Strategic Leadership Programme, Saïd Business School, University of Oxford

Ron Emerson, Associate Fellow, Saïd Business School University of Oxford; chairman, British Business Bank; chairman, Fairfield Energy

Anthony Fitzsimmons, founder and chairman, Reputability LLP

Dr Wolfgang Grulke, founder, FutureWorld, fellow of the Centre for Management Development, London Business School

Piers Ibbotson, founder, Directing Creativity

Simon Jordan, founder and managing director, Jump Studios

Olivier Oullier, consultant; Professor of Behavioural and Brain Studies, Aix-Marseille University

Karen Phelan, business author; consultant; co-founder Operating Principals

Peter Rawlins, founder, Rawlins Strategy Consulting; former Chief Executive, London Stock Exchange

Jonathan Stebbings, proprietor, Stebbings Ltd; associate at Olivier Mythodrama

Robert Rowland Smith, philosopher, author and business advisor

Dr Roland Valori, consultant physician and clinical director for service accreditation, Royal College of Physicians; founder, Quality Solutions for Healthcare

John Willshire, founder, Smithery Ltd

"And let it be noted that there is no more delicate matter to take in hand, nor more dangerous to conduct, nor more doubtful in its success, than to set up as a leader in the introduction of changes.

For he who innovates will have for his enemies all those who are well off under the existing order of things, and only lukewarm supporters in those who might be better off under the new.

This lukewarm temper arises partly from the fear of adversaries who have the laws on their side, and partly from the incredulity of mankind, who will never admit the merit of anything new, until they have seen it proved by the event."

Niccolò Machiavelli (1469–1527),
The Prince

PREFACE

Several years ago, Mark Powell, one of the authors of this book, was leading an executive development programme at Saïd Business School, at the University of Oxford, when he experienced something that had a profound effect on his thinking about organizations, and the relationship between organizations and the people that work for them. That experience led directly to the writing of this book.

It was a simple thing: a session with a poet, encouraging 'courageous conversations' about different aspects of the executives' lives, touched a sensitive spot with one highly stressed senior executive, who sought Mark out after the session, asked if he could have a word, and quickly collapsed in tears.

As Mark told his co-author, Jonathan Gifford:

We were running a leadership programme for a group of senior project managers for a global company. As part of a one-week programme, we had a half-day session with a poet around the importance of the need to have what he termed "courageous conversations" with the different aspects of your life.

The session had a huge impact on everyone, as it made them reflect on the balance and tensions between their personal and work lives. After the session, one of the participants approached me. He was in his mid-thirties and pretty easy-going. He said: "Can I have a word?" and then proceeded to break down into little pieces. The session with the poet had had a profound effect on him.

Over the next hour he explained his problem. He had been working 60–70 hours a week for many months to meet the huge expectations his company had of him. He was working evenings and some weekends just to keep all his balls in the air. When he finally did get home, he faced the huge expectations of his wife and two young children who then assumed he was now "theirs".

As he put it: "I just don't know who I am anymore. I cannot remember the last time I even had a drink with a friend, or sat down and read a book."

Between his work world and his personal world, he had simply disappeared.

Part of any coach's job is to help executives to deal with the stress of their roles. Picking up the pieces after the occasional breakdown is arguably an occupational hazard. But the encounter stuck in Mark's mind:

If I look at the human misery I was seeing – if I look at the broken people that I've tried to put back together, coming through leadership programmes, who have been sent to be fixed by the organization – the conclusion I've come to is that it's not the people who need to be fixed.

Leadership development programmes have become a safety valve for organizations that are fatally, structurally flawed and are desperately trying to find ways of trying to fix the problem by fixing their people.

We have to build a more human organization, because the modern organization is so out of alignment with the evolution of our social and psychological understanding about what drives human beings. Ultimately, we are organic, emotional beings. The ability of modern organizations to actually leverage that – rather than destroy it – will be the secret of success for those organizations in the rest of this century.

This book explores 10 paradoxes – 10 things that organizations do that, paradoxically, prevent them from achieving the very goals that they have set for themselves. All of these paradoxes revolve around the relationship between the organization and the people who make up the organization. It is the authors' fundamental belief that this constantly shifting collection of people *is* the organization: that organizations have (or should have) a distinctive and continuing purpose – the reason for their existence – but that this purpose only has meaning in a human context and can only be served by the various people who make up the organization as it endures over time.

It is these people who should be entrusted – as a whole – with the organization's continued success, and its ability to fulfil its purpose.

This book will argue that a very primitive approach to management, inherited from our early industrial past, has persisted long after it became disastrously unsuited to the needs of the modern world and the needs of the people who work for modern organizations – or, rather, the people who *are* modern organizations.

More importantly for the organizations themselves, the failure of this heavy-handed, hierarchical 'managerial' approach – the failure to make intelligent people happy and fulfilled in the service of the organization – means that the industrial-era organization is doomed, sooner rather than later, to fail.

Fulfilled, self-motivated, ingenious, collaborative, social human beings will ensure the survival of any modern organization. But an unhappy, demotivated, disenfranchised workforce spells an organization's doom.

Don't take our word for it: think about the last time you had any dealings with an organization whose workforce was unhappy, demotivated, and disenfranchised. Will you be going back there in a hurry? See what we mean?

This book argues that the failure to change the industrial-era organization is due partly to inertia but more fundamentally to the sheer scale and importance of most modern organizations: these are the enterprises that have created huge wealth, prosperity, and wellbeing in the modern era. It takes a very brave caretaker to change them in any way that might put that huge prize at risk.

But the organization must change. Not because it would be "nice" if the organization was less damaging to its members, but because modern organizations will begin to fail – quite soon, very dramatically, and in large numbers – unless they change. This is already beginning to happen.

We are now in the Age of Ideas, not in the industrial era, and organizations that do not reflect this will be left behind. Their members will turn up for work, go through the motions, and leave their energy, ingenuity, and commitment at the factory gate. In a modern world where the pace of change is constantly accelerating, this will not produce the cutting-edge, ahead-of-the-race, innovatory results that an organization needs simply to keep its head above water.

Industrial-era organizations will be trampled underfoot by more agile and intelligent enterprises whose members are fully signed up to their projects and are firing on all cylinders. People who see the organization's success as their success — in every sense of the word. What else could possibly prevail in the global marketplace: a bored, indifferent, uncommitted workforce, dully doing what they are told? Are you serious?

This book highlights 10 things that industrial-era organizations unthinkingly do that we believe are at the heart of the problem. They do these things because people have been doing things that way for a century or two, and because it has worked in the past. But it's not working now.

My Steam Engine Is Broken suggests a number of different approaches that would dramatically improve the situation — things that are simple to grasp and easy to put in place. There are a number of different options suggested by a wide variety of people; some might work for you, others might not. We're not being prescriptive, and we don't believe that there is any one-size-fits-all solution. But there is a solution, and it doesn't look like the industrial-era organization.

These things, taken in themselves, are not hard to do, and will not bring an organization crashing down. But the effect of these several, fundamental changes of attitude, implemented over a reasonable period of time, will be nothing short of revolutionary. The industrial-era organization — which this book will call the "steam-engine organization" — will be transformed.

The organization will be well served by its people, and people will be well served by the organization, because people will be allowed once more to *be* the organization. How radical — and how simple — is that?

DR MARK POWELL AND JONATHAN GIFFORD, AUGUST 2014

INTRODUCTION

MY STEAM ENGINE IS BROKEN
WHY THE ORGANIZATION IS NO LONGER FIT FOR PURPOSE

At the heart of this book is a metaphor. It is a light-hearted metaphor, but it has a serious point.

The modern organization came into being toward the end of the 18th century, during the Industrial Revolution in Britain: a revolution in the means of production, fuelled by coal and symbolized by the steam engine, a remarkable new source of power that allowed us to pump water out of deep coal mines, giving us access to more of the precious black stuff. Later innovators put steam engines on wheels and in boats, and new forms of transport were devised.

For the first time in history, mankind was no longer reliant for its power on what nature provided: the power of animals, wind, or water. The manufacturing companies that sprung up, using the heat of coal and the power of steam to create an ever-increasing range of goods in unprecedented volumes at reducing costs, set the foundation of all modern economies.

The way in which those organizations were structured and managed has remained in place to the present day. It has been refined by "management science" and made ever more efficient, but it is has essentially the same old management and workforce, command and control, reward and punishment structure that would still be recognisable to a factory worker in Manchester, England, in the closing decades of the 18th century.

Let's call this kind of organizational structure the steam-engine organization, in homage to the Industrial Revolution's iconic new source of mechanical power. But the steam-engine organization was designed and built for a different era. Our steam engines are no longer fit for purpose. They must be transformed.

✩ ✩

The Industrial Revolution changed the world, immeasurably and for the better. Similar revolutions are still happening around the world today, as nations make the radical and turbulent shift from agrarian to industrial economies. These industrial revolutions are still driving huge increases in standards of living.

In the 18th century, Britain's population tripled over the course of a few generations; and, for the first time in history, this surge in population was not reversed. Up until the 1740s, Britain's population, like that of every other nation in the world, had been subject to periodic famines caused by the disasters that have afflicted mankind through the ages (typically drought, flood, war, and pestilence). But after the middle of the 18th century, though Britain suffered from the usual economic downturns, wars and epidemics, things began to get better. The wealth created by the revolution in manufacturing – combined with Britain's enviable potion as the world's leading trading nation and financial centre – began to take the country out of the previous cycles of want and plenty, dependant entirely on the productivity of the land. The newfound wealth sustained an increasing population and drove huge improvements in living standards and in public health. The country entered the modern age, soon to be followed by the rest of the world.

In the early 19th century, the young United States of America expanded into the huge, undeveloped territories to the west of the pioneers' original settlements on the Eastern Seaboard at a time when the core innovations of the Industrial Revolution had become common knowledge: steam power, iron and steel production, the techniques of mass production. The combination of a wealth of natural resources and the means to transform them into manufactured goods for a rapidly expanding population quickly created the world's largest economy.

Other countries around the world soon followed suit. The modern world is the strapping, healthy, privileged adolescent child of the Industrial Revolution. But there is a cost.

It is a subtle cost, and soon after the early days of the revolution, it probably seemed a small and perhaps inevitable price to pay. In the early days, people whose lives had been tied to the land had lived by the rhythms of that land. Their lives were governed by the cycles of daylight, and of seasons; by the life cycles of crops and of livestock. With the coming of the "manufactory", all of this changed.

LEARNING TO LIVE WITH "INDUSTRIAL TIME"

Life on the land was not, is not, and never has been easy. People who worked on the land often suffered great hardship; most lived in poverty. The opportunity to earn a wage drew people in their millions to the rapidly emerging cities dominated by new source of wealth: the factory.

When these people got to the cities, however, their lives changed. "Industrial time" was a new reality that people struggled, at first, to live with. Now there was always work, regardless of the weather or the time of day or the season. Overseers enforced punctuality and diligence. People were required to service the wonderful powered machines that produced the goods that brought the wealth, and the people were obliged to become more machine-like.

The effects were soon obvious to all. Writing in 1929, the Victorian essayist and historian, Thomas Carlyle, observed: "Men are grown mechanical in head and heart, as well as in hand." The Industrial revolution had changed everything.

As we moved away from the old "craft" model of making things – home weavers, carpenters' shops, jewellers, leather-goods manufacturers – so there was an increasing division of labour. People were employed to perform a particular task within an organization, and as work became more mechanized, so it became more mechanical. Workers of all kinds were managed and assessed, rewarded and punished, in attempts to increase their efficiency.

By the start of the 20th century a new discipline of "management science" sprang up to help to systemize ways of ensuring that people served the machines and the organization as efficiently as possible, epitomized by Frederick Winslow Taylor's meticulous measurement of the time taken to perform each activity in a manufacturing process – down to one hundredth of a minute – and his insistence that there was and should be a complete divide between management (who planned a task) and workers (who carried it out).

Most managers had relatively little freedom of action themselves; they followed the instructions of their superiors. A handful of top "executive" managers took strategic decisions about the company's overall direction and mode of operation.

In his book *What Matters Now*, business thinker Gary Hamel cites the remarkable fact that in America in 1890, nine out of 10 white males worked for themselves. Hamel points out that the inevitable result of industrialisation was that "unruly and independent-minded farmers, artisans and day-labourers had to be transformed into rule-following, forelock-tugging employees." And we are still at it today, he argues: "working hard to strap rancorous and free-thinking human beings into the straightjacket of corporate obedience, conformity and discipline."[1]

But times have changed. Or, rather, they should have.

As economies mature and production is increasingly mechanized, people are freed from the need to perform unrewarding, repetitive tasks, so that what is needed from workers is not their unthinking maintenance of mechanical processes but their knowledge, their ideas, their uniquely human attributes. Put another way, there is a huge opportunity to stop using people for something that they are not suited for – mindless, unrewarding, repetitive tasks – and to use them instead for things that they are uniquely good at: collaborating, problem-solving, having flashes of insight, inventing clever new devices and processes.

Despite a growing awareness of this essential truth, the modern organization has failed to change in order to seize this great opportunity. It clings stubbornly to its old, steam-engine structure.

Just as we see steam engines as quaint and rather charming reminder of days gone by, so we should see the old organizational structures as quaint (though, sadly, not charming at all) and no longer fit for purpose. The industrial-era organization – once the great driver of wealth and progress – is beginning to stifle progress.

We are leaving the industrial era and we are entering the Age of Ideas. This book will argue that we are all knowledge workers now, and that what is needed from us is our ingenuity – but steam-engine organizations are perfectly (and deliberately) designed to stifle ingenuity.

Steam-engine organizations seek to control the workforce to ensure the efficient production of a known process. Modern organizations can and must empower their workforce to astonish and surprise – to find new solutions and brilliant innovations.

WEALTHIER BUT NOT HAPPIER

The effects of the 18th century Industrial Revolution are still with us today. Many countries are still going through their own industrial revolutions, shifting their economies from an agrarian to an industrial/manufacturing base. The end result is hugely increased economic growth and dramatically improved living standards, leading to wealthier, healthier nations. But as is increasingly clear, these wealthier, healthier nations are not happier. Work, it seems, has taken over our lives. The organizations for which so many of us work seem to have become oppressive masters, demanding all of our time, leaving us richer in material goods but poorer in spirit.

New perils have entered our working lives: devoting most of our waking hours and energies to the organization is no longer a guarantee that the organization will continue to employ us. In the name of efficiency, the vast majority of modern organizations will quickly "downsize" when profitability is threatened.

This, we are assured, is one of the prices that we pay in order to benefit from the miracle that is the modern industrial economy. We must work as hard as is necessary to compete in the global market, and job security is a luxury that we must forgo in order to keep our organizations operating at maximum efficiency through rapidly changing economic circumstances. The end result is an increasingly stressed and anxious workforce, striving for maximum productivity in the face of global competitors who are straining every sinew to take over their market and put them out of a job.

Organizations that are surviving would claim that they are winning the battle. But there is a catch here. It is a very big catch, and that is what this book is about.

The skills and outcomes that the modern organization needs from its workforce cannot be provided by an over-stressed and anxious workforce. The organization used to assume that people were like slightly more nimble and possibly more intelligent versions of the machines that powered their output. The successful mechanization of many production lines seemed to prove the point: you only employed a human being if there wasn't a machine that could do the job. Machines, after all, don't get tired, don't need comfort breaks, and don't go on strike.

As computing power increases, managers look forward to the day when many white-collar skills can also be mechanized: for example, absorbing and analysing data, and then making a report; perhaps, with a good enough algorithm, even using that analysis to select an optimum solution to a particular problem.

Oh, brave new world, that hath such creatures in it![2]

This could, indeed, be a brave but benign new world – a world in which any human function that can be replaced by a device is, and should be, so replaced. The real skills of human beings are, after all, far superior to any skill that human ingenuity may be able to programme into a device. This is not to denigrate the likely future capabilities of devices: humans will continue to devise machines capable of carrying out increasingly complex tasks; devices that will accomplish things that seem astonishing to us today; things that tax even human abilities.

But no inorganic device will be able to do what human beings do best, and effortlessly: work in large social groups; intuitively understand the social nuances of that group; individually conceive of brilliant new innovative ideas; collectively create complex solutions based on our shared experiences. Unfortunately – and this is the catch – steam-engine organizations are custom-built to repress all of these abilities.

MARK POWELL
"STRUCTURES OUT OF THE INDUSTRIAL AGE"
Organizations talk a lot about individuals and the human importance of their people, and yet their entire approach is like our metaphor of the steam engine.

We are applying organizational approaches and structures that are out of the industrial age, which were set up in a world where we were trying to organise mechanised production. But human beings are about processes of creativity and innovation and engagement and energy – the very things that modern organizations struggle to understand.

When they send people on executive development programmes at business schools to learn to behave differently, they are proceeding on the fundamental assumption that the individuals are broken and need to be fixed.

Over the many hundreds of hours I've spent talking to people attending these programmes, I've come to realize that what really needs to be fixed is the organizations themselves and the basic assumption they are working on – the assumption that people need to be aligned to the organizational requirement rather than the organization needing to adapt to the requirements of human beings, if they want to really get the kind of energy and the focus, and the creativity that human beings are capable of.

Everybody increasingly recognises that these organizations are archaic, are out of the industrial age; they're like steam engines. Steam engines were amazing in their time; they fulfilled a phenomenal function and were a great advancement. But over time, other technologies and approaches develop. The steam engine became an archaic symbol of a bygone age – as modern organizations are today.

Mark Powell in conversation with Jonathan Gifford

We need to focus on the things that only human beings can do; things that – remarkably – we do naturally, and willingly.

MARK POWELL
"WHY HAVEN'T THEY DONE ANYTHING ABOUT IT?"
In a situation where it's quite obvious that most modern organizations are fundamentally not fit for purpose, in terms of the human side of energy and creativity and innovation – the things that really drive performance – the question you have to ask yourself is" "Why haven't they done anything about it?"

The conclusion I've come to over many years of working in this space, is that because it's just too damn difficult. Changing a steam engine by throwing it away and starting again is too difficult – it's too hard. So what tends to happen is, organizations find a myriad sticking plasters, if you like, to kind of patch up the age-old steam engine and then pretend they've actually done something fundamental. They pretend that by putting those plasters on the steam engine they've transformed it into a rocket ship, when all available evidence indicates that this so far away from the truth, it's laughable.

They will talk about human beings as being important to the organization; they will paint the walls in an office to make it colourful for people. But, fundamentally, they are recognising that they know the model is broken, but all they are actually doing is putting patches on the steam engine and hoping that people will believe that they've actually changed something – when the truth is they haven't changed anything at all.

Mark Powell in conversation with Jonathan Gifford

THREE THINGS THAT ONLY HUMAN BEINGS CAN DO
- **Innovate:** individually generate radical, new, disruptive solutions
- **Socialize:** work together in large social groups
- **Collaborate:** create solutions based on the collective understanding

The second of these natural human abilities – the instinctive ability, evolved over millennia, to work collaboratively in large social groups

– reminds us of another set of uniquely human attributes that inorganic devices will never emulate.

FOUR THINGS THAT COLLABORATIVE HUMAN SOCIAL BEHAVIOUR GIVES RISE TO

- The ability to inspire and be inspired
- The instinctive ability to trust and mistrust
- Feelings of shame and pride
- The willingness to make sacrifices for the greater good

It is these uniquely human characteristics that allow us to work together successfully in organizations: to be inspired by a common purpose, to trust our colleagues and to want to be seen to be doing our bit, to feel pride in being part of something bigger than ourselves, and to be prepared even to make personal sacrifices to achieve this. These human qualities are at the heart of any emotionally healthy organization – and only emotionally healthy organizations will survive in the modern age.

Steam-engine organizations assume – implicitly or explicitly – that these emotions have no place in the workplace – that they are confusing distractions from the rational business of running an efficient enterprise. How wrong they are. These "emotional" reactions are the very stuff that binds people together in common endeavours.

The modern organization has become completely outmoded, but we have failed to notice this. We behave as if organizations are still "manufactories" whose only aim is to produce a unit of output as efficiently and cheaply as possible, using human beings as cogs in the wheels of the machine, because – sadly, as steam-engine thinking would have it – no machine has yet been devised that can replace the troublesome humans.

It is time to transform our steam engines: to improve their every function, every mechanism, little by little, to the point where the steam engine has been transformed.

TRANSFORMING THE STEAM ENGINE, BIT BY BIT

The steam engine must be transformed into something fit for the age of ideas.

There is a growing groundswell of thinkers who have been saying exactly this for many years now: many of them will feature in the pages of this book. More importantly, ordinary working people have been clamouring, for many long years, for a change to their working lives; calling out for the opportunity to use their unique talents for the benefit of everyone; asking to feel more involved, more appreciated, more fulfilled by the working lives.

We have now reached a point of crisis – a tipping point in the history of the organization. Organizations will have to change, or

☆ ☆

MARK POWELL
THE AGGREGATION OF MARGINAL GAINS
Several years ago, I was very privileged to see a session run by Dr Steve Peters, psychological coach for the British cycling team. What he talked about in terms of what transformed a potentially interesting team into probably the greatest Olympic team in history, certainly for Britain, was two things. One was around reprogramming people's psychology, in terms of allowing individuals to not let the emotional get in the way of the rational as they try to perform at a high peak. But the thing I thought was even more interesting was the recognition and the focus on the process of improving performance and changing things through the aggregation of marginal gains – the recognition that the idea that we live in a world where anybody can suddenly achieve huge step changes in performance has long since passed, and that the aggregation of many small incremental steps is the only way that you can transform performance or, indeed, organizations.

For me, that's the key – that if you transformed enough elements of the steam engine over time, you would actually change it. The problem we have at the moment is that the organizational challenge around steam engine practices is so fundamental: it's around structures, it's around processes, it's around philosophy, it's around culture, it's around measurements, it's around the notion of "efficiency". It's all of these things, and when you look at it in its entirety, that's just too big a deal. Which is why we effectively put plasters on the steam engine.

But if you rethink it in a different way, what we need to do is to break this whole problem down into a number of component parts, each of which is small enough to get your head around, and to say, "I can change they will begin to fail – suddenly, and in large numbers. The old steam-engine way of running organizations is no longer able to deliver the outcomes that these organizations desperately need in order to prosper, or even to survive.

Organizations need to be innovative and agile; they need to respond quickly to change in a world where the very pace of change is constantly increasing. The old command-and-control structures,

✩ ✩

this one thing." If it was to do with cycling, one of the things may simply be to change the material of the helmet. It's a small thing, but if I combine it with enough other elements, maybe I can change something quite fundamentally.

Maybe that's where we've been going wrong with the organization. We've been trying to say: "How do we change the whole steam engine, how do we throw the steam engine away today and create a rocket ship tomorrow?" The answer is that you cannot do that, because it's just too big and too difficult. But if we go back to that philosophy that the only way of radically changing performance is to aggregate multiple small gains, several things together might give you one second off your time. I'm a great fan of motor racing, where people spend millions of dollars chasing 0.1% of a second on the track. But chasing 10 or 15 or 20 times 0.1% of a second through different things – through the engine, through aerodynamics, through driver training, through whatever it may be – and by aggregating it all together, they can actually find a second on the track.

With the organization, it seems to me that we need to work out what are the 10, 15, 20 marginal gains that if we could achieve these individually and then aggregate them, we could start to re-baseline, and to change the steam engine into something far more different than just a steam engine with a few bolt-ons attached to it on the side.

This book is about rethinking the model; understanding what are the individual elements that together could give us an accumulation of marginal gains that might, just might, transform the steam engine.

Mark Powell in conversation with Jonathan Gifford

the old divisions of labour, the old "jump when I say 'jump!'" mentality will not deliver this.

The organizational structure that *is* capable of delivering this is something completely different. It is made up of genuine communities of independently minded people, striving willingly to achieve common goals and taking great pride in their work, and deriving a deep sense of reward and fulfilment as a result.

That's not going to happen with the old way of doing things. We all recognize this. But organizations don't seem to be changing. Why not?

In this book we argue that the primary reason for a lack of significant change is that the organization, as whole, is a daunting apparatus to change. It is, after all, a great juggernaut of a steam engine. Where do you start? Which bits do you change? Who should be responsible for bringing about the change? Even small, supposedly agile organizations find themselves quickly slipping into the bad, steam-engine habits of hierarchy and control, of systems and efficiencies and a lack of genuine human community.

The answer, the authors believe, is not to try to dismantle the steam engine and build a new, modern organization from the ground up. That's a nice idea, but it won't happen – not with small to medium-sized enterprises, and absolutely not with great multinational enterprises or large institutions.

The answer is to transform the steam engine bit by bit. To recognize the fundamental issues that are preventing us from using our astonishing human skills and abilities to deliver what is needed, and to start to change the structures that are responsible for this, little by little.

THE TEN PARADOXES OF STEAM-ENGINE ORGANIZATIONS

In the following chapters, 10 key "paradoxes" are identified and explored: things that steam-engine organizations do that are actively preventing them from achieving the outcomes that they desperately need if they are to succeed, or even to survive in the age of ideas. This represents a powerful force for change: the organization must change or fail.

There may be many different ways of tackling these paradoxes: each chapter will present the thoughts and practices of a wide range of business people, change leaders, management coaches, and innovators. This book doesn't have all of the answers, but you, collectively, do. That's what's so great about the age of ideas.

Control: Organizations set out to control processes and people, but control stifles ingenuity, sharing, and innovation – things that the organization needs in order to survive and thrive.

Measurement: Organizations have become obsessed by measurement, but the metrics cannot reveal whether or not the organization is fulfilling its real purpose. Too much focus on measurement can actively prevent the organization from achieving its real goals.

Efficiency: Efficiency is important, but short-term efficiencies can destroy long-term potential; petty efficiencies destroy human energy and commitment, and "efficiency drives" can reflect mere lack of ambition – the inability to think of positive solutions.

Innovation: Organizations know that they must innovate or die, but most are still designed to replicate a known process as efficiently as possible. A focus on control, measurement, and efficiency cannot create the conditions needed for innovation.

Communication: We are communicating more than ever; dealing with "messages" takes more and more of our time, but is a very poor form of communication. Real communication within organizations is suffering as a result.

Physicality: Organizations feel the need to have a physical manifestation – a symbolic place where the organization lives and its people come together – but these physical spaces can prevent real communication and reinforce hierarchies. Attendance at the symbolic place of work has become an end in itself.

Democracy: Organizations are, actually, still based on command and control; they profess that they should be more "democratic", but democracy is a good political system and a bad way to run an enterprise. What is needed is self-organization based on shared objectives and a forged consensus, which is far more radical – and effective.

Leadership: The "hero" leader is dead, but radical change needs heroic leadership. The new generation of strong leaders who will change the organization will encourage other leaders to spring up throughout the organization. Paradoxically, we need more leadership, not less.

Networking: Organizations think that they have a network, which can be useful to them, but real networks involve real membership: we contribute to our network and it gives something back. This involves a loss of control, which steam-engine organizations cannot tolerate. Organizations are themselves also networks, but they do not understand this or allow the network to function.

Diversity: Organizations have devoted much time and effort to being "diverse", but this is an empty, politically correct form of diversity. Organizations are still effectively homogeneous. What is needed is a genuine diversity of human talents, opinions, and capabilities, which in turn will drive change and innovation.

TRANSFORMING THE STEAM ENGINE, ONE STEP AT A TIME

Radically changing the way that any organization is structured and run – even a small organization – is a daunting task. The sheer scale of the task prevents us from tackling the root-and-branch change that is needed.

It's not as if there is a lack of recognition of the problem. This book is full of contributions from business thinkers who are in full agreement about the problems facing our unreconstructed, steam-engine organizations – problems that will inevitably lead to a failure to leverage the human energy and ingenuity, which are the only things that will guarantee our continued prosperity.

Exploring these 10 fundamental paradoxes – things that steam-engine organizations continue to do that are directly preventing the outcomes that they most need – reveals possible routes to change: new ways of experimenting with the organizational structure that might, just might, aggregate to the point where the old steam-engine organization has been transformed beyond all recognition and become something fit for the modern age.

The paradoxes are all interconnected. An improvement in one area will help to make things better in other areas: less control will lead to more self-organization; better use of our physical and virtual spaces will lead to better communication; more communication, diversity, and networking will lead to more innovation; better leadership will remove the need for obsessive measurement and "efficiencies"; more emergent leadership and better networking will remove the need for tight control; and so it goes, in a virtuous circle. Or, to put it another way, in an interconnected, organic, self-sustaining network.

We will not be able to transform the steam-engine organization in one almighty "restructuring" – and it would be foolhardy to attempt this. But we can change it, little by little, bit by bit, until it has been transformed beyond all recognition. We have, after all, progressed from real steam engines to space travel. But not overnight. And not all in one go.

CHAPTER 1

LEARNING TO LET GO
HOW CONTROL IS KILLING THE ORGANIZATION

The great majority of modern organizations are not modern at all. They are still following a model that was created to suit the first great manufacturing companies that sprang up in the early 20th century as part of the Second Industrial Revolution – and these companies are not that different from the very first "manufactories" spawned by the first Industrial Revolution in the 18th century.

The principles of "scientific management" were laid down by an engineer called Frederick Winslow Taylor, very early in the 20th century, and they have stuck with us ever since. These principles are still at the heart of steam-engine organizations. They delivered important improvements in efficiency in their day, but in the modern workplacethey are damaging – they are making people less efficient and less productive.

According to scientific management, the best way to carry out any task must be the subject of scientific analysis. People should then be selected, trained and developed to be best suited to perform their particular task; the performance of that task should be subject to detailed instruction and strict supervision; workers should carry out the tasks while managers ensure that instructions are strictly adhered to (and, by the way, you need a lot of managers).

It sounds like hell on earth, but it worked – especially at a time when America was driving the Second Industrial Revolution, manufacturing the goods that the created the consumer society. So we keep doing it. And, if it works, why should we not carry on applying this brutal, dehumanizing process?

Because it isn't working any more. The steam engine is broken.

THE PARADOX OF CONTROL

The paradox of control is the most pernicious of organizational paradoxes. It is also the very essence of steam-engine management. By attempting to control every aspect of the organization, we are actively preventing the organization from succeeding.

The main aim of early modern industry was, quite correctly, to manufacture goods with increasing efficiency. Since it was assumed that people would not willingly be servants of corporations, systems of rewards and punishments were devised to keep people motivated to behave in the right ways, and fearful of behaving in the wrong ways. "Command and control" was the prevailing management model. Sadly, it still is.

Early managers turned, quite deliberately, to the best-known models of successful command and control, which happened to be the military and the Catholic Church. "Unity of command" was the paradigm (any member of the organization must have only one superior); obedience to command was the essence. This classic, hierarchical structure is said to have served the organization well for a century or so. That is debatable. What is clear is that it is not working any more.

Control of organizations has been achieved in the obvious way – by measuring the outputs of the organization and noting discrepancies between current and desired outputs. New, improved outputs (those that came closest to the defined intentions of the organization) were achieved by adjusting – controlling – the behaviour of management and workers. Any other kind of output was, by definition, a deviation from the ideal.

By attempting to exert such control, steam-engine managers were also, to deepen the paradox, losing real control. Human beings are genuinely motivated by things that reward them at an emotional level: a sense of purpose, of belonging, of taking part in a meaningful common effort, of making a difference. The desperately old-fashioned techniques of steam-engine control touch none of these emotional triggers. People see through the simplistic attempt to "control" them and begin to disengage. As a result, the organization loses their commitment, and their potential contribution. It has succeeded in making them mere cogs in an unchanging machine.

There have been a few companies in the history of the modern organization to have ripped up the command-and-control handbook and actively encouraged colleagues to be genuinely innovative, or to behave in "out of control" ways – the early Hewlett Packard and 3-M spring to mind – but they, and the handful of companies like them, are the exceptions that prove the rule. But surely this old-fashioned, command-and-control model of management can't still be happening – especially in the innovation-driven, high-tech companies of today?

FROM "LEAN COMPETITION MACHINE LED BY YOUNG VISIONARIES" TO "BLOATED AND BUREAUCRACY-LADEN" – IN ONE GENERATION!

If you had to name the companies most associated with the white-hot creativity that drove the microcomputer revolution in the last decades of the 20th century, Microsoft would surely be on your list, as personified by the alarmingly intelligent, hard-driving and barely socialized young Bill Gates. Unsurprisingly, despite his lack of social graces, Gates attracted a group of likeminded, brilliant young people – people who wanted to play their part in the revolution in personal computing that was happening before their eyes.

Microsoft started up in 1975 in an atmosphere of anarchic creativity, with world-changing results. It should be inconceivable that the same organization was described by a leading journalist less than 40 years later as "bloated and bureaucracy-laden". But, as they say, stuff happens.

Microsoft's work environment, in its earliest days, was driven, barely managed, and highly creative. Young programmers worked insanely long hours, driven by the heady feeling that they were making history. They worked themselves to a standstill, ate some pizza, played basketball in the corridor, and maybe nipped out to take in a movie. And then they went back to work. "We noticed the long hours," one Microsoft veteran from the early days recalled, "but it wasn't a burden. It was fun" (see panel).

As the company grew into a mighty empire, its managers – fearful of losing control of a rapidly growing and hugely profitable organization – imposed the usual steam-engine control systems. By so doing, they destroyed its vital force.

There is a dreadful, gravitational pull back toward the basic precepts of the industrial-era steam-engine organization. As companies grow and become valuable – immensely valuable, in the case of Microsoft – so the organization's guardians, its senior executives, become (understandably) obsessed with control: "We've been put in charge of this hugely successful organization," they think, "and, whatever happens, we mustn't foul up! We mustn't let it get out of control." But the inevitable outcome of this essentially conservative (and timid) attitude toward being the caretakers of a successful organization is to destroy its vital force.

The rules and regulations and petty bureaucracies that "control" an organization inevitably begin to sap its creative energy and to destroy the vitality of its once insanely committed workforce, who no longer feel that they are creating something new and wonderful, and have been reduced to turning up and following instructions. As the journalist Kurt Eichenwald wrote of Microsoft in 2012: "What began as a lean competition machine led by young visionaries of unparalleled talent has mutated into something bloated and bureaucracy-laden, with an internal culture that unintentionally rewards managers who strangle innovative ideas that might threaten the established order of things" (see panel overleaf).

THE ILLUSION OF CONTROL

The really insidious problem with control is that we all wish we were more in control, not less. We can't help ourselves. Life is chaotic, unruly, and unpredictable. Control is what we crave.

But our attempts to control people, rather than things, are doomed to end in failure. Ask any parent. You love your children; you nurture them and enable them. You attempt to control them through advice and guidance. Parents who genuinely try to control their children are seen, rightly, as monsters. It always ends badly. So why do organizations imagine that they can behave differently, and get different results?

MICROSOFT: THE EARLY DAYS
"IT WASN'T A BURDEN, IT WAS FUN"
Microsoft was created in 1975 by Bill Gates and Paul Allen, two driven, brilliant pioneers in the world-changing personal computer revolution. Bright young people flocked to work for the new company. They became known as "Microkids".

They worked insane hours in a chaotic environment; sometimes breaking off work to play ball games in the corridor and eat pizza, before going back to work through the night.

They shared a common goal, and they were creating a new world.

As Steve Wood, Microsoft employee No. 6 said of those early, heady days:

"There were times, not that infrequently, that I'd be going home for a few hours of sleep about the time [my wife] was getting up.

"We'd often be there 24 hours a day, trying to meet a deadline for another OEM or getting a new product out. We noticed the long hours, but it wasn't a burden. It was fun.

"We weren't doing it because someone was standing over us with a whip saying, 'You guys have to do this.' We were doing it because we had stuff to do and we had to get it done."

James Wallace & Erickson *Hard Drive, Bill Gates and the Making of the Microsoft Empire*, **John Wiley & Sons, Inc, 1992, p 129**

In many companies, there is, quite literally, a whole manual devoted to travel expenses (to choose one example from the many "manuals" that exist in steam-engine organizations). A weighty tome that attempts to codify every possible scenario in which the unwary executive might find him or herself, agonizing as to what the correct procedure might be. The very existence of the manual also makes the executive vulnerable to the accusation that he or she has transgressed, or broken "the rules". Manuals and sets of instructions are the joy and treasure of steam-engine organizations.

KURT EICHENWALD REPORT ON MICROSOFT CEO STEVE BALLMER'S KEYNOTE ADDRESS AT THE 2012 INTERNATIONAL CONSUMER ELECTRONICS SHOW, LAS VEGAS

"BLOATED AND BUREAUCRACY-LADEN"

Amid a dynamic and ever changing marketplace, Microsoft—which declined to comment for this article—became a high-tech equivalent of a Detroit car-maker, bringing flashier models of the same old thing off of the assembly line even as its competitors upended the world. Most of its innovations have been financial debacles or of little consequence to the bottom line. And the performance showed on Wall Street; despite booming sales and profits from its flagship products, in the last decade Microsoft's stock barely budged from around $30, while Apple's stock is worth more than 20 times what it was 10 years ago ...

How did this jaw-dropping role reversal happen? How could a company that stands among the most cash-rich in the world, the onetime icon of cool that broke IBM's iron grip on the computer industry, have stumbled so badly in a race it was winning?

The story of Microsoft's lost decade could serve as a business-school case study on the pitfalls of success. For what began as a lean competition machine led by young visionaries of unparalleled talent has mutated into something bloated and bureaucracy-laden, with an internal culture that unintentionally rewards managers who strangle innovative ideas that might threaten the established order of things.

James Wallace & Erickson *Hard Drive, Bill Gates and the Making of the Microsoft Empire*, John Wiley & Sons, Inc,, 1992, p 129

Ricardo Semler, in his remarkable book *Maverick: The Success Story Behind the World's Most Unusual Workplace*, tells of how he began to tear up the manuals, procedures and regulations that governed the business that his father had formed and which he then took over (see panel). These rules and regulations, he argues, "divert attention from a company's objectives, provide a false sense of security for executives, and create work for bean-counters".[3] Semler got rid of them all, and says that the company benefited as a result. And he owns the company, so he should know.

The authors of this book have worked with one medium-size manufacturing company in the UK that also dispensed with its substantial travel and expenses manual and replaced it with this

RICARDO SEMLER, MAVERICK: THE SUCCESS STORY BEHIND THE WORLD'S MOST UNUSUAL WORKPLACE

In their quest for law, order, stability and predictability, corporations make rules for every conceivable contingency. Policy manuals are created with the idea that, if a company puts everything in writing, it will be more rational and objective [...]

Sounds sensible, right? And it works fine for an army or a prison system. But not, I believe, for a business, and certainly not for a business that wants people to think, innovate, and act as human beings wherever possible. All those rules cause employees to forget that a company needs to be creative and adaptive to survive. Rules slow it down.

Semco had a particularly complicated set of rule on travel expenses. Our auditors often spent hours arguing over whether someone on a business trip should be reimbursed for movie tickets. Well then, what about theatre tickets? What would we do if an employee went to a concert that cost $45? $100? And what about calling home? How often should the company pay? Was a five-minute call reasonable? What if an employee had, say four children? Are 75 seconds per child sufficient?

... Without rules all answers are suggested by common sense. No, I can't define what common sense is, but I know it when I hear it. Some of our people stay in four-star hotels and others, sometimes with much higher salaries, choose lesser digs. Some people spend $200 a day on meals; others get by on far less.

Ricardo Semler, *Maverick: The success story behind the world's most unusual workplace*, Random House Business Books, 1999, p 92 little algorithm:

- We are a frugal company; please do not waste company money.
- Winning new business and impressing our customers is our top priority; please do not turn up for an important meeting tired or travel-stained, or fail to entertain clients in a reasonable way.
- We leave it to your good judgment which combination of flights, hotels, meals, taxis, and so on allows you to achieve the best compromise between these two principles.

With these simple principles in place, and having thrown away the previous 50-page Corporate Travel and Expenses Manual, the company's expenses bill went down.

A FAILURE OF TRUST

At the heart of the mania for control is a failure of trust. People understand that they have a job to do. They understand that they need to create value, and that they should not needlessly waste money. If they forget this, a good manager can gently remind them. If more forceful reminders are needed, it sounds as if that person is not a good fit with the organization.

It's not rocket science – and it doesn't need a time-consuming set of rules and regulations to ensure that people understand the spirit of what is required of them. In healthy organizations, all of this stuff comes naturally, as it should do. The very attempt to set up complicated bureaucratic controls over people's behaviour is a clear sign that an organization's culture is beginning to fail.

One immediate casualty is, indeed, trust. People instantly recognize when they are not actually being trusted to use their own judgment or, more damningly, when they are not even trusted not to pocket the company's silverware.

In the same way, people are immediately aware if they are not being trusted with the best use of their time. Steam-engine managers want to control the input of the workforce, very much in the tradition of Frederick Winslow Taylor. If they can control the input, they feel, they will guarantee the output.

They are very wrong.

WHAT CONTROL KILLS

When industry adopted the command-and-control model two centuries or so ago, it was moving away from the old "craft" model, in which one person or a small team of people would build an item – a piece of furniture, a saddle, or even an automobile. It moved toward the assembly line model, where individuals were required to perform specific tasks in sequence. Creativity, it was wrongly believed, was not needed; people were required to fulfil their tasks in

KATHRYN BISHOP, ASSOCIATE FELLOW, SAÏD BUSINESS SCHOOL, UNIVERSITY OF OXFORD

Loss of control is perceived as a problem, but actually it only acknowledges the reality. The problems that are now being faced in most organizations are so complex that they aren't being managed from the centre, even if top management like to think they are.

People in the thick of things—people in the front line, if you like – are just trying to get things done, they're activating bits of their network , making decisions on the spot and doing whatever they can to get stuff done. It's not controlled centrally; it is a complex, adaptive system, whether top management like it or not.

People have to make decisions rapidly. They don't have time to go through the processes, and those organizations that are still insisting on that have become sclerotic, they're sort of bunged up; they can't get stuff done.

So it's a very uncomfortable reality, but for some of the clients we work with, one of the reasons they're prepared to invest in high quality, focussed and expensive executive development is actually a tacit recognition that this is the only way they have to ensure that the decisions that are made moment by moment on the front line are consistent and sensible -- because they can't do it with procedures and tick lists and approvals and terms and rules and regulations. I truly believe that.

Kathryn Bishop in conversation with the authors

as machine-like a manner as possible.

It is possible to argue that this was appropriate at the time: that the success of Henry Ford and General Motors' Alfred P. Sloan proves the efficacy of the management model that they helped to create.

But we now know that creativity is needed, even on assembly lines. We also know that the world has moved on: that the revolution represented by assembly line manufacturing and "modern" management processes that made Ford, General Motors and others a success in the early 20th century will absolutely not guarantee the success of any 21st-century business.

It is not the efficiency of our assembly lines that will allow us to create world-beating products, but the brilliance of our ideas.

Ever-improving efficiency is merely a given – a tool that allows us to bring our ideas to market at a competitive price. Creativity – innovation – is the driving force of successful organizations.

Innovation is everything. And innovation can never stop, or even pause for breath. Even the most brilliant product or process is quickly imitated, with or without patent infringements. Remarkable innovations are quickly commoditized. Constant innovation, at every level, is the only thing that will keep alive any organization that is exposed to market forces.

A substantial body of research – and almost everyone's experience of working for large organizations – confirms that working in rigidly hierarchical structures and experiencing various degrees of control does not make people happy or fulfilled in their working lives. More importantly, command and control actively stifles creativity – sometimes intentionally but often unintentionally.

Attempts to control the members of any organization destroy the creativity and energy that drive, or could drive, the organization's success. Strangely, pretty much everyone agrees with this. You don't find many management gurus proclaiming that what modern organizations need is more command-and-control management.

The paradox of control is infuriatingly clear – so why aren't we doing something about this? Why are we not seeing a bonfire of control systems?

We are persisting with a failing model only because there are not yet enough examples of successful organizations that are using radically different management (or lack of management) techniques to give us the confidence to try a new approach. The number of such organizations is growing, and we believe that the tipping point will come relatively soon.

If you can examine your own organization and look for examples where the comfort blanket of management control is stifling the natural creativity of people in the organization (you are unlikely to have far to look) and simply begin to let go – to learn to let stuff happen – then you will be helping to move all of us toward that tipping point.

Let's remind ourselves of what management thinkers have been saying about the benefits of self-motivation, as opposed to coercion by management, for the last 50 years or so. Let's consider the way everyone says: "That's right, I really do believe that" – and yet we still don't seem to have actually done anything about changing our working environment.

SELF–MOTIVATION – OR, "HELLO, HELLO, IS ANYBODY LISTENING?"

We have known for a long time that people work best when they are self-motivated. In 1960, Douglas McGregor, management professor at MIT Sloan School of Management, published *The Human Side of Enterprise*. In it he argues, correctly, that rewards and punishments of the kinds used in steam-engine management work at a pretty low level of behavioural needs. If I am desperate to keep my job, I will be motivated by fear of being sacked. If my quality of life absolutely requires that I make the next pay grade, I will be motivated by the fear of not getting a promotion. But if I am living quite comfortably – if I have a lovely partner, delightful children, and a circle of close friends; a good chance of finding a new job if my currently employer "lets me go", and especially if I do not trust my current employer not to "let me go", for business reasons beyond my control – then these low-level carrots and sticks really will not ring my bell.

As McGregor writes:

*The philosophy of management by control ... is inadequate to
motivate, because the human needs on which this approach relies
are relatively unimportant motivators of behaviour in our society
today. Direction and control are of limited value in motivating
people whose important needs are social and egoistic.*

McGregor's shorthand for the old-fashioned control model is
"Theory X". He goes on to paint a bleakly compelling picture of what
we might expect from it:

*People, deprived of the opportunities to satisfy at work the needs
which are now important to them, behave exactly as we might
predict – with indolence, passivity, unwillingness to accept
responsibility, willingness to follow the demagogue, unreasonable
demands for economic benefits.[4]*

McGregor's alternative approach to management, "Theory Y",
argues that people are inherently self-motivating. Daniel Pink picks
up on this theme in Drive, his bestselling book from 2011:

*If your starting point was Theory X, your managerial techniques
would inevitably produce limited results, or even go awry entirely.
If you believed in the "mediocrity of the masses", as [McGregor]
put it, then mediocrity became the ceiling for what you could
achieve. But if your starting point was Theory Y, the possibilities
were vast – not simply for the individual's potential, but for the
company's bottom line as well.*

Pink devised his own name for self-motivated behaviour: "Type
I" (for "Intrinsic"). Type I kinds of people, he writes, "usually achieve
more than their reward-seeking counterparts":

*Type I behaviour is fuelled more by intrinsic desires than extrinsic
ones. It concerns itself less with the external rewards to which
an activity leads and more with the inherent satisfaction of the
activity itself.*

OLIVIER OULLIER, PROFESSOR OF BEHAVIOURAL AND BRAIN
SCIENCES, UNIVERSITY OF AIX-MARSEILLES
"LEARNING STRATEGIES BY HEART"
Many top people are trained in a way similar to pre-season training
in America football: learning strategies by heart. You know that you
needed strategy 2b, and you apply 2b. And there is 2b(i), 2b(ii), 2b(iii),
because there are parameters that are changing.

This is very fine if you're involved in an environment that is pretty
stable; that is not volatile, and where there are no new risks.

New risks have emerged that are not in the books. Nobody can
manage these things because they are not trained for them. Nobody
can be trained for the impossible.

Training people in a way that is so classical also minimised the
propensity and the ability of people to improvise.

These days, whether we are talking about individuals or
institutions, what is super important is to have some kind of "adaptive
governance", because all sorts of things that you will have to deal with
will have adaptive properties, whether we are talking about markets
or individuals, will evolve over time in a ways that is more and more
unpredictable and more and more volatile.

Olivier Oullier in conversation with the authors

*If we want to strengthen our organizations, get beyond our
decade of underachievement, and address the inchoate sense
that something's gone wrong in our businesses, our lives, and our
world, we need to move from Type X management to Type I.[5]*

The really strange thing is that the writings of McGregor and Pink
– and those of a myriad of other social scientists, business analysts,
and neuropsychologists – are generally accepted to be pointing in
the right direction. Business and management gurus are not writing

magazine articles saying that what really motivates people is the old-fashioned command-and-control model.

Think about that for a moment.

There is a general consensus of opinion that old-fashioned, hierarchical control is not a good way to run a business – especially if you want creativity from your colleagues. And these days, creativity is absolutely what businesses need. So what's going wrong? Why are we so resistant to these ideas?

McGregor – writing way back when Ronald Reagan was still an actor, and a popular beat combo called the Beatles were just starting to perform under that name – probably had it right at the time:

> *Someone once said that fish discover water last. The "psychological environment" of industrial management – like water for fish – is so much part of organizational life that we are unaware of it. Certain characteristics of our society, and of organizational life within it, are so established, so pervasive, that we cannot conceive of their being otherwise.*[6]

It is becoming increasingly and urgently clear that successful organizations need to move toward a "networked" model (see chapter 9), where teams of people work together to achieve a common goal, new ways of thinking are encouraged, and leadership exists at many levels within the organization.

Olivier Oullier, Professor of bBehavioural and brain sciences at the University of Aix-Marseilles, argues that we need "adaptive governance" – a form of leadership that is able to adapt to markets and social conditions that are themselves constantly shifting and adapting (see panel).

Rigid, steam-engine management assumes that it knows the answer, and insists that everyone applies the familiar solution. This isn't even likely to work in a rapidly changing world. We need to try to make the move. We're already about 50 years late.

THE BONFIRE OF CONTROLS

One company, the video-game developer Valve Corporation, has already made the move. It has done away with management, and allows its employees to pursue the projects that they feel they add most value to – and, ultimately, to be driven by the market, learning what the market likes and does not like by the simple method of shipping products, seeing what sells, and reacting quickly to the results. They are doing very well.

Valve Corporation has taken the bonfire of controls to its logical conclusion. At Valve, there is no management. Not "just a little bit of management", but seriously, NO MANAGEMENT.

Employees are given desks with wheels – which is pretty cool in itself, but also, as the company itself says, serves as "a symbolic reminder that you should always be considering where you could move yourself to be more valuable".

The wheels have an entirely practical function. Employees have to choose the project that they want to work on. If they think they could add more value to another project, they wheel their desk over to the other project, plug in their computer, and start working there.

"You'll notice people moving frequently; often whole teams will move their desks to be closer to each other," the company's Employees' Handbook points out. "There is no organizational structure keeping you from being in close proximity to the people who you'd help or be helped by most."

Valve employees have their own ideas about what games they want to develop. That's the point. They create the idea, develop it, and ship it. Nobody from management steps in to evaluate the project, because there is no management. Only one person gets to evaluate the project: the consumer. As the company says:

Nobody has ever been fired at Valve for making a mistake.
It wouldn't make sense for us to operate that way. Providing
the freedom to fail is an important trait of the company—
we couldn't expect so much of individuals if we also penalized
people for errors. Even expensive mistakes, or ones which
result in a very public failure, are genuinely looked at as

EXTRACT FROM VALVE CORPORATION EMPLOYEES' HANDBOOK
WELCOME TO FLATLAND
Hierarchy is great for maintaining predictability and repeatability. It simplifies planning and makes it easier to control a large group of people from the top down, which is why military organizations rely on it so heavily.

But when you're an entertainment company that's spent the last decade going out of its way to recruit the most intelligent, innovative, talented people on Earth, telling them to sit at a desk and do what they're told obliterates 99 percent of their value. We want innovators, and that means maintaining an environment where they'll flourish.

That's why Valve is flat. It's our shorthand way of saying that we don't have any management, and nobody "reports to" anybody else. We do have a founder/president, but even he isn't your manager. This company is yours to steer — toward opportunities and away from risks. You have the power to green-light projects. You have the power to ship products.

A flat structure removes every organizational barrier between your work and the customer enjoying that work. Every company will tell you that "the customer is boss," but here that statement has weight. There's no red tape stopping you from figuring out for yourself what our customers want, and then giving it to them.

Valve Employee Handbook http://bit.ly/17iYJul

opportunities to learn. We can always repair the mistake or make up for it.

Screwing up is a great way to find out that your assumptions were wrong or that your model of the world was a little bit off. As long as you update your model and move forward with a better picture, you're doing it right. Look for ways to test your beliefs. Never be afraid to run an experiment or to collect more data ...

There are still some bad ways to fail. Repeating the same mistake over and over is one. Not listening to customers or peers before or after a failure is another. Never ignore the evidence; particularly when it says you're wrong.

LEARNING TO LET GO

The answer to the paradox of control is not the absence of any form of control; it is not total anarchy. What we are seeing at Valve is a form of self-organization – an absence of controlling government (which, technically speaking, is the correct definition for the much-maligned political system called "anarchy", which we will talk more about in chapter 7).

Organizational leaders need to identify the very few things that really matter – the things that will allow the organization to fulfil its fundamental purpose. They need to ensure that the organization is aligned with these goals. And then they need to let go. Attempting literally to control the organization's progress toward those goals will end in failure.

It is quite clear why this must be true: if the leadership knew *exactly* how the organization would progress from where it is today to its desired state of being in the future, then they could draw up a detailed road map. They could *manage* the organization toward the desired future, and leadership would not be needed (which is, of course, exactly what steam-engine managers attempt to do).

But the future is unknown. Which means that the best route to the organization's desired future is also unknown. This optimal route can only be discovered by the organization as a whole, through experimentation and debate.

Leaders, having set the direction in which an organization should be moving, should literally stop controlling. Progress toward key objectives should be measured in some way, of course. Many supposedly essential metrics are probably not useful, and may even be misleading, but the organization's general state of health certainly needs to be carefully monitored, as we will discuss in the next chapter. But if things begin to drift off course, the answer is for the leader to alert the organization and encourage and enable it to find solutions, rather than to put a new set of controls in place.

Strong leaders who succeed in "letting go" and creating an environment in which people can organize themselves to meet the challenges that they face will find that their organization will largely shape itself to meet its challenges. This natural social process will leave the members of the organization feeling happy and rewarded as they work together to achieve the common goal.

Companies that control their employees to the extent of taking over, in effect, their whole lives, are actively destroying a precious resource. People become unable to function at all, let alone creatively, when an organization demands all of their time, and all of their energies. Lives are ruined, and the potential for creativity is destroyed.

The paradox of control is brutally clear. There are no half measures. Letting go is the answer. Start today.

TAKING THE ORGANIZATION FROM THE INDUSTRIAL ERA TO THE AGE OF IDEAS
Transforming the steam engine, one step at a time

- Control is an illusion
  - We can try to control things and processes, but not people
- Like fish in water, we fail to see the old-fashioned, carrot and stick psychological environment of our organizations
  - Command and control creates a stressed and unhappy working environment that destroys natural enthusiasm and creativity
  - People work best when they are self-motivated
- Most policy manuals serve no useful purpose
  - Forget about the rule books; ask people to behave sensibly
- Some organizations and many departments can function better without management
- What matters most is not the efficiency of our organizations but the brilliance of our ideas
- The global environment changes rapidly and cannot really be controlled
  - Organizations need 'adaptive governance'
  - Only the organization as a whole knows how to adapt to changing circumstances to achieve its goals
- The organization is not actually under the control of any one person
  - Learn to let go

CHAPTER 2

WHAT GETS MEASURED IS WHAT GETS DONE
BUT ARE WE MEASURING THE RIGHT THINGS?

In the previous chapter we explored the way in which steam-engine organizations are persisting with an outmoded model of management – one that insists on a rigid distinction between managers and the managed, and which believes that the role of management is to control the behaviours of the managed to ensure peak efficiency.

The very idea of organizational control is merely a comforting illusion, and attempts to control every aspect of an organization will prevent a large number of desirable outcomes. People who feel 'controlled' are prevented, both institutionally and psychologically, from contributing fully to the organization's efforts. Their self-motivation is quashed, along with their creativity.

A thousand tasks that could have been performed in a thousand better ways are performed in exactly the same way, over and over again, following the template set up, some time ago, by some supposedly omniscient "scientific" manager. A thousand unique human beings have been successfully prevented from engaging in a normal, constructive, and adaptive way with the other members of the organization.

This chapter explores a closely related paradox: the paradox of measurement.

WHAT DOESN'T GET MEASURED DOESN'T GET MANAGED – MAYBE THAT WOULD HELP?

"What gets measured, gets managed," writes business guru Peter Drucker. This is quite an interesting thought, though not in the way intended by Drucker: since this book argues that steam-engine organizations are suffering from a surfeit of old-fashioned management, it may well be that we should stop measuring some things to prevent managers from managing them.

It's a thought. A rather radical thought, but a thought nevertheless.

Are we, after all, even measuring the right things? By definition, we can only measure things that are quantifiable. Some important things about a company's overall state of health are very hard to quantify, and are therefore difficult, if not impossible, to measure: an organization's general culture, for example; its spirit; its "buzz" – the discernible level of liveliness and creativity within an organization; the degree of willingness to help customers and each other; the sensitivity to outside events. We all recognize these things: walk into any organization, and you will immediately pick up the vibe of the place. Either people will be welcoming, engaged, outgoing, and excited, or they will be unwelcoming, disengaged, inward-looking, and bored – or even, in the worst cases, cowed and anxious.

Can we measure these things? Well, yes – but the first point is that these are not the things that steam-engine organizations even attempt to measure. What gets measured is, of course, "metrics" – because metrics, by definition, can be measured. But the obvious (and measurable) metrics will tell you nothing about these other, far more interesting and important things that are hard or impossible to measure.

There are some other problems with measurement. What gets measured is indeed what gets done. People are not stupid. If they know that they will be appraised against certain measures, they will try very hard to deliver. Unfortunately, this drives some very strange, often unproductive, and sometimes downright bad behaviour.

There are several other very major problems with the whole culture of measurement. One is that the numbers can definitely lie – or at least mislead. Some "key performance indicators" may be perfectly on target, and yet there may be issues festering at the heart of an organization or a project that will ensure its ultimate failure. Those, of course, will be the "people issues". Things that we supposedly can't measure.

And then, of course, there is the issue of who is observing what, and what they hope and expect to see (and what they will be rewarded for "discovering"). There are, of course, to quote a phrase that Mark Twain attributed to the 19th-century British prime minister Benjamin Disraeli, three kinds of lies: lies, damned lies, and statistics. Most metrics fall into the last category.

Metrics are devised by people, measured by people, and interpreted by people, and people have a well-established capacity for self-delusion. We are likely to find what we want to find, or at least to interpret it as what we wanted to find. It is also unlikely – and this opens a whole new area for discussion – that even the most alarming piece of data will persuade us to abandon our prejudices and to take truly radical, brave, and effective action.

Metrics are, in general, a comfort blanket. They help to give steam-engine managers the illusion of control – enabling them, in theory, finally to realize that something might be going wrong; something that should almost certainly have been very obvious if the managers had got their noses out of the metrics dashboards on their computer screens and talked to a few people in their organization instead.

Finally, there is the inescapable fact that any measure lags behind the underlying reality. Metrics are a snapshot of the now: they cannot tell us what is going to happen in the future. By measuring outputs, and ignoring inputs, we see only the results brought about at a particular moment in time by a myriad of inputs. It is, in fact, the inputs that really matter: the intelligence, energy, and creativity that people are bringing to their individual tasks in the first place. To get to heart of the matter, we need to find the pulse of the organization – its very heartbeat.

"GET THE METRICS RIGHT AND SUCCESS WILL SURELY FOLLOW"

Metrics do have a purpose. Every successful company has a good grasp of the numbers that reflect its current position and its apparent progress. It is important to know if you are manufacturing too many widgets, or too few. It is important to know if the costs of a project exceed its likely income. It is important to know if your operations are slower and more expensive than those of your competitors.

Most of the metrics that we really need to know are common sense. But the obsession with metrics – the belief that the most important part of management is to control certain key measures that supposedly define the health of one's organization – is a key part of steam-engine thinking. The machine will continue to run, we tell ourselves, if the readings on all of these gauges are all green. The metrics become the solution: "If only we can get the metrics right, success will surely follow. Keeping the metrics on track is the key role of management."

This is another illusion, like the illusion of control.

Organizations, like the people who make up the organization, are complex and full of surprises. Success is to be found by exploring and dealing with complexity, nuance, and subtlety, not by attempting to distil such delightfully complex issues into a few idiotic simplicities.

Let's explore a few of the problems with the steam engine obsession with measurement.

ARE WE MEASURING THE WRONG THINGS?

The answer, usually, is yes.

At the most fundamental level, we tend to assume that some simple measure of "success" is the correct thing to measure. Is the company profitable? Is it making money? It's a good measure. If you're not profitable, you won't be around for long. A fall-off in profitability is an alarm call to everyone. But, as David Packard, founder of Hewlett Packard, pointed out to a group of Hewlett Packard managers back in 1960, even profits are not the central point (see panel).

According to Packard, profitability is "an important result of a company's existence", but not "the real reason for [its] being". Neither is a company's share price.

Apple's rising share price saw it become the world's most valuable company in August 2012, with a market capitalisation of over $620 billion, but its success as a company is best measured by

DAVID PACKARD, *THE HP WAY*

"MAKE A CONTRIBUTION TO SOCIETY"

I want to discuss *why* a company exists in the first place. In other words, why are we here?

I think many people assume, wrongly, that a company exists simply to make money.

While this is an important result of a company's existence, we have to go deeper and find the real reasons for our being.

As we investigate this, we inevitably come to the conclusion that a group of people get together and exist as an institution that we call a company so that they are able to accomplish something collectively which they could not accomplish separately.

They are able to do something worthwhile – they make a contribution to society (a phrase which sounds trite but is fundamental) ... . You can look around and still see people who are interested in money and nothing else, but the underlying drives come largely from a desire to do something else – to make a product – to give a service – generally to do something that is of value.

Speech by Dave Packard to HP managers March 8, 1960, quoted in David Packard, *The HP Way*, Harper Collins, 1995, p ix-xx

the extent to which it stays true to its mantra of "Think Different". Apple's success is the result of its astonishing run of groundbreaking, innovative products. Its profitability and its share price is a measure of its success, but the fundamental source of Apple's success is its continued ability to produce remarkable devices that enhance people's lives. If Apple's ingenuity dries up and it loses its intuitive grasp for the way in which people relate to new technologies, its profitability and its share price will also falter. But the downward shift in these measures will be mere symptoms of the disease (should Apple ever fall sick in this way), and not the disease itself. You can't, after all, measure a company's capacity for creativity. So we measure the things that can be measured, but by the time we see some outward symptoms of the important, underlying problem – a fall-off in creativity and innovation – it is often too late.

Even the most obvious and essential metrics do not measure what really matters. Karen Phelan, author of *I'm Sorry I Broke Your Company: When Management Consultants Are the Problem, Not the Solution*, argues that what she calls "measurement madness" replaces long-term, meaningful objectives with short-term objectives that have the advantage of being measurable, but have little else to recommend them. Measures, she points out, can't make good decisions; only people can make good decisions, and only then when they understand the organization's long-term goals, not the short-term metrics.

Karen worked for many years as a management consultant for prestigious consultancy firms in the US. She began to believe that the various "solutions" that she had been trained to apply to organizational problems were not, in fact, what was solving the problem. What was solving the problem was her ability to get people together to recognize the issues and to work together to find a solution.

Karen realized that it wasn't the "methodologies, models, metrics, processes, and systems" that she was implementing on behalf of her consultancy that were doing the trick. It was her social skills in helping to bring people together to work better. But, as a management consultant, Karen wasn't able to say that her expertise lay in her social skills. Management consultants don't *do* social skills; what they do is bring highly complex technical corporate solutions that only a few initiates can hope to understand. That's what you pay consultants for.

For Karen, that was becoming a problem.

MAKING PEOPLE BEHAVE LIKE MACHINES

We spoke to Karen at her home in Hewitt, New Jersey. Most management consultants, in our experience, are careful to present themselves as being pretty formidable characters. This is a serious business, their body language tells you, and they themselves are uber-intelligent, mind-bogglingly hard-working, and pretty buttoned-down. This is not the time for idle chatter. They don't smile. They don't do jokes. They are here to get down to business. After all, time is money. And finally, just to get things clear on the issue at hand, they are much cleverer than you are. Much. Now, how can they help?

Karen Phelan is clearly highly intelligent and dauntingly hard working. You don't get to work for Deloitte's and other blue-chip consultancies unless those boxes are clearly ticked. But she is also warm, approachable, and generous with her time. She has wavy, shoulder-length blond hair that is only nominally under control. To meet Karen is to realize immediately that she is a very nice person. This, as you have probably noticed yourselves, is not the usual first impression given by management consultants.

'LOFTY, INTANGIBLE, CONTINUOUS GOALS'

When talking about organizations' obsession with short-term metrics, Karen draws an analogy with a person wanting to lose weight. A short-term goal, she writes, might be "to lose twenty-five pounds in six months". But a short-term obsession with achieving this result could lead to damaging results:

> To achieve this goal you could diet, but afterward, you'd likely gain the weight back. If you choose to exercise, then you run the risk of gaining weight by building muscle because muscle weighs more than fat. If you aren't anywhere near your target weight at five months, you may become tempted to starve yourself. This has the harmful effect of ruining your metabolism, making you more prone to weight gain. Or you may try a more extreme form of exercising, which makes you more prone to injury.

It's much better, Phelan suggests, to stay focussed on the long-term objective: "I want to improve my overall level of health and fitness." This objective is not time-bound, and nor, interestingly, is it "achievable". There will never be a moment in time when the objective has been achieved; it represents a process of continuous improvement.

KAREN PHELAN, AUTHOR, *I'M SORRY I BROKE YOUR COMPANY*
CONFUSING A MAP WITH THE TERRAIN
I went into consulting with very much the mind-set that people are logical. The world behaves in a logical fashion and there were cause and effect relationships between things – very much that sort of logical perspective of the world. I quickly realized that's not the way the world works. After a client made an illogical decision, I started getting interested in more of the people side, and how people made decisions, how people learn, how people assimilate information.

I do think that a lot of our methodologies are still rooted in Taylorism [the principles of scientific management set out by Frederick Winslow Taylor], and it's very much the machine approach: we need to make people act like machines in order to be more productive. And my philosophy is that people aren't broken.

Businesses love measurement because they mistakenly believe that numbers are real data. I have likened it to confusing a map with the terrain. Instead of watching where you're going and looking at what you're stepping on, you've got your face in the map. It's a representation of what is, and the map can't give you the fuller picture of the terrain you're in.

I think the whole measurement mind-set has gotten out of control. I mean it seems so easy. It is so easy in some ways. But when you look behind the measures, you forget that its people who are doing the data collection, people who are creating the measures, there's so much room for fudging it, but because it's a number, people automatically assume that it's true.

Karen Phelan in conversation with the authors

This is the kind of objective that companies should embrace, Phelan argues: "lofty, intangible, continuous goals". Any short-term metrics that we measure in an attempt to ensure that we are on track to achieve our lofty, intangible, continuous goals are not the real goals, and they must not become the management process itself:

The way to help people make good decisions is to ensure that

they understand the company's overall goals and priorities and
that they have the tools and knowledge to help them improve
their judgment. Measurements can probably help with that, but
replacing management with measurement is nothing short of
measure-mental. [7]

EVALUATING INTANGIBLES

Metrics, by definition, tell us only about things that can be measured
in a fairly straightforward way: units, costs, speeds, variances,
margins, returns on investment – that kind of thing.

But what really matters to the success of any organization will
be far less tangible: things to do with that messiest of arenas –
the relationships between the people in the organization, and the
relationship between the organization and the outside world.

Intriguingly, Jim Stengel, former marketing director for Proctor
and Gamble, one of the biggest companies in the world, also
believes in intangibles. In fact, he argues that the most successful
companies in the world are successful precisely because they focus
on intangible ideals.

In his 2012 book *Grow: How Ideals Power Growth and Profit at the
World's 50 Greatest Companies*, Stengel reminds us that even stock
markets have to acknowledge the importance of intangibles. Most
of the value of major companies, he writes, does not reside in their
physical assets, but in their intangible assets, such as skills, abilities,
people, and the power of brands:

> *In 1980, virtually the entire market capitalization of the S&P 500*
> *companies consisted of tangible assets (cash, offices, plants,*
> *equipment, inventories, etc.). In 2010, tangible assets accounted*
> *for only 40–45% of the S&P 500 companies' market capitalization.*
> *The rest of their capitalization consisted of intangible assets, and*
> *about half of that – more than 30% of total market capitalization –*
> *came from brand.*[8]

So, interestingly, big business and Wall Street acknowledge the
existence of powerful intangible forces at work in the world's most

significant businesses. Brands have a value. A glass of Coca-Cola is not just a glass of flavoured soda water; for the loyal consumer, it is the sum of all of the emotional messages that Coca-Cola has disseminated over the years. It's "the pause that refreshes"; it's Santa Claus in a Coca-Cola-themed red-and-white outfit; it's "the real thing"; "things go better" when you are drinking Coca-Cola.

Brain scans reveal that tasting Coca-Cola while blindfold triggers brain responses that relate only to basic responses like thirst and taste. Under these conditions, people tend to prefer the taste of Pepsi (embarrassingly for Coca-Cola) – a well-documented effect that has been dubbed the "Pepsi Paradox".

But when the Coca-Cola brand livery is revealed, a part of what we tend to call our "conscious" mind (the ventromedial prefrontal cortex, since you ask) takes over, bringing a whole range of associations and expectations to the taste of the drink. With the brand visible, people say that they prefer the taste of Coca-Cola.

What we "taste" is a construct our mind concocts from a range of sources. People with damage to their ventromedial prefrontal cortex don't experience this effect – they judge their colas on taste alone, and their preferences do not change when brand names are revealed.[9]

The same "added value" applies to a TAG Heuer Watch, a Prada bag, or a Ferrari automobile. The perceived value of these goods is more than the sum of their parts. This value resides "out there" in the collective unconscious of the brands' consumers (and would-be consumers).

The skillsets and capabilities of an organization also have value. Companies like Dyson, Samsung, Pfizer, and Google have a market value with a built-in mark-up that springs from our belief that the talented people in these organizations will continue to come up with brilliant new ideas and products. We try to put a monetary value on these intangibles, because we can't stop ourselves (oh, how we love a metric!) and because these things do, demonstrably, have immense value.

So, intangibles like "brand value" and "this company's proven ability to come up with innovative new products" and even "this company's can-do attitude" are known and proven to have real, cash money value. *But none of these things are capable of being measured on the typical steam-engine dashboard of metrics.*

MEASURING THE WRONG THINGS

Stengel takes his thinking about intangibles further. When he analysed the performance of the world's top 50 companies, he came to the conclusion that what set them apart from the competition was that their brands embodied an ideal: that there was a promise to the consumer that went beyond mere benefits, and which offered customers an experience that would improve their lives in some way.

This is interesting, because it is quite a philosophical point, and Stengel is not a very philosophical kind of guy. We don't mean to be rude, but Stengel is a big business, big bucks, "show me the money" kind of guy. He just is. So when he says that what really creates the success of the world's 50 greatest companies is something as intangible as a "brand ideal", we are entitled to sit up and take notice.

Here's what Stengel writes in *Grow* about brand ideals:

The Stengel Study team and I analyzed each business in the top 50 to identify its ideal, and we found all brands had an ideal of improving life in some way appropriate for their category. Some brands, like Google and IBM, have obvious life-improving ideals. Google exists to immediately satisfy every curiosity, IBM to help build a smarter planet. Other brands, like Moët & Chandon and Diesel, bring an extra dimension to life, providing their consumers with a special experience that enhances life. Moët & Chandon's ideal is to transform occasions into celebrations, and Diesel's ideal is to inspire imagination and endless possibilities in style. So when I use the phrase "improving life" when I discuss brand ideals, there is, of course, a continuum in how deeply these 50 brands impact life. But they all do impact life in their own ways.[10]

What Stengel is saying goes beyond just clever marketing. These ideals represent the reason for the companies' existence; they inform everything that they do.

You may choose to be cynical about this, but we believe it this is an important truth. Businesses do not exist simply to make money; they have a purpose. If they don't, they tend to fail, because nobody wants to do business with a company that has no purpose. So when IBM says that it wants to help build a smarter planet, it means it, and we like and respect IBM for it.

Stengel realized that this was the key to the resurgence of Proctor and Gamble's Pampers, the disposable diaper brand that had been suffering as a result of heavy competition from Kimberly Clark's revitalized Huggies brand. (We realize that British readers will be reminding themselves that a "diaper" is actually a "nappy", but since the rest of the world probably has no idea that a nappy is a diaper, we will stick with the American term).

A "BRAND IDEAL" FOR A DIAPER?

What could be less glamorous than a disposable diaper? This, surely, is the ultimately functional product: it does its job well, or less well. End of story. As a result of this thinking, the Pampers team, quite sensibly, focussed on "dryness". *Will this diaper keep my baby's wee off its clothes and bedclothes for a reasonable length of time?* That was the question the team they expected parents to ask, and to be most concerned about.

But then Stengel, working with the advertising agency Saatchi and Saatchi, saw that parents had a deeper relationship with the brand, and one that involved that most precious of things: their babies' health and development. A diaper that keeps a baby dry helps the baby get a good night's sleep, for example. The quality of a child's diaper is part of that child's quality of life.

The advertising campaign that resulted from this way of thinking was crystallized in the slogan "Inspired by babies, created by Pampers". This approach to the brand led to a new stated brand ideal of "partnering with moms in their babies' development". As Stengel writes:

> *Trust, honesty, respect, caring, warmth, and humour aren't the criteria most companies use to develop and measure their communications. But they are the criteria the most successful businesses use. When we evaluated the P&G businesses that were growing far faster than average, we found that those with a trust advantage over competitors had a huge market share advantage.*[11]

In other words, intangibles like trust, honesty, respect, caring, warmth, and humour are the things that matter most for some of the world's most powerful and profitable brands. Stengel believes that these intangibles can and should be measured to ensure the continued health of these brands – but then, he's a died-in-the-wool, old-school marketing man. You can't do marketing without measuring things!

Stengel is not entirely wrong, though; as he well knows, such entirely human measures as truth, honesty, respect, caring, warmth, and humour will require a qualitative, not quantitative evaluation. We can *evaluate* these things but not measure them, just as we can evaluate the strength of someone's friendship but not measure it.

We have to realize and accept – as Stengel has implicitly accepted – that what really matters about an organization's relationship with the outside world is, actually, intangible – and, truly speaking, immeasurable. We can get some kind of *assessment* of degrees of "trust, honesty, respect, caring, warmth, and humour", but let's not kid ourselves – these are not measurements.

Intangibles matter. Intangibles drive success and create or destroy billions of dollars of value. They are not really measureable – because they are intangible. Our Enlightenment-driven, rational, emotionless minds don't like that, so we invent "measures" for these things.

But try the same thing in the personal sphere:

Exactly how much, on a scale of one to ten, can we trust this person? Six? What does that mean, "six"? Do we go into business with a six? Supposing they're really a five and it's, like, random?

"She thinks you're warm and funny." Really? Cool. Exactly how warm and funny? I'm not going on a date with someone based on some woolly notion of "warm and funny". I need numbers.

Maybe not.

Let's remind ourselves about a couple of other inconvenient truths about metrics.

MARK POWELL
TAKING THE PULSE OF THE ORGANISATION
I think about the concept of the pulse – so, if you take large capital projects in the oil and gas industry as an example, I've worked within a number of project teams where, about half way through the project, all the standard metrics would have told you that everything was going brilliantly. The project was on time. The project was on schedule and all the weekly, monthly dashboards around where everything was, were looking really good.

But I sat in some of those projects in that situation and I can tell you, categorically, it was painfully obvious that the project was in trouble. It was in trouble because you could see that the relationships were fractured between the team and other stakeholders. You could see that there were political issues on the horizon, none of which was being reflected in the metrics.

So the metrics that had been reported, actually, were giving a completely false view about the situation that the project was actually in. As it turned out, that particular project actually ended up in court.

Another way these things link together, I think, is the issues around inputs and outputs. If you go back to the capital project example, what a project really needs to understand at any given time in the project, is 'What are the things, what is the *pulse* that could affect the ability to deliver to time and schedule?'

That's much more important than where you are in time and schedule, in many cases. Issues around relationships and human energy and creativity and conflict – lots of things that are hard to measure, which is why people don't want to go there. But there is a real and hugely valuable opportunity going forward for organisations to start thinking around developing ways of diagnosing and measuring pulses in organisations – things that are driving success but are not necessarily being translated into physical output measures.

You might then get a much more sensible connection between inputs and outputs. I think organisations should think around saying: 'These are our output metrics and these are our input metrics', but they talk about metrics in a much more generic sense, so I think we are measuring many of the wrong things.

Mark Powell in conversation with co-author, Jonathan Gifford

MEASURES CAN DRIVE THE WRONG BEHAVIOURS

There are any number of examples of the way in which choosing any one metric and using that to drive the "right kind of behaviour" nearly always goes horribly wrong. You know the kind of thing:

- Bus companies decide to measure and reward bus drivers' ability to keep to the timetable. The result: bus drivers drive past bus stops full of waiting customers, because stopping to pick up passengers will make them miss their deadline.
- The British government tasks the country's National Health Service with ensuring that no patient waits more than 18 weeks for an operation. Hospitals begin to cancel operations for people who had already waited for more than 18 weeks, since the hospital can only meet its targets by treating patients who are still within the 18-week period. For the first group of patients, waiting times for operations become even longer.
- Within the same NHS's "18 weeks" initiative, there are some get-out clauses for hospitals; patients who refuse to accept an appointment for surgery go back to the beginning of the queue, for example. Hospitals start to offer patients appointments at short notice at inconvenient times in the hope that they will not accept.
- Loan officers at banks are rewarded by the number of home loans that they issue. Loan officers begin to issue loans to borrowers who are highly likely to default. Banks pay bonuses to sales people who will cost them money; customers are given loans that will end in misery and debt.

The list goes on, and every example is driven by the same thing: a mistaken belief that focussing on any one measure will drive overall success. At the heart of these broken incentive systems lies the same steam engine assumption: that you cannot allow people to use their best judgement. As Karen Phelan writes in *I'm Sorry I Broke Your Company*: "Given the direction – emphasis is on direction and not directive – humans are usually able to judge what to do. Funny thing, when you remove human judgment from decision making, you get decisions that are not judicious."[12]

METRICS LAG REALITY

Very few business metrics happen in real time. Those that do (such as production figures or resource consumption) are still a reflection of previous decisions and previous actions. It may well be very useful to see that a certain metric has gone "orange" or even "red". But it's much better to have one's finger on the pulse of what is driving the organization, and to sense a problem in the making.

The verb "sense" is used here with great deliberation. There are no metrics that will prove where the problem lies; this is a matter for well-informed human intuition.

THE NUMBERS DO LIE

There is no agreement on what some of our most straightforward financial measures should actually measure. What is included in a unit cost? What represents capital expenditure as opposed to an expense? What constitutes an asset?[13] These are things that keep teams of accountants happy for days, working away to produce the answer that somebody (probably a stock market analyst) wants to see in a quarterly report.

There's another important thing to remember: measures are invented, collected, and interpreted by people, and this gives people a lot of room for manoeuvre. With a bit of creativity, it is nearly always possible to produce the "right" figure – the one that justifies our decisions, or gets the result that we hoped for (like a rise in the share price).

These measures should never be taken as a true sign of the organization's health: let's all remember Enron, which, with a lot of help from its auditor, Arthur Andersen, kept producing remarkably good sets of corporate figures right up until it imploded in 2001.

TAKING THE ORGANIZATION FROM THE INDUSTRIAL ERA TO THE AGE OF IDEAS

Transforming the steam engine, one step at a time

- We are wrongly obsessed with measuring relatively simplistic metrics
  - Metrics are useful but they are not the full picture
- Metrics are what can be measured

- The most important indicators of an organization's health are intangible – they can be evaluated, but not measured
- Organisations focus on measuring outputs
  - Evaluating inputs is harder but more meaningful
  - Take 'the pulse' of the organisation as a whole
- Intangibles lie at the heart of success or failure, from the "lofty, intangible, continuous goals" that will inspire success, to the subtle breakdowns in relationships that will doom a project to failure
- What really matters is the pulse of the organization or project – the general state of health that will allow it to deliver its purpose
- Focussing on simplistic measures can drive bad behaviours
- Metrics lag reality
- The numbers do lie

CHAPTER 3

LOSE THE FRUIT BOWL
WHEN "EFFICIENCY" MASKS LACK OF AMBITION

In the earlier chapters about steam-engine organizations' obsession with control and measurement, there are many references to "efficiency".

Efficiency is the end, the justification, the *excuse* for all of the initiative-sapping but supposedly scientific management programmes that are put in place from time to time, especially (but not exclusively) in times of crisis.

The people who make up any organization (and let's remind ourselves that organizations are collections of people brought together for a common purpose) are often required to jump through various infinitely tedious bureaucratic hoops, to forgo various small pleasures, to cut costs to the point where product or service quality is compromised, and to work themselves and their colleagues to an unproductive standstill – typically as a result of a piece of steam-engine dogma that managers have swallowed hook line and sinker, without question or examination. These measures, steam-engine managers repeat by rote, will make the organization more *efficient*.

The steam engine will run more efficiently, we are told, if only we would stop doing a number of things that we had previously done, many of which typically involve extracting a small amount of enjoyment from our work, either in terms of producing something of which we can genuinely feel proud, or of deriving a small amount of pleasure from the process of work itself: like having a chat and perhaps even a cup of coffee while we discuss an interesting aspect of work with our colleagues.

And, of course, if business looks really bad, steam-engine managers will decide (often surprisingly early in the process) that the only solution to the problem is a *real* efficiency drive – which of course entails "letting go" large numbers of people.

The organization is now not only in an adverse business position, it has lost a proportion of its key resource – its people – and the people that remain feel vulnerable, demoralized, and demotivated.

Efficiency, like measurement and control, is a favoured comfort blanket for people of the steam-engine mentality.

Management must at all times be in control of every aspect of the organization, otherwise efficiency will suffer. This can only be achieved by measuring our progress against a number of key performance indicators. When these indicate that our business performance is suffering, we must act quickly to maintain our competitive edge.

We've all heard that said so often, possibly in exactly that form of words, that we no longer even question its sense or meaning.

Of course an organization needs to be efficient; *of course* we need to be in overall control of its operations; *of course* we need some key measures of our progress toward the desired result. But for steam-engine organizations, these concerns become ends in themselves. The real goal – to achieve the organizations' long-term purpose – is subsumed to the more easily managed but ultimately insignificant goal of operating "efficiently". It is the exact equivalent of having an army that is perfectly turned out, behaves impeccably on the parade ground, and is very careful not to spend too much on equipment, but which is incapable of winning a real battle. After all, things get messy on the battlefield. Uniforms get messed up. Ammunition is wasted. Soldiers and equipment get destroyed. It's all terribly inefficient. But the army that has the will and the resources to fight and win is the one that achieves the purposes for which it exists. There is literally no point in having the other, "efficient" kind of army.

No organization can afford to waste money, but neither can it hope to achieve its real purpose if it obsessed by efficiency and has no appetite for risk and investment, or if its people are demoralized and cowed. There are few better investments in the modern world than investment in a talented and motivated workforce.

The unthinking drive for "efficiency" typically does four, quite terrible, very steam-engine things:

- It assumes that the cheapest way of achieving any particular result is the best and indeed the only acceptable way
- It sees people as an expense to be avoided if at all possible, so that "efficiency drive" has become synonymous with "wage cut" and "layoffs"
- It destroys people's energy by imposing small-minded, supposedly money-saving impositions, or by withdrawing motivational "luxuries" because they are "non-essential"
- In its most dangerous form, steam-engine efficiency stifles opportunity – it fails to seek out the positive actions that could transform the situation and focuses instead on the negative actions that attempt to limit the damage. Steam-engine organizations cut their costs (and especially their "people costs") to match the new reality, rather than trying to use their resources (including their people) to take the organization to a new and better place.

Let's have a look at each of these steam engine 'efficiencies.'

CHEAPEST IS BEST, AND PEOPLE ARE EXPENSIVE

"There is scarcely anything in the world that some man cannot make a little worse and sell a little cheaper."

This delightful quotation is attributed to the 19th-century British art critic and writer, John Ruskin. The same principle could now be taken as a kind of definition of globalisation: the mad dash to manufacture our goods wherever in the world they can be made most cheaply. If we do not do this, we tell ourselves, the price of our goods will become uncompetitive.

Sometimes the labour force elsewhere in the world is more affordable because the standard of living is lower, and it takes fewer dollars to pay someone a living wage. Sometimes the labour force is more affordable because it is desperate, and will accept any level of wage, any number of working hours, and any standard of workplace health and safety – pretty much the conditions that existed in the first manufactories in 19th-century Britain. So much for progress.

All right-minded global corporations ensure that they do not exploit labour forces that fall into the second category. Many highly successful businesses also do not buy into the "cheapest is best" philosophy, whether in terms of the steam-engine business philosophy that says "I am driven by economic forces that I cannot resist to pay the workforce as little as possible" or in terms of the equally outmoded idea that there is no alternative to offering the cheapest possible version of any product or service.

There is, as John Ruskin remarked over a hundred years ago, always a market for something that is less well made but cheaper. There is also always a market for a product that is better made, or a service that is better delivered, but which is also slightly more expensive. There is also always a market for any customer-facing organization whose employees are well trained, enthusiastic, and happy in their work.

A key argument of this book is that it is not hard to find examples of businesses that have chosen to move away from the old, 19th-century ways of running organizations. Many academics, business thinkers, and entrepreneurs have been pointing out for quite some time that there is an alternative way of doing business; that the 19th-century organizational model is not the only show in town.

These examples are out there, staring us in the face, reported regularly in the mainstream business press. "That's interesting," we seem to say, "but it wouldn't work for our own organization."

It is time to recognize that there is an alternative way to do business to the outmoded steam-engine model – or, more likely, that there are several alternative ways to do business, and that every one of these is almost certainly a better, more effective alternative.

Let's look at two well-documented examples, Costco and Zappos.

COSTCO: YOU GET WHAT YOU PAY FOR

Costco, the major international "big box" discount retailer, pays higher wages to its staff than the industry average, because it believes (and can prove) that the benefits in improved staff retention and motivation mean that its total staff bill is lower as a percentage of sales than rivals such as Walmart.

In a 2004 interview with *Businessweek* online, James Sinegal, co-founder and former CEO of Costco, talked about his organization's approach to staff wages and staff morale and retention:

> *In every country where we conduct business, we pay good wages. Not just the US. We have Costcos in the UK, Canada, Mexico, Japan, South Korea, Taiwan, and Puerto Rico. We always strive to be the best in the wage package. We think it's good business. In the final analysis, you get what you pay for. Better employees mean higher productivity. We've proven that with our business model. We want to turn our inventory faster than our people. We are a company that promotes 100% within the company. So it's even more important to hire good people and give them good jobs and good wages. They are the people who are going to run your business.*
>
> *[Paying low wages] doesn't pay the right dividends. It doesn't keep employees happy. It keeps them looking for other jobs. Plus, managers spend all their time hiring replacements rather than running your business. We would rather have our employees running our business. When employees are happy, they are your very best ambassadors.*[14]

Costco's wage policy is still in force and is still producing good results today. At the end of 2013, Costco posted profits of $537m, up 36% over the same period for the previous year. The current CEO, Craig Jelinek, has defended the company's policy of paying higher wages to its own workforce and supported calls for a nationwide raise in the US minimum wage. "At Costco, we know that paying employees good wages makes good sense for business," he said in 2013. "Instead of minimizing wages, we know it's a lot more profitable in the long term to minimize employee turnover and maximize employee productivity, commitment and loyalty. We support efforts to increase the federal minimum wage."[15]

ZAPPOS: TO MAKE CUSTOMERS HAPPY, YOU NEED A HAPPY SALES TEAM

Tony Hsieh, co-founder and CEO of online shoe retailer, Zappos, always believed that Zappos was "a service company that just happened to sell shoes". His point was that the focus is on service. If you kept your customers happy, they would come back for more. More importantly, they would tell their friends about your wonderful service. Your business would grow through word of mouth without expensive advertising.

To make a happy customer, Hsieh believed, you needed happy sales people. Hsieh's genius was to accept, in the face of all conventional steam engine wisdom, that the typical "battery farm" approach to sales call centres does not breed happy sales people.

Hsieh removed most of the rules and regulations – there was no longer a set sales script, and no time limit on how long a customer service call should take. Sales people were empowered to do whatever it took to make a customer happy. A new record for the longest call was set in December 2012, when Customer Loyalty Team member Shaea Labus spent 9 hours and 37 minutes on a call to customer named Lisa. "Sometimes people just need to call and talk," Shaea said. "We don't judge, we just want to help."[16]

Well – how inefficient is *that*?

Sales staff at Zappos are given free food and drink, and are offered a free dry-cleaning service. There is a "nap room", encouraging team members to take a break and have a snooze, which Hsieh believes promotes productivity. Teams are encouraged to spend time together outside the office, even on "company time", to create team loyalty. Team members are encouraged to decorate their workspaces any which way they want, to express their individuality. Something of a party atmosphere seems to be norm, and is clearly encouraged.[17] The company motto is "Deliver WOW! Through Service".

Zappos accepts returns for a period of twelve months after the initial order, and covers postage costs both ways. You order as many shoes as you want, try them on, and return the ones you don't want – maybe eleven months after you bought them.

Insanity!

This certainly isn't "efficient", in the steam-engine sense, but in the broader, more holistic, more organic view of business, Zappos's crazy "happy sales team = happy customer" philosophy makes hard-nosed business sense. Zappos gets to charge a premium price for its shoes and its service; its ecstatic customers do Zappos's marketing for them through word of mouth, saving millions in advertising costs.

Zappos was bought by Amazon in 2009, with a valuation of $1.2 billion, on the express condition that Amazon would respect and preserve the unique culture of Zappos, which it has.

LOSE THE FRUIT BOWL

A classic example of steam-engine thinking is often revealed when times get tough. A financial crisis reveals the need for urgent change; the first reaction of steam-engine organizations is to remove small perks and privileges. It may have been company policy to provide tea and coffee at business meetings, and perhaps even pastries and biscuits; in these health-conscious days, there may even have been a fruit bowl.

Faced with a financial problem, the first reaction of most steam-engine organizations is to take away the free tea and coffee, and definitely the expensive fruit bowl.

"We have a serious problem here," the managers presumably reason. "We are down against target. We can't afford to squander money on unnecessary items."

A few hundred dollars have been saved, when in fact the size of the financial crisis is, by definition, considerably larger. People's motivation has been reduced at a time when highly motivated people are most needed. The future looks bleak for everyone at exactly the time the organization needs people to imagine a brighter, better future.

A FAILURE OF AMBITION?

In a broader context, the fruit -bowl effect poses a different question about the focus and ambition of organizations. Organizations may need to take a billion dollars out in cost reductions, yet it never seems to occur to them to ask the question: "What would we need to do to find another billion in top line revenue? Maybe that would be a better way of focusing our resources."

Steam-engine organizations tend to default to the least ambitious option – something they can control and measure and monitor as you would if they were running a cotton mill, such as: "I sit here and the demand for cotton has gone down, so the question is, which machine do I shut down first?" – rather than looking outwardly and thinking: "How do I actually grow this organization? How do I deal with the market challenges? How do I refocus the efforts and the

☆ ☆

MARK POWELL

I've been a consultant for 25 years and I've designed and taught executive development and leadership programmes for probably more than a decade, so I'd like to flatter myself that this has given me a pretty good opportunity of looking at organisational issues from both sides – both as someone who has sat in many organisations and someone who also has observed the results of other organisations. I've become increasingly aware of something which I call The Fruit Bowl Effect, which I think summarises some of the inherent challenges and issues for steam engine organisations.

I remember, a number of years ago, I worked for a large global company; for reasons that will soon become obvious, I won't say who it was. I was a senior managing director in the organisation and a number of things happened in the market that meant that the organisation went through a huge market transformation in terms of its economics. It went from making more money than it knew what to do with to suddenly having to face some really serious financial challenges. What I witnessed absolutely shocked me at the time. I'm going to say exactly what happened, in a kind of compressed time scale. This was exactly what happened, but I'll put it in the context of a week, whereas this happened over two or three months.

So, the bottom fell out of the market that this organisation was in and the reaction was, on day one, they did take the fruit bowls away! They started removing all the free food and the free coffee and the free tea. It's kind of odd that you'd start there in an organisation that was in serious trouble, but that's exactly where they started.

So that was on Monday. On Tuesday, they fired approximately 3,000 people. So these are 3,000 human beings with mortgages and families energy of the individuals that make up the organization?"

The fruit-bowl effect has two insidious effects.

When organizations focus first on cutting costs, they are already focusing on the wrong thing. Cutting costs may be essential in the end – nobody is immune to the need for cutbacks in difficult business conditions – but the first focus should be on cause of the business problem, and on the positive steps that that could be taken

☆ ☆

and school fees to pay who are effectively reduced and taken out of the organisation incredibly quickly, with no great thought in reality for what that meant for them, let alone for the organisation itself. On Wednesday, they finally got rid of the first corporate jet, but not before the first 3,000 people had been fired. So you sit there and think: that's quite interesting – that they were more interested in trying to keep a corporate jet on the tarmac than 3,000 people's livelihoods; and you think, 'That tells you an awful lot about the fundamental organisational psychology'. On the Thursday, about 5,000 more people were effectively fired and on the Friday, the second corporate jet went. So, at the end of that week they'd taken away the fruit bowls, fired 8,000 people and taken two corporate jets out – but the two corporate jets were very much the last things that they wanted to take out.

It makes you realise increasingly that organisational approaches to efficiency are strange. The Fruit Bowl Effect starts at the bottom, looking for things that are easy to cut out, but without any recognition of what this actually does to people and how it affects them. Interestingly, many years later when I was running leadership programmes and I saw many organisations going through the same process, I was stunned to recognise that they did exactly the same thing – the fruit bowls always went first. Organisations have become so focussed on an efficiency mindset that when push comes to shove all they know how to do is to cut costs. They don't actually think about value. They don't think about the top line, because they can't control it, but they can control the fruit bowls or the size of the fruit bowls.

Mark Powell in conversation with Jonathan Gifford

to re-create the missing revenue.

The other effect is the damage that misguided "efficiencies" do to what matters most of all – the human energy of the organization.

The recent history of the consumer products giant Procter & Gamble offers a perfect example of the dangers of an inward-looking focus on "efficiency" and of the great benefits that can come from an outward-looking focus on growth.

PROCTER AND GAMBLE: LOOKING OUTWARD

When A.G. Lafley took over as CEO of Procter & Gamble in 2000, the company was in considerable trouble. As *Time* magazine reported in 2002: "P&G had repeatedly failed to deliver expected earnings, and its stock tumbled 50% in six months."

With most of the company's resources and best people focused on developing the next blockbuster new product, sales for the established brands were stagnating, market share was eroding, and morale was sliding. Lafley's predecessor, Durk Jager, had been asked to leave the company after what the *Time* magazine reporter described as "an overly aggressive, ill-timed restructuring program" left a good number of P&G's 110,000 employees in new jobs, "disoriented and distracted."[18] As you have probably guessed, this "aggressive restructuring" involved the closing down of plants and the elimination of many jobs.[19]

What Lafley did was not to embark on another "restructuring program". In fact, his big realization was that P&G had developed an unhealthy, steam-engine-like obsession with its own internal operations, and had lost its focus on the real, outside world – the world of consumers. Lafley's outward-looking collaboration programme opened up the company to anyone who thought they had a good idea that P&G might be able to take to market. Constant innovation was seen as the key to developing and extending the company's array of established and successful brands.

Lafley also made a number of key acquisitions, including the purchase of Clairol's hair-care business in 2001 and the massive, $57 billion acquisition of Gillette in 2005. But even this was driven by innovation. "We didn't buy Gillette because we wanted their male shaving business," Lafley explained in an interview with *Smart Business* magazine in 2011. "We bought Gillette because we thought Gillette would be a fabulous platform for male personal care innovation for the next 50 or 100 years. Innovation drove everything."[20]

What Lafley did with Procter & Gamble after 2000 was to refuse to succumb to an inward-looking, steam-engine mentality. Rather than trying to fix the steam engine with the usual approach of "imposing efficiencies" to match costs to the organization's reduced circumstances, Lafley encouraged the organization to look for new opportunities in the outside world. He did undertake one entirely sane "efficiency" measure: he rationalized the company's product range to focus on household products, baby care, health and beauty, and male grooming. Now that *is* efficiency: focus on your company's purpose, get rid of distractions, and fulfil your purpose excellently.

When Lafley took over P&G in 2000, the company had 10 $1 billion brands; when he retired in 2010 (Lafley was subsequently asked to return to the company in 2013), P&G had 24 $1 billion brands, sales had doubled, and profits had quadrupled. What *BusinessWeek* had described as a potential "death spiral" for P&G[21] had been turned into a period of focussed growth.

MAINTAINING THE ORGANIZATION'S HUMAN ENERGY

The second insidious effect of a knee-jerk search for efficiencies in difficult times is the huge impact that this has on the people in that organization – like P&G's "disoriented and distracted" team in the wake of A.G. Lafley's predecessor's "aggressive" restructuring programme.

Organizations are ultimately collections of human beings with a finite amount of energy. The ability to manage that energy in a positive way to achieve the organization's purpose is the key task of the organization's leadership. The fruit-bowl effect, with its focus on efficiency at the expense of all other things, destroys huge amounts of human energy. If an organization succeeds in taking out 10% of its operating costs, but at the cost of losing 20% of the human energy that drives its success, they have almost certainly made a very bad bargain indeed. Even if the organization survives the crisis, a legacy of mistrust is left among staff who see that they and their colleagues are regarded as dispensable – that they are indeed the first things to be let go – as soon as the organization meets difficulties.

In one study, Harvard Business School professor, Teresa Amabile, and researcher and writer, Steven Kramer, looked at management behaviour in a company that professed to embrace innovation as a core principle: they noted that the company's annual report featured the word 'innovation' three times in the first five sentences.

But, in practice, the company's actual focus on prioritizing cost reductions 'drove new-product innovation into the ground'.

As one of the company's engineers wrote in the diary that employees had been asked to keep for the researchers: "Today I found out that our team will be concentrating on [cost savings] for the next several months instead of any new products. ... It is getting very difficult to concentrate on removing pennies from the standard cost of an item. That is the only place that we have control over. Most of the time, quality suffers. It seems that our competition is putting out new products at a faster rate. ... We are no longer the leader in innovation. We are the followers."

When they had finished collecting their data, the researchers found that many employees had become "completely disengaged" and that "some of the very best had left."[22]

Addressing business problems by losing the fruit bowls and starting "efficiency drives" that destroy people's energy and trust is not the route to business success.

TAKING THE ORGANIZATION FROM THE INDUSTRIAL ERA TO THE AGE OF IDEAS
Transforming the steam engine, one step at a time
- Being efficient is a means to the end, not the end in itself
  - Wasting time, money or energy is inefficient;
    doing everything possible to achieve a goal is not
- In times of stress, increasing 'efficiency' is a natural reflex
  - Focussing on using resources to drive improvements
    to the top line is more productive
- The cheapest solution is not necessarily the best

- Offering the cheapest product or service is a choice, not an obligation
- Rewarding colleagues well is an investment
- People are not resources
  - Selling the company jet is painless; sacking people has consequences for them and for the organisation
- Keep the fruit bowl
  - And the coffee and the tea and the free lunches and the dry cleaning ...
- Think positively; look for new opportunities
  - The best way out of decline is growth, not managed decline

CHAPTER 4

THE INNOVATION COMMITTEE
BE DISRUPTIVE: YOU HAVE TWO HOURS

At the heart, the very core, of all of the paradoxes that beset the steam engine, is innovation. If the organization's focus is on control, measurement, efficiency, predictability, lack of variation, then innovation is the last thing that the organization wants.

Innovation is inherently risky – it's different. We don't know where innovation might take us. This creates a very deep paradox for the steam-engine organization, because it knows that it needs innovation. The biggest threat to any industry is commoditisation: the increasing likelihood that people will not care whether they buy your particular product or service or somebody else's, in which case they will buy only on the basis of price. The process is visibly speeding up.

Even in the 20th century, if a company established a successful brand of soap, or breakfast cereal, or range of clothing, there was a good chance that their brand would dominate the market for decades. The BlackBerry mobile device, launched in 1999 by the small Canadian company Research in Motion, brought email and mobile telephony to a grateful business community, desperate to be able to access their emails and voice messages anytime, anywhere. A decade later, in 2009, *Fortune* magazine named BlackBerry as the fastest-growing company in the world, with an annual growth rate of 84%. But by then the company had already failed to spot the potential of the consumer market for what would become known as smartphones, with their sexy swipe screens and an ever growing library of downloadable third party apps: a devastatingly innovative development that turned the smartphone into a platform – a kind of blank canvas – for the innovatory genius of thousands of developers out there in the wild, unmanageable, uncontrollable world.

BlackBerry was out-innovated by the Apple iPhone and by a range of other smartphones – and with frightening speed. In the autumn of 2013, BlackBerry shed 4,500 jobs, 40% of its workforce, in the face of huge losses.[23]

The smartphone itself is already at risk of commoditisation: while there is strong brand loyalty to Apple, Samsung, Nokia, and others, there is the growing risk – or likelihood – that a new generation of consumers will be happy to buy any device that delivers the same functionality at a lower price. In the meantime, and quite rightly, smartphone manufacturers continue to add various bells and whistles to their smartphones in order to differentiate themselves from their competitors, But one day, of course, someone will develop something that radically disrupts even the smartphone: a device that is a step-change ahead of the smartphone.

Constant innovation is the only hope to survival. But steam-engine organizations can't do innovation.

THE INNOVATION COMMITTEE

This chapter is called *The innovation committee* because, as we will discover in the next few pages, and as you may already have noted, steam-engine organizations tend to think that innovation is something that can be *managed* in exactly the same way that these organizations try to manage everything else that crosses their path.

"We clearly need more innovation," they sagely note, "so it is essential for us to set up a reliable innovation process. As a first step, we will create an innovation committee, which will be charged with the business of making us more innovative as an organization."

But innovation, like creativity, doesn't happen that way. If there was a process for generating breakthrough innovations, then all of mankind's problems would have been solved we would already be living in utopia.

Innovation is produced, by definition, by mavericks; by people who do not fit the current mould. By geniuses, screwballs, weirdoes, and freaks. It is not possible to create something radically different by

WOLFGANG GRULKE, *LESSONS IN RADICAL INNOVATION*
Evolutionary innovation is relatively risk-free and companies that innovate at this level generally focus on improvements at the "product" level – making them faster, better, cheaper.

Going up the innovation/risk ladder ... you enter the domain of innovation at the total business level, but of course risk increases exponentially. Beyond this, the company enters the domain of radical innovation ...

Here it is typical to encounter high-risk innovation that will change an entire industry ... Ultimately, radical innovations have the power to change global markets.

Brand Pretorius, CEO of McCarthy Retail, puts it succinctly: "Today, competition is no longer between products, it's between business models. And you can't get there through evolutionary change."

Wolfgang Grulke, *Lessons in Radical Innovation*, Financial Times/ Prentice Hall (Pearson Education Ltd), 2002, p 45

following a step-by-step process from the familiar; what is needed is the very essence of the creative act: a flash of brilliance; a leap into the unknown; a sudden spark of genius.

Call us pessimistic, but we haven't noticed any of these things emerging from the steam-engine committees that we have witnessed (and endured) in the last few decades, so we don't expect the current batch of innovation committees to crack this fundamental problem any time soon.

RISK, EVOLUTIONARY INNOVATION, AND RADICAL INNOVATION

Wolfgang Grulke, author of *10 Lessons from the Future and Lessons in Radical Innovation*, is the founder and chairman of FutureWorld, a networked global business and technology think tank. A former IBM executive, he is passionate about disruptive, radical innovation: the kind of game-shifting innovation that changes all of the rules.

He also believes that the very nature of steam-engine organizations condemns them to be unable to embrace such innovation.

"One of the functions of an organizational structure is to limit risk – to stop people doing things wrong; the opposite of innovation," he told us, his fluent and forceful English revealing faint traces of his family ties to both Germany and South Africa.

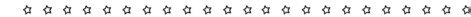

MARK POWELL
THE INNOVATION PROCESS
I've been working with an organization recently, a very successful organization in its sector, but increasing evidence from both its staff and customers made it very clear that it was not seen as being innovative. They were good at what they did but they did the same old stuff – they did it very, very well, but the market made it very clear that they were looking for new ideas from this organization.

So the organization said: "We must innovate." I went to a session where they were talking about innovation and I was presented with a process – "This is our process for how we're going to innovate." And I sat there and I thought: "You've already killed it." You can't innovate through a process. By definition, a process seeks to control, seeks to govern, seeks to limit what you can do; the mind-set of the organization was so endemically around control and focus and structure that it actually missed the whole fundamental concept of innovation, which is that innovation is something that is much more organic – it's about people being able to take risks, it's about people being able to be prepared to fail.

The second conversation that was had around this particular idea, which I thought was interesting, was: "Well, the best way of getting this off the ground is to make it look and feel as close to something we already do, so it's not so difficult." So, you sit there and you think: "So, what you're basically telling me is, you like the idea of a radical innovation but only if you can make it radically un-innovative and as close to what you do anyway, i.e. 'We'd like to radically innovate if you could make it more like a process innovation.'"

I think that's at the heart – there's this incredible paradoxical force between organizations that desperately do actually want and understand the need to radically innovate but there is this force like the Earth's gravity pulling you back to make it as close to process innovation, so that the organization can be happy

Very few people want to take risks with an existing successful organization, so the design of the organization is usually to limit risk, not to increase it. Everything escalates to the point where somebody says, "Gee, that's a risk" – and it stops.

The structure is actually designed to stop *innovation – you just can't innovate from an organization that is geared to reduce risk.*

☆ ☆

about it; so they can see that the risks they're taking are manageable; that it's not seen as a personal risk for individuals – and so they will process innovate again.

I'll give you another example that I think is quite interesting – another organization, same issue. What they were facing was that the internet was effectively destroying a big chunk of their business because it enabled other people to supply their services incredibly cheaply and to access a massive global market in a way that they simply couldn't with their much more traditional offering. So they accepted that they needed to rethink and be much more innovative and they started off with great thoughts and they actually created a very interesting incubation process whereby people would just bring completely bizarre ideas and say: "How about this?" – and actually it was working really rather well, I think, from what I was seeing.

It was really genuinely opening up new ideas and different conversations and trying to challenge a lot of conventional thinking, but it became increasingly clear that those running the organization were becoming more and more and more uncomfortable with it, because there was no obvious process that was going on. So they stopped that and put in an innovation process – "This is the process by which we will now innovate."

The irony was lost on them, although not on many others, that what they'd actually done had killed any opportunity to genuinely innovate. Not surprisingly, a number of months later, this organization is probably less innovative than it was six months ago. The natural gravitational pull of doing today what you did yesterday but maybe slightly better was just too strong and it was unable to overtake the governance, the control, the structures, the processes.

Mark Powell in conversation with co-author Jonathan Gifford

In my experience with FutureWorld, over the last 20 years, I don't think we've seen one organization that managed to do it. They can tinker at it, improve process and the usual stuff, but serious, radical, step-change innovation just doesn't happen in an organization steeped in the old school of management. They want things to be predictable: they want to set goals, they want to deliver to them, they want to meet targets — and that is the antithesis of innovation.

In *Lessons in Radical Innovation*, Grulke differentiates between evolutionary innovation, disruptive innovation, and radical innovation. Evolutionary innovation is the nice, gentle kind: we improve things bit by bit, but everything stays reassuringly familiar. Disruptive innovation can be brought about by a new technology (in the way that cellular networks disrupted the old fixed line telephony system), or by disrupting what Grulke calls "market linkages" (in the way that the development of the internet — a technological disruption — disrupted travel agencies' hold on flight and holiday bookings, allowing consumers to book direct or via a growing number of price comparison sites).

Radical innovation, argues Grulke, goes even further. It disrupts both technologies and market linkages; it is not merely disruptive but genuinely destructive, though it also offers immense creative potential. The eBook is a good example, threatening to destroy old markets and technologies (the bookshop and the printed book) while creating whole new markets and technologies (the book downloading market and eReaders and apps).

No organization can be blamed for being frightened of such radical innovation. This is exactly the kind of stuff that puts companies out of business overnight — which is genuinely scary. The solution is not, however, to put our heads under the blanket and hope that it does not happen to us. The solution is to be innovative ourselves. Even radically innovative.

LIVING WITH RISK

At the heart of steam-engine organizations' problem with innovation is, of course, the problem of risk, with the consequent possibility of failure. And you can't entirely blame them.

Steam-engine executives have been schooled in the notion that they are in charge of the machine; that their job is to analyse it and maintain it to ensure that it is running at peak efficiency. What you do not do, because the machine cannot be allowed to break down, is to try something risky. You might have a special "Research and Development" department who explore this kind of risky change, but it is very likely that even these people – supposedly removed from the day-to-day concerns about keeping the steam engine on the rails, going about its business and earning the organization's money – are probably focussing on how to make the steam engine go faster, or run more efficiently.

R&D might even be working on a diesel-powered locomotive to replace the steam-driven variety, but history confirms that it was not the America's 20th-century railroad companies, to choose one example, who developed the commercial airplane. That task fell to, among others, William Boeing, who was running a forestry business in Washington State when he just happened to fall in love with the first, rudimentary and life-threatening airplanes. Many years later, Boeing's model 247, the world's first modern passenger airliner, flew from Los Angeles to New York in 20 hours, making seven stops en route. The commercial airliner began to seriously disrupt the railroads' core business, but it was not developed by the railroads themselves.

Even organizations that are trying to innovate will usually fail to innovate disruptively, let alone radically. Steam-engine organizations' attitudes toward risk are clear and unsurprising: risky behaviour can lead to failure, and failure is inefficient, expensive, and also generally forbidden. Organizations are very good at rewarding success. They are also very, very good at dis-rewarding failure: failure is bad, and not generally to be embraced.

But by refusing to embrace the possibility of failure, even at a controlled, manageable, don't-bet-the-company-on-it level, organizations are cutting themselves off from the lifeblood of change and innovation.

Anthony Fitzsimmons, founder and chairman of Reputability, is an expert in risk. After graduating from Cambridge University with a degree in engineering, he became a lawyer, working in the corporate fields of risk, crisis, insurance, and reinsurance. He spent over 20 years as a partner with a leading firm specializing in the handling of international disasters before founding Reputability, a consultancy that advises large organizations and senior leaders on behavioural, organizational and reputational risk.

We talked to Antony near his firm's office in London's Covent Garden. Fitzsimmons is slim, youthful-looking and bespectacled, with a schoolboy- fringe to his smartly trimmed hair. He also has the rather formidable air of the barrister that he once was. He concentrates intently on his "brief" and then answers precisely and with enviable fluency. Only when the meeting has been brought to a successful conclusion does he relax into an infectious grin.

Fitzsimmons's work at Reputability looks at risk though the other end of the telescope: he looks for behavioural and organizational risks hiding – unappreciated, unrecognized, or ignored – at the heart of many organizations, not when they are attempting to be innovative, but when they are going about their usual business. These risks, argues Fitzsimmons, can be both the root causes of organizational crises and what tips a crisis into a full-blown reputational catastrophe. The risks, he believes, are often unrecognized because they are not "hard, measurable facts" staring senior executives in the face from their familiar metrics, but rather "soft issues" – issues of culture, of leadership, of incentive, of character and communication.

"What's measurable and measured gets managed," he says, ruefully, while confirming that, in his experience, the fond hope of many managers that significant elements of human behaviour can be measured and managed in good, old-fashioned, steam-engine ways is "a pipe dream".

He talks about his belief, based on years of experience, that many leaders fail to grasp and to work with what he argues is the *organic* – not machine-like – nature of organizations:

"It is sad that so many leaders don't really understand the extent to which organizations are organic things made up of people, and what makes organizations successful is fundamentally the people,

and what makes organizations fail *is basically the people – and I mean people right up to the very top level."*

It is perfectly possible for organizations to take on risk, he argues, provided they address the risks comprehensively, openly and clear-headedly, give the right leadership and governance, and address the very human issues that such an approach to risk would entail:

I find it rather depressing that larger organizations can get themselves into a psychological *bind – and I think it is a psychological bind as much as anything else – that prevents them from being able to take the risks involved in innovation, because it's not something that the outside world can't understand. If you say – "Our model is that we are going to innovate; we're going to take risk and we're going to manage risk; some of these things will fail and some of them will succeed but our aim across our portfolio is to succeed" – that should be a perfectly understandable position.*

Talking about organizations' internal attitude to experiment and failure, Fitzsimmons argues again that this should be a straightforward issue, but it has in fact become clouded by misplaced notions of "infallibility":

It's not just valuing failure, it's dissecting it and learning lessons. If you think you have messed up, you should 'fess up immediately, work out the consequences and the root causes, then share them and deal with them. But most organizations find that incredibly difficult, and they find it very difficult to lead *on it, because there's a damaging culture, in a way, in society, which implies that leaders have to be infallible and that failure is something that should be beaten out of the organization. That culture drives mistakes underground and prevents learning from mistakes.*

In stark contrast, Fitzsimmons talks about the healthy and successful culture that exists with the commercial airline industry. Because a major disaster involving an airplane is so appalling, the industry has trained itself to take any failure, however small, incredibly seriously, and to turn it into a learning experience:

The missed opportunity for many organizations is that they do not learn from the myriad of small mistakes that are made throughout the organization all of the time. Because those mistakes are typically swept under the carpet. And the result is that there's a huge reservoir of information that most organizations deny themselves. Aviation is the best example by far where small mistakes are lit on as a learning experience which prevent you from making big mistakes later on. They have thousands to tens of thousands of small mistakes reported for every big mistake that happens that has very nasty consequences. They relish looking into lots of mistakes; it's culturally embedded. There's no other industry that I know of that gets remotely near to having a universal global culture, whether it be the operators, or the supply chain, including the local service people, the local manufacturers – absolutely everyone buys into it.

GERARD KLEISTERLEE, FORMER CEO, ROYAL DUTCH PHILIPS
"FAILURE IS PERMITTED"
We have tried to create a culture where people are encourage to take risks, and where failure is not something never permitted.

The only thing I always say is: "Don't make the same mistakes twice, because then you have obviously not learned."

We have also tried to move away from big single initiatives to more small experimental initiatives. There is no one big bang that is suddenly going to get us into growth mode. In our organization, each of our leaders has to learn to take calculated risks, and work on several initiatives. Some will fail and some will succeed. You nurture the ones that promise to be successful.

So it's about getting away from a culture in which people are risk averse.

Gerard Kleisterlee, interview with *European Business Forum*, Spring 2007, Issue 28, p60-63

It is not, despite what the steam-engine mentality accepts, impossible to innovate within a large organization, or to embrace the certainty of occasional failure that accompanies the process of innovation, or to turn the small, everyday failures that occur in any enterprise into learning opportunities that lead to further innovation.

EMBRACING FAILURE ON THE ROAD TO SUCCESS

The paradox of innovation is a very dangerous paradox: organizations understand the need for innovation, but they are reluctant to take huge leaps into the unknown – for the very understandable reason that they do not want to be responsible for destroying the organization. Small-step "process" innovation is much easier to contemplate (and to manage) than radical innovation.

But such a cautious approach to innovation leaves companies open to being overtaken by events; to the risk of waking up one morning and finding that the rug has been pulled from under one's feet (just as the revolutionary BlackBerry found that the smartphone had stolen its glory and its market). There is no simple solution.

One line of thought says that large organizations are incapable of radical innovation and should reconcile themselves to receiving regular kicks in the teeth from smaller, entrepreneurial companies. This seems like a council of despair.

Some organizations – even some of the largest – have succeeded in acknowledging that failure is an inevitable part of progress: that all progress results from a large number of attempts, most of which will fail, to find the successful solution.

- Gerard Kleisterlee helped to enable the giant electronics conglomerate Philips to embrace a culture of experimentation and to accept the inevitability of failure (see panel), preferably with a multitude of small projects, from which those with the most potential could be selected and nurtured: a kind of Darwinian process, encouraging the natural selection of the best ideas.
- A.G. Lafley at Proctor and Gamble reached out to the wider world with his "Connect and Develop" project, inviting anyone with a good idea to share it with P&G and to use the company's marketing clout to try get the new idea to market. Lafley also

embraced the inevitability of failure. "You're going to fail, and you're going to fail multiple times," he told *Smart Business* magazine in 2011. "I always encouraged fast failure, and I always preferred cheap failure."[24]

- 3-M, founded in the early 20th century as a sandpaper-manufacturing company, famously encouraged its workers to experiment with pet projects on company time, even when management could not see the project's potential. The results were breakthrough products such as masking tape, Scotch Tape, and the famous Post-it note. 3-M today is a highly diversified technology company that still puts innovation at the heart of its business.

- In 1943, the Lockheed Aircraft Corporation was charged with developing the US military's first jet fighter – very quickly. Clarence "Kelly" Johnson led the hand-picked team that designed and built what was to become the XP-80 fighter in just 143 days, working in a rented circus marquee outside a manufacturing plant. Johnson insisted on a number of special rules under which the team would operate, all of which avoided bureaucracy and facilitated creativity. The maverick operation became known as the Skunk Works. "Johnson's rules" included giving the Skunk Works manager complete control of the project, reporting only to a divisional president or higher; the use of very small teams of hand-picked engineers; a minimum of reporting (but a sharp focus on important work being recorded thoroughly); and a pay system that would reward people in a way that was "not based on the number of people supervised".[25]

It is perfectly possible for a large organization to be innovative, but not in the context of the usual steam-engine management practices.

A number of the contributors to this book – academics, consultants, coaches, and business people – shared with us their thoughts on encouraging the creative, innovative process. They are intriguingly consistent. At heart, their ideas involve a form of letting go – in exactly the same way that was recommended when discussing the paradox of control in chapter 1 of this book.

ROBERT ROWLAND SMITH, PHILOSOPHER AND CONSULTANT
STEPPING INTO THE UNKNOWN
Innovation comes from stepping into the unknown; the new cannot come from what is already known and what is already familiar.

The most typical medium in which innovation takes place in organizations today is the brainstorm. But having sat in dozens of brainstorms I've come to the conclusion that they are probably the least creative environment there is.

I'll give you a list of words – if you had a brainstorm today in any organization in the Western world, all of the following words would come up in the first hour: app, digital, viral, scalable, gaming, social media, street, interactive, sustainable ...

So what you're getting is not any kind of creation, what you're getting is a recreation of the zeitgeist; you're getting a recycling of the air that everyone is already breathing.

The medium of innovation should be anything but brainstorming, which is a very cognitive, ideas-based activity. It seems to me that innovation is not about ideas. I know that's a very paradoxical thing to say, but it's about stepping into the unknown, and the source of the unknown is not an idea-based unknown, it comes from somewhere else. It comes from the phenomenological; it comes from the felt; it comes from feelings ... that sort of embodied feeling that changes in relation to other things.

Robert Smith in conversation with the authors

Only the organization's leaders can create the freedom that allows this kind of letting go, and it will require a radically different way of running at least parts of the organization. But the results are likely to be profound.

What are we letting go of? Constraints, inhibitions, excessive rationality, preconceptions, fear of failure ...

"INNOVATION IS NOT ABOUT IDEAS"
Robert Rowland Smith began his career as a philosopher at Oxford University, where he was prize fellow of All Souls college, specializing

in the crossover of literature, philosophy, and psychoanalysis. After 15 years at Oxford, he moved into management consultancy in London, specializing in organizational development, leadership, creativity, and innovation. He now divides his time between consultancy and writing: his books include *Breakfast with Socrates* and *Driving with Plato*, which explore the application of philosophy to everyday life, and *The Reality Test*, on business strategy.

We spoke to Robert about his thoughts on organizations' capacity for innovation.

One tends to imagine former fellows of Oxford colleges as being a rather crusty, distinguished and rarefied bunch. Robert is disturbingly fresh-faced, looking more like a student than an established author and business consultant. He talks clearly and measuredly, not so much in paragraphs as in whole chapters. His philosophical background is evident, but his focus is always on the practical.

He talked to us about his belief that creativity and innovation are not "ideas based": that they cannot result from the kind of rational discussion beloved of process innovators, but are rather 'felt'. In layman's language, this might translate as "gut feeling". It reminds the authors of Steve Jobs's famous statement about creativity: "When you ask creative people how they did something, they feel a little guilty because they didn't really do it, they just saw something. It seemed obvious to them after a while."

Smith makes the same point: he is especially scathing of "brainstorming", which, he argues, just "recycles the air that everyone is breathing" (see panel).

SHARING FAILURE

Olivier Oullier is professor of behavioural and brain sciences at Aix-Marseille University in France and a 2011 Young Global Leader of the World Economic Forum.

Olivier is very French: charming, debonair, handsome, voluble, philosophical, demonstrative, excitable, passionate. He talked to us (passionately and excitedly) about some practical ways of removing people's fear of failure, building trust, and trying to ensure that the mistakes of the past are not repeated (see panel).

OLIVIER OULLIER, PROFESSOR OF BEHAVIOURAL AND BRAIN
SCIENCES, AIX-MARSEILLE UNIVERSITY
SHARING FAILURE, BUILDING TRUST
Of course you don't want to encourage failure, what you encourage is
that failure is not the end of the story. There is this obvious thing that
you don't hire people who never fail because what you want is people
who regardless of failure, etc etc – this is one thing.

I have been working in close cooperation with people who have
been working for a long time together to organise "failure meetings"
where people share about how they failed, in total trust – and this
requires trust! – but we frame it an a way so that by sharing your failures
you're going to help the organization – because then your colleagues
are unlikely to make the same mistake. You're not knocking, of course,
at the personal level; it accepts that others could make the same
mistake; it shows that it's not only your fault and the aim is to prevent
the organization from repeating the mistakes of the past.

People vote on their favourite failure – and it can be fun!

So this is a way where you facilitate the expression of some failing
voices. And in terms of trust built, it's very productive.

Oliver Oullier in conversation with the authors

SERIOUS PLAY

Organizations need entrepreneurial spirit, but the idea of an
organization of entrepreneurs is an oxymoron: entrepreneurs are
not "clubbable" – they will not be "members".

Organizations can turn to outside entrepreneurs for their ideas
and input (as Procter & Gamble did with Connect and Develop) or
they can build special teams of people charged with innovation, and
shelter them from the rest of the organization – as Lockheed did
with the Skunk Works. The team comes first – ideally a team with
wide-ranging talents and abilities – and it needs an atmosphere of
relative freedom from the usual bureaucratic restraints.

Olivier Oullier's ideas about the centrality of trust – that establishing
genuine trust within a team is the first step toward creating an

atmosphere of potential creativity, is echoed by Tracey Camilleri, a former investment banker and management consultant, now an Associate Fellow at Saïd Business School, University of Oxford, where she focuses on leadership development and innovation.

Camilleri looks like an unfeasibly attractive version of the investment banker that she once was – elegant, poised,

☆ ☆

TRACEY CAMILLERI, ASSOCIATE FELLOW, SAÏD BUSINESS SCHOOL, UNIVERSITY OF OXFORD, ON HER TIME AS A TEACHER AT ST PAUL'S GIRLS SCHOOL, LONDON

"THIS IS PLAYING!"

If we are to achieve consistently great results,we either create an environment that is essentially dependent upon the teacher, where we do too much and create dependency, or we think about innovation; we think about: "When were our best moments as teachers and learners?" And we realized these moments cme through the creation of high-performing groups – when we created "organizations" – where everybody's difference was the point of being together; was maximised. And then we thought: "Well, how have we done this?" And the answer was: "By luck, in the past – and only occasionally!"

And then we realized that to create these high-performing groups, we had to play together, we had to put a lot of energy into tribe forming. And so we decided as a department, as a group – there were eight of us – that we would spend half a term with these incredibly bright, driven kids, with the parents beating at the door, and anxious that they should get into the best universities, essentially playing. And so we cut up recipes and made poems out of them; we acted bits of *Hamlet* as if it was a comedy and bits of comedy as if they were tragedy; we went out and made pictures of metaphors; we all composed first paragraphs, anonymously, always including the teachers, and then critiqued one another. We team-taught and disagreed with each other.

And about halfway through this process, which is I think what happens in organizations, both the parents and the head of school started to become very worried. They said: "This is playing; these young people have got to get good grades, they've got to pass – what are you doing?" And we absolutely sharp, and business-like – but she talks like a revolutionary. She believes, passionately, that we need to shake ourselves out of our ingrained corporate habits in order to achieve breakthrough results.

We talked to her about her current work at Saïd Business School with various corporate clients.

☆ ☆

stuck to our guns until a long half a term had gone by. And, miraculously, what happened was, everybody ended up respecting everybody else in the group, and respecting them. We had the historians in the class thinking about context; we had the people who were really mathematicians demanding logic; we had the musicians who understood rhythm and metre; we had the children who were less able, who were valued for asking the questions that everyone was too clever to ask but wanted to. And the brighter students realized that if they left their ideas in the room, and other people took them, they got to go out of the room with new ideas. And we got this incredible group of people who trusted each other, essentially, and what happened at the end of the first year was that all of them got top grades. That was extraordinary – we couldn't believe it!

And then what happened was – this ends badly – we got somewhat hubristic as a department and of course everyone started to want to do our subject – which threatened the balance of the whole larger organization. What we should have done was to say: "This is a fantastic methodology!" and share it out. But of course we were too young and inexperienced to do that.

But that upfront, conscious establishing of trust and relationships rather than thinking about tasks, which is essentially how a lot of organizations do things – it's tasks to be done rather than trust to be created – and also honouring people's difference. If you put a paintbrush in people's hands [in a leadership development session], they think: "Oh my gosh, if anyone saw me – we're playing!" The idea that work could be enjoyable or could be playful, and we could enjoy working with each other ... occasionally one does do that, but by luck rather than anything else.

Tracey Camilleri in conversation with the authors

I think a lot of innovation investment is just wasted money; it simply dies. I sat in a meeting the other day and someone said: "What we've got to think about [for this client] is evolution." And I said: "I'm sorry, what we have to think about is revolution!" And he said: "Well, our clients can't cope with that word."

And, actually, how do you change the system, because it's the system that kills all these things at birth. It's the way people are evaluated, it's the way people are allocated to teams, it's the way we just accept objectives without having proper beginnings; proper ends; real interrogation of what these objectives are. It's in the way we fail to know each other as human beings; to recognise our strengths and weaknesses and to be fine with that.

Camilleri talks about the central idea of building real teams ("of mature, grown-up people"), working with the differences between individual team members and creating an environment where creativity is possible (and even likely), *before* setting any objectives: the absolute converse of "innovation process" and the dead hand of "the innovation committee".

She talks about the vital importance and the potential of playful exploration, suggesting that highly valuable work might even be imaginative and fun (we warned you that she was a radical.)

In our conversation, Camilleri talked about her unconventional – but highly successful – teaching methods during her time as a teacher of English literature at St Paul's Girls School in West London, and about how these ideas still inform her executive development programmes (see panel).

DEVELOPING TRUST AND VULNERABILITY

Piers Ibbotson is an actor who has worked with both the Royal National Theatre and the Royal Shakespeare Company, where he became Assistant Director. He has appeared in films and on television. He runs Directing Creativity, which was set up during his time at the RSC and which continues to offer development and consultancy services to business, based on techniques used to develop acting and improvisational skills, and on other approaches and attitudes that are possibly unique to the theatre. Ibbotson is also the author of *The Illusion of Leadership*.

Ibbotson has an actor's face: good-looking, engaging, animated – and able, it seems, to rearrange itself into an infinite variety of different expressions at a moment's notice. Ibbotson's face can look serious, sombre, excited, or concerned within the space of one sentence. When acting, he has the unnerving capacity to turn himself into a variety of different people merely by putting his body and face into very subtly different arrangements.

Ibbotson takes established techniques – used routinely in the world of theatre to turn a group of individual actors into a powerful theatrical ensemble – and transplants them into the world of business, using the same techniques to turn groups of people thrown together by the organization into real, trusting, potentially creative ensembles. As Ibbotson told the authors in the course of a recent conversation:

> There are some directors who work to create ensemble companies – Peter Brooke being the outstanding example in British theatre – and that was a specific way of working together as a group that has evolved into a set of very sophisticated techniques for bringing a group of people together, developing the kind of trust and vulnerability and security within the group that allows people to then improvise together and innovate together.
>
> There's a lot of technique behind it; it's a well-established practice. There's a certain body of techniques and practices which will bring about the respect within a group of people that allows them to improvise and that produces a fantastically productive way of working. My best experiences, both as an actor and as a director, were where that work had been done with the group, and that produced not just innovation but also extraordinary ownership and commitment. And how you create those groups and direct those groups was the core model – what I've been doing is really going into organizations and saying: "Look, I'm going to pretend you are actors and I'm going to sort of stitch you through how I would go about turning you into a creative

PIERS IBBOTSON, ACTOR AND FOUNDER OF DIRECTING CREATIVITY
REHEARSING SUCCESS
The notion of rehearsal in the theatre doesn't exist within
organizations, as far as I can see – the acceptance that you might
have five or six weeks failing to succeed before you emerge with an
effective solution.

It's quite different from the idea of planning and implementing,
which is what the engineering model of the organization is; we are
trying to bring back human behavioural change instead of using an
engineering model – which I don't think works, because you can't
plan and implement human change in the organization, you have to
practise that, you have to rehearse it.

The army understand this perfectly well; they spend most of
their time doing [military exercises], they are rehearsing war fighting
because they know they can't do it in a lecture theatre. Anybody who
goes that route is all over the place, but for some reason organizations
imagine that they can decide how the new structure needs to look,
and then implement it and it will work, which the army will tell you is
bonkers.

Piers Ibbotson in conversation with the authors

*ensemble and beginning to improvise solutions and try and get
creative with you."*

One of Ibbotson's most interesting insights concerns the complete
absence of the concept of "rehearsal" in modern organizations.
Theatre ensembles rehearse for weeks – making many mistakes,
going down various blind allies, trying out ideas that really do not
work – before they venture onto the stage before an audience.

The military, he points out, does the same thing: spending a lot of
time "rehearsing" war in exercises, because it is very expensive, and
potentially disastrous, not to discover what does and does not work
until you are on a real battlefield.

Organizations, suggests Ibbotson, could take a leaf out of the actor's (and the army's) handbook, and try to "rehearse" various scenarios that an innovative idea might create, rather than attempting to use the old steam-engine approach of "planning and implementation" which, as he points out, never works where human behaviour is involved.

This kind of organizational rehearsal could physically enact various real scenarios: if the organization adopted a certain innovative procedure, or an innovative product, how might that play out? How would the organization have to react? What new demands would the organization face? What internal forces and pressures within the organization would be created by that new scenario?

INNOVATE OR DIE

The paradox of innovation is very real. Steam-engine companies are institutionally risk averse; their first priority is to do what they do as efficiently as possible and to make as few mistakes as possible. This is an understandable position. Sadly, however, any organization that effectively stands still, failing to innovate in any significant way, will quickly be overtaken by younger, nimbler companies who are prepared to take a chance with something that the steam-engine company considers to be "too risky".

Over time, unless we begin to move away from steam-engine practices in a systematic way, these new, once nimble companies will become bogged down in the swamps of control, measurement and efficiency, and will themselves be overtaken by another generation of new, more agile companies.

As the pace of change accelerates, so companies will be left behind and eventually replaced, on shorter and shorter timeframes: BlackBerry is a current example of this. There is nothing unimaginable about this scenario; companies will simply have to accept that their lifespan will be relatively short.

Unless, of course, organizations begin to move away from steam-engine practices and begin to create working environments where people's natural curiosity and creativity is allowed to drive the innovation that every organization needs in order to survive.

TAKING THE ORGANIZATION FROM THE INDUSTRIAL ERA TO THE AGE OF IDEAS

Transforming the steam engine, one step at a time

- Steam-engine organizations attempt to manage innovation along with everything else, turning innovation into a process
  - Innovation is not a process, it is a state of mind
- "Process" innovation is merely "gradual improvement", not innovation
  - Innovation is a leap into the unknown
  - Encourage truly radical ideas; try them out; see if they work
- Disruptive innovation disrupts, radical innovation destroys – but also creates
  - Radical innovation creates different business models, not just different products and services
  - If you don't do it, somebody else will – get ready to play catch-up
- Organizations hate risk – risk involves failure
  - Failure is inevitable, desirable, and manageable
- Innovation is not a rational process
  - Look for connections; follow gut instincts
- Building teams comes first
  - Create real teams, seek out diversity, take off restraints, encourage creativity
- Play, improvise, rehearse
  - Build real trust, mutual vulnerability, and common purpose
  - Imagine a number of different futures
  - Try them out and rehearse them

CHAPTER 5

EVERYBODY'S TALKIN' AT ME
I DON'T HEAR A WORD THEY'RE SAYING

The paradox of communication within the organization is very clear. In theory, we are 'communicating' – with our colleagues and our bosses, with our friends and family, and with a bunch of near strangers to whom we happen to be connected via social media – more than ever before. We are accessible, via various devices, at any hour of the day or night and on any day of the week. And yet in the truest sense of the word, we seem to communicate less and less.

We know that you know this, so we don't need to labour the point: communication, in both our work lives and our social lives, has gone (to use a technical term) bonkers.

In our social lives, where we can exercise choice, this is generally a good thing. We can stay in touch with people at the click of a "like" button, by typing a few words with an anarchic disregard for either spelling or grammar, by posting something that just caught our fancy somewhere else in cyberspace – or a photograph of ourselves, or of what we are looking at right now, or of a cat that looks like Hitler.

It's fun! It might lead to a dark world where the next generation have only virtual friends and no real human contact, but that seems highly unlikely. Various forms of social media will change, morph, die, and be replaced by something new and better – or at least different. Facebook was down in the UK for a few hours recently, triggering a flood of tweets with headlines such as "Facebook down; nation deprived of pictures of cute animals for several hours", and also this interesting tweet by a well-known television actor: "People are still using Facebook? What is this – 2010?!"

In the hectic, virtual world of social media, nothing stands still. After all, somebody somewhere is always keen to make a few billion dollars by launching whatever will turn out to be the next big medium to bring us all together in the virtual world and create a new marketplace for the exchange of gossip, ideas, advertising, and goods.

This should be applauded. The exchange of gossip, ideas, advertising, and goods is what has driven human progress for the last few millennia. Ideas are rattling around the world at an unprecedented speed: brilliant ideas and idiotic banalities criss-cross the globe within minutes via a shifting network of media. This is all good. It aids the flow of ideas around the planet.

So what about our work lives? What about the world of business? Well, the world of business got email. And then it kind of stuck with email.

Of course, top executives and analysts will be wired into a flow of information about the outside world that hopefully keeps them supplied with a flow of data and new ideas that may benefit the organization. And traders have market data streaming across their screens in real time.

The information revolution has reached parts of the steam-engine organization, too, but only a few elite or specialized parts. Members of steam-engine organizations will be wired into their own networks of potentially priceless information sources, but the organizations are not giving them the opportunity or the technology to share that information — because to do so would be "inefficient".

In a networked world, the average information worker is not "networked" to his or her organization in any meaningful sense (as we explore further in chapter 9). Instead, the typical knowledge worker has become a slave to email.

It is perfectly possible to fill a day simply reacting to the stream of emails that flood into the average inbox. When other work — meetings, phone calls, that report we are trying to write — "interrupts" us, the emails pile up. Increasingly, people are spending what should be their leisure time simply coping with the flow of emails. To fail to respond to an email, preferably within an hour, is seen as rudeness, and implies that one is not coping with one's workload.

109 BILLION BUSINESS EMAILS A DAY

Steam-engine organizations really liked email when it first arrived, because it was a bit like a memo, only much faster: you could get it on everyone's desk within seconds. Managers could now send out their directives at the click of a mouse. In fact, steam-engine organizations loved email so much that they stopped communicating in almost any other way.

And, as you will have noticed, we are still at it today.

According to a 2014 report by the research organization the Radicati Group, 196.3 billion emails are sent worldwide every day. The bulk of these are business emails: 108.7 billion. This volume of business emails is forecast to grow to 139.4 billion in 2018.

The same report estimates that the average business email user sends 36 emails per day and receives 85 emails per day, of which about 10 are spam.[26] That's an average of 111 meaningful emails each and every day that have to be dealt with in some way: written, read, analysed, digested, ignored, responded to, noted for later action, or filed.

If every email received or sent took one minute of our time, that would be 111 minutes per day: nearly two hours of our time. If, on the other hand, we spent an average of, not one, but five minutes composing each of the thirty-six emails sent, that would take another one hundred and eighty minutes – three hours – out of our working day. And if we spent that average of one minute per item just reading the seventy-five non-spam emails received, this would represent a total of four hours and fifteen minutes out of what is supposed to be an eight-hour working day.

Half of our working day spent dealing with emails?! That sounds about right, in our experience. And the sad fact is that, since most effective people choose not to spend half their day handling email traffic, they extend their working day – and their working week – in order to cope with it.

If email was the perfect medium for communication, this could be seen as a good use of our time. But, in practice, email is one of the worst forms of communication imaginable.

Email is excellent as a way of sending a file. If you want to send something to someone, send an email with an electronic

MARK POWELL
EMAILING FIFTEEN FEET
I was working with an organization once and I was interviewing both
of the directors. They were complaining about how difficult it was to
get communication time with the CEO and the chairman who owned
and ran the company – and this was not a small company, it was a
very, very large company.

The directors were trying to work out when the chief exec and the
chairman were in their offices, and they'd worked out that when they
were in their offices there were certain times when they would look at
their emails.

They worked out that the key to communicating whatever issue
they wanted to discuss was to get an email into the top 20 emails in
their inboxes, because they knew that as soon as it went off the top 20
and was not visible on the screen, the communication went down.

So we have this bizarre reality of two very senior executives
spending their time trying to work out how to get their email into
the right place on the screen of someone who is literally 15 feet from
where they were sitting.

And you have to think: "When it comes to communication, we
are mad!" The easier it is for us to communicate, the easier it is for
us to be connected; human communication is very important to us,
because we are ultimately social animals. But the apparent ease of
digital communication is actually reducing the amount of human
communication that organizations really, really need.

Mark Powell in conversation with Jonathan Gifford

attachment. The paperless office was, and is, a great idea.

But it is very hard to have a dialogue by email. If it is an exchange
between two people, then it is at least no worse than an exchange
of letters, though it is far less efficient than a phone call. If several
people are involved, we wish you well. You may well have received
one of those emails where a colleague copies you in on an email
chain saying, not very helpfully: "This will bring you up to speed on
the issue – what do you think?"

Since the email chain often stretches back toward the birth of the internet, this is always a hugely time-consuming process, to which the honest answer, after much puzzling about *exactly* what so-and-so seems to be on about, might be this:

The issue raised by Jane in her original email is perceptive and challenging. John's initial response is, as ever, evasive and indecisive. Martin has offered a potentially interesting answer, but to an entirely different question. Garry has completely missed the point. It looks as if it is time for Peter to take his medication again. Henry, I see, is busy trying to score points at the expense of his colleagues. Gail has introduced an entirely different and completely unrelated issue – which is, of course, the issue that she always raises, regardless of context. Henrietta wants us to know that she thinks top management are doing a wonderful job. The brief intervention from the senior manager who was copied into the original email is intimidating but not illuminating. Your own contribution is dull, mistaken, and craven, yet probably career-enhancing. If you want my honest opinion, the answer to Jane's original question is: "A brilliant idea: let's try it and see what happens!" but I see that no one has had the guts to say so.

Sadly, while one tends to write such responses, one never sends them. One doesn't want to seem sarcastic.

This little example may be facetious, but we suspect that it will ring a few bells with you. The problem, sadly, is very real: is it surprisingly difficult to get people in any organization to communicate properly, and email is one of the least good ways of achieving this.

It is hard enough to get a group of people to see the problem as it really is and not as they would like it to be, but beyond that there are two more fundamental steam-engine problems that get in the way of good communication: "hierarchies" and "silos".

COMMUNICATION ACROSS HIERARCHIES
People are very wary of what they say in front of their superiors, because steam-engine managers seem to imagine that their main

KAREN PHELAN, MANAGEMENT CONSULTANT AND AUTHOR
OF *I'M SORRY I BROKE YOUR COMPANY*
AN EXPENSIVE WAY TO COMMUNICATE
The more comfortable your organization is with open and honest
conversations between all layers of the hierarchy, the more likely
problems and issues will become visible quickly and resolved quickly.
In my experience, many business problems are due to a lack of
communication, and often my real value as a consultant is in being a
communications vehicle between functions or levels.
  That's an expensive way to communicate.

**Karen Phelan, *I'm sorry I broke your company*, Berrett-Koehler
Publishers Inc. 2013, ch. 8**

function is to "catch people out" – to be constantly alert to the
possibility that someone is not "on message" or is having "bad" ideas.

As a result, many – if not almost all – steam-engine managers
remain completely unaware of the problems that their organization is
facing. Sometimes the problem is one of literal non-communication.
Often, people do not tell management things that they should know
because to raise a "problem" is seen as an implicit criticism of the
manager, or because of deeply ingrained cultural habits of deference
to superiors – or for the very good reason that bad managers have a
habit of shooting messengers.

Sometimes there is a genuine attempt to communicate, but our
very real habit of hearing only what we want to hear prevents the
message from being received. Good communication is very difficult.
Bad communication can be disastrous.

Anthony Fitzsimmons, founder and chairman of the risk-
assessment consultancy Reputability, discussed the communication
problems caused both by hierarchies and by "group blindness" in the
course of our conversation with him:

*In our research, we identified one of the fundamental problems
as the fact that the people who can see a particular problem can*

*often see it better than those above them. Those below can't do
anything about itand they daren't even try and talk about it with
those above them.*

*Basically, people don't learn from experience, because nobody
dares to tell their boss why the project went wrong, and the
boss doesn't know himself, so everyone keeps making the same
mistake over and over again. And the organization never learns."*

Even if the top leadership does recognize the challenge of
creating strong, clear channels of communication, the problem
of our unrecognized biases still remains. "There are all sorts of
psychological traits which keep groups of people blind to what's
really going on around them," says Fitzsimmons. "We all have very
commonplace biases that stop us from seeing things as they are."

Conversely, he sees good communication within an organization
– and between the organization and the outside world – as a sign
that many other aspects of the organization are in good shape:

*We regard the effectiveness of communication as a 'canary in the
mine' as to what's going on in the organization If communication
– particularly about systematically recognizing and learning
from non-dramatic mistakes - is flowing freely, it gives a benefit
because the information is flowing, but it also indicates that a lot
of other things are probably set to allow the information to flow
freely. The free flow of information and lessons from mishaps is
fragile and easily blocked, for example by all kinds of incentives,
the culture of the place and the way leaders behave.*

The problem with bad communication is that its consequences
can be disastrous. In *Roads to Ruin*,[27] a special report produced
by Cass Business School for the Association of Insurance and Risk
Mangers in Industry and Commerce (AIRMIC), Fitzsimmons and
his fellow authors identify a number of previously un-catalogued
key risks to which organizations are exposed. These include
board-member skills and levels of risk awareness; leadership ethos
and culture; defective communication; excessive complexity;

inappropriate incentives and "risk glass ceilings" – the hierarchy effect in reverse, where managers who are charged with risk-management are unable to comment on risky behaviour that emanates from executives who are more senior than the managers carrying out the report.

At the risk of sounding simplistic, we are going to argue that all of these factors (except those that reflect individual attitudes or competencies) can be described as issues of communication.

It is perfectly possible to deal with extreme complexity, for example, provided the possible consequences of that complexity have been communicated and understood. We also assume that no leadership team intentionally sets out to offer inappropriate incentives, but there are indeed many cases where a well-intentioned incentive sends out the wrong message and encourages unwanted behaviours. "Defective communication" is the very subject of this chapter, and "risk glass ceilings" reflect exactly the problem of communicating effectively across hierarchies that we are currently discussing.

Roads to Ruin analyses several infamous corporate disasters, including the appalling Texas City refinery explosion of 2005, which

ATKINS, FITZSIMMONS ET AL, *ROADS TO RUIN*
FATAL FAILURES OF COMMUNICATION
The Baker Report on the Texas City Refinery explosion criticized BP's board for the "disconnect" between its high ideals and the day-to-day practice of its operations ...

The background to the Texas City Refinery fire included poor vertical communication, which meant that there was no adequate early warning of problems and no means of understanding the growing problems on the site. BP's approach to decentralisation also meant that top management had not effectively communicated its priorities, including those on safety, to its operating units.

Atkins, Fitzsimmons et al, *Roads to Ruin*, report by Cass Business School for AIRMIC, http://bit.ly/1kJ1SFC

killed 15 workers and injured at least 170 others. Poor, absent, or defective communication played a part in every one of them.

TEXAS CITY REFINERY EXPLOSION: COMMUNICATION FAILURES AT MANY LEVELS

"On March 23, 2005, BP employees and contract workers began an especially dangerous procedure: restarting a unit that had been down for repairs," reported CBS News in October 2006, as proceedings against the oil giant BP began in a court in Galveston, Texas, in connection with the deaths caused by the explosion 18 months earlier. The report continued:

> They began to fill a tower with gasoline. The tower overflowed, and the excess gas flowed into a back-up unit, which then also overflowed and sent a geyser of gasoline into the air. Pat Nickerson, a 28-year veteran of the Texas City refinery, was on site that day, driving his truck to an office trailer.
>
> "I looked down the road. It looked like fumes, like on a real hot day, you see these heat waves coming up and then, I saw an ignition and a blast. Then my windshield shattered. The roof of the vehicle I was driving caved in on me," Nickerson recalls.
>
> The plume of gas had formed a massive vapor cloud on the ground, and an idling truck likely had ignited the fumes. The blast pulverized several office trailers full of workers parked nearby.
>
> Nickerson began digging through the wreckage looking for survivors. "Out of the corner of my eye, there was somebody on the ground," he remembers. "A guy named Ryan Rodriguez, and he was just kind of staring at me. He couldn't move because his face was so, you know, deformed and everything from the blast." ... Rodriguez eventually died in the ambulance.[28]

Tragic accidents like the one at the BP refinery in Texas City do not come out of nowhere. The CBS report said that they had "found evidence that BP ignored warning after warning that something terrible could happen at Texas City". CBS News was not alone in forming that conclusion (see panel).

It could be argued that the route to BP's Texas City Refinery explosion began with its merger with Amoco. As *The Roads to Ruin* report notes: "BP's Texas City Refinery explosion was partly the result of the BP's merger with Amoco, which had a very different culture. The merger made BP's management structure overly complex, and the Texas City Refinery came with a long history of poor maintenance."

With hindsight, it seems that BP, the refinery owners, had failed to sustain a corporate culture in which safety was given the highest priority at every level of the orgnaization.

This disconnect between BP's high ideals about safety and the reality of the day-to-day operations was noted by the 2007 report on the incident, led by former US Secretary of State James Baker. BP's top leadership had clearly failed to communicate its real concerns about safety to its key executives and to its operating units.

Arguably the worst communication failure, however, was the most mundane: workers at the refinery had been aware of a growing number of safety issues at the site, and none of these concerns got transmitted up the "vertical communications" channel. It seems nobody "upstairs" was listening.

COMMUNICATION BETWEEN SILOS

Another major barrier to communication is represented by the "silos": those parts of the organization that come to feel independent of each other, standing together but unconnected, like a collection of grain silos in a giant wheat field; departments or divisions that have developed their own mini-culture – their own microclimate – and now struggle to communicate with other silos.

"The bane of my life was silos," Peter Rawlins, founder of Rawlins Strategy Consulting and former CEO of the London Stock Exchange, told us.

> *People would speak to and deal with their own, but would be blindly ignorant of the rest of the organization.*
> *In my experience, there is no substitute for doing a lot of it physically, that is to say, physically reorganizing who sits where and who is in whose proximity.*

It's quite staggering how a staircase between floors might as well be an iron curtain, and in modern dealing rooms, just walkways between different trading floors, between different trading desks, could be chasms. So physical organization is always something I've paid a lot of attention to and that tends to force people to readdress who they deal with; who they interact with. ... People kid themselves that they are communicating by sending emails around the place.

On the other hand, Rawlins says, organizations that manage to bring together different parts of the enterprise, each with their own distinctive culture – organizations that succeed in creating meaningful communication between what would previously have been silos – can generate a huge organizational advantage.

Getting what I think the modern phrase is "cluster organizations" to work effectively is far more demanding, but ultimately far healthier: cross-functional, multi-cultural, multi-functional organizations that are much more dynamic, much more effective, with much better reach, better ideas. But of course it's rather hard to portray that model on an HR organization chart!

There is a very good reason why communication between silos is so difficult: a significant part of how we behave is defined by the group that we feel we belong to. Piers Ibbotson, the Royal Shakespearean actor turned business coach, uses his experiences as an actor and a director to work with organizations in creating teams that are capable of good, open communication. In his experience, there is no substitute for time and effort: different communities can only truly be brought together if they are forged into a new community by taking time to break down barriers and build trust (see panel).

THE FLOW OF IDEAS

Communication – the successful flow of new ideas through groups, organizations, and societies – is arguably the most significant factor

PIERS IBBOTSON, FOUNDER OF DIRECTING CREATIVITY,
AUTHOR OF *THE ILLUSION OF LEADERSHIP*
BUILDING NEW COMMUNITIES
Because everyone is invested in the structure of their own little part
of the organizational universe, they are not freelance contractors, so
they don't bring themselves to the project; they refer and position
themselves with regard to their own most stable community within
the organization.

The longer you are in a community, the more you project your
survival needs onto the members of that community – survival in the
sense of "supplies your most basic needs". You come to believe that
your survival and career success depend on this group.

If you are put together with various other people and other groups,
there isn't any way that you can make it work – unless you task the
community, work with them for a long time, a week or two at least,
breaking down barriers, building trust, forming an ensemble out of
them – and then you might be able to begin to have some creative
conversations.

You have to build a new community from scratch. And I know from
theatre, because we do it every day, that that takes about three weeks.
But of course what you get when you pull together a community of
experts to challenge something is two hours on Wednesday, four
hours a fortnight later, three hours another month later – and then
we've got to get down and write a report.

It's a complete waste of time, because nobody appreciates that the
way in which the social, psychological work that needs to be done to
prepare an ensemble for creative work is quite extensive. It can be done.
Any drama teacher can show you how to do it. But it takes time. It takes
time devoted to forging the relationships before you can set them to
the task. And that is what people in organizations just don't get.

Piers Ibbotson in conversation with the authors

affecting the success of those groups. The flow of ideas, after all, is
what got us from the flint hand axe to the 3D printer.

On this basis, encouraging a dynamic flow of ideas into, around,
and out of the organization could be said to be the organization's
core function. The steam-engine organization, in stark contrast,

sees itself as the hoarder and guardian of the core idea that got the organization started in the first place: it diligently manages the original process that was created when the organization first came into being, and it actively resists the flow of new (and clearly dangerous) ideas.

Alex Pentland, author of *Social Physics*, is a professor at MIT and a director of the research university's Human Dynamics Laboratory. He is a pioneer of computational social science, crunching big data gathered about human behaviour from "the digital breadcrumbs we all leave behind us as we move through the world—call records, credit card transactions, and GPS location fixes, among others". In order to record details of human interactions on a smaller scale, Pentland and his team sometimes use a clever gizmo: "sociometric badges" that track when people are talking, their tone of voice, their body position relative to other people, and their body language, including arm and hand movements and nods of the head.

The collection of such data, often over extended periods of time, provides a far richer source of material than any of the previous techniques used by social scientists to measure human behaviour: surveys involving relatively few people over relatively short periods of time, measuring only a few variables. Pentland has done pioneering work on both the practical and the legal aspects of collecting electronic information from what he calls "living laboratories" – which, he argues, will soon be giving us "incredibly rich data ... about virtually the whole of humanity, on a continuous basis".

One of the most interesting aspects of Pentland's work is his argument that it is the "flow of ideas" though any social group that most significantly affects our behaviour, and that the flow of ideas is a better indicator of our likely behaviour than, for example, the flow of money – making Pentland's proposed new discipline of 'social physics' arguably more useful (and certainly more interesting) than economics. "Rather than study how economic agents work and how economies function," he writes, "social physics seeks to understand how the flow of ideas turns into behaviours and action. Put another way, social physics is about how human behaviour is driven by the exchange of ideas – how people cooperate to discover, select, and learn strategies and coordinate their actions – rather than how markets are driven by the exchange of money."[29]

Or, to quote Pentland again in what is a profound, though deceptively simple-looking observation: "We are traders in ideas, goods, favors, and information and not simply the competitors that traditional market thinking would make us."[30]

The flow of ideas, he argues, happens in a very believable and common-sense kind of way: it is not that a very few people have very bright ideas, it is rather that people have new ideas all of the time, and some very active people, whom Pentland calls "explorers", constantly collect and spread these ideas among their extensive network of connections, where the ideas are tried and tested by a wide range of minds. Only the best, most useful ideas get to survive.

GOOD COMMUNICATION MAKES BETTER TEAMS

Pentland's work on smaller groups of people, using his sociometric badges, has produced some very interesting ideas about how groups interact and, particularly, what makes a successful, high-performing team – a collection of people who are clearly "buzzing". Pentland believes he has the answer, and that it has everything to do with *how* we communicate.

Groups that communicate in the right way, he says, do better. A kind of "group intelligence" emerges, and is greater than the sum of its parts:

Unexpectedly, we found that the factors most people usually think of as driving group performance – i.e., cohesion, motivation, and satisfaction – were not statistically significant. The largest factor in predicting group intelligence was the equality of conversational turn taking; groups where a few people dominated the conversation were less collectively intelligent than those with a more equal distribution of conversational turn-taking. The second most important factor was the social intelligence of a group's members, as measured by their ability to read each other's social signals. Women tend to do better at reading social signals, so groups with more women tended to do better ...

RON EMERSON, ASSOCIATE FELLOW, SAÏD BUSINESS SCHOOL, UNIVERSITY OF OXFORD

ENGAGING THE EMOTIONS

I did quite a lot of research in this area about change and communication. A huge amount of time is spent at the top analysing what the company should do, looking at strategies, hiring consultants, and then in the space of a few PowerPoint presentations, they expect the rest of the organization both to understand it and buy into it.

And what they do is they dump a lot of data and then what you get is a reaction. If it's change that is on the agenda, the problem with change is it creates fear. People are frightened, often, of change, so it becomes emotional, but what they do is they engage with the information cascade with their own interpretations of the data.

So they'll argue about the data. "Well, that's not the right data; I've got some different data." Or: "That's not the conclusion I would draw from that data." And actually what they're really saying is: "I'm frightened of this change. I got to be successful in this organization through the old ways. How do I know that I can survive and be successful in this new world?"

So you have to engage with them at an emotional level, and with the fear.

Ron Emerson in conversation with the authors

What these sociometric data showed was that the pattern of idea flow by itself was more important to group performance than all other factors and, in fact, was as important as all other factors taken together. Think about it: Individual intelligence, personality, skill, and everything else together mattered less than the pattern of idea flow ...

This group problem-solving ability, which is greater than our individual abilities, emerges from the connections between the individuals. In particular, a pattern of interactions that supports the pooling of a diverse set of ideas from everyone, combined with an efficient winnowing process to establish a consensus, seems to form its core.[31]

How a group interacts and behaves determines its success as a group, Pentland argues, a *Harvard Business Review* article entitled "The New Science of Building Great Teams".

The data also reveal ... that successful teams share several defining characteristics:
1. *Everyone on the team talks and listens in roughly equal measure, keeping contributions short and sweet*
2. *Members face one another, and their conversations and gestures are energetic*
3. *Members connect directly with one another – not just with the team leader*
4. *Members carry on back-channel or side conversations within the team*
5. *Members periodically break, go exploring outside the team, and bring information back.*

Perhaps the most telling factor in creating a successful group is the first: teams where dominant members of the group – often entirely unconsciously – dominate proceedings, reinforcing each other's ideas, are less successful. Pentland has developed a way of visually displaying the flow of ideas between group members and says that he and his team can now spot the less successful teams just from the pattern of the flow of conversation, without having any idea about the content of the conversation. They have successfully predicted, based only on the visual evidence of the pattern of communication, which teams will win a business-plan contest, or which teams of investors would make better investments. Pentland and his team can also spot a team that will report that it has had a "productive" or "creative" session just by looking at the visual representation of the flow of conversation.[32]

What is even more fascinating is something that is vehemently denied by all steam-engine managers but well known to most human beings: that "social" time is critically important to the success of any team. "Social time," Pentland writes in his *HBR* article, "turns out to be deeply critical to team performance, often accounting for more than 50% of positive changes in communication patterns."

This, of course, is part of Pentland's process of "exploration", whereby people try out new ideas, using other people as sounding boards. Interestingly, it doesn't work very well if the social time is forced. Pentland reports that a young software company tried organizing "beer meets" without much success in improving communications within the team, whereas putting longer tables in the company's lunchroom worked like a charm, encouraging people to chat to a wider and more random selection of colleagues over lunch.

Pentland and his team made one profoundly non-steam-engine recommendation to the manager of a call centre that they were studying. The manager, in pursuit of efficiency (what else?), had staggered the coffee breaks of the team in order to prevent timewasting chatter and debilitating socializing. Pentland recommended that employees should be allowed to mix more during breaks. Pentland's gizmos revealed that the level of engagement between employees subsequently went up as a result and – hey presto! – so did productivity. By about $15 million per year, apparently.[33]

Who would have thought it? Well ... you, probably. And us.

This is a truly perverse example of steam-engine managers' obsession with measurement: if Pentland and his "sociometric data" had not "proven" to the call centre manager that it would be a good idea to let the team members get together during their coffee breaks, the manager would presumably have persisted with the unpleasant and inhuman policy of staggered breaks, never noticing that he had a collection of miserable, demotivated, dehumanized individuals answering his customers' invaluable phone calls, rather than a real, self-motivating team.

It is possible to argue with Pentland's central notion that massive data crunching will help to point humanity in the right direction because it will give us (oh, joy!) a *science* of human behaviour, but many of his observations confirm the vital importance of face-to-face communication. He notes, for example, that the number of face-to-face communications between team members – in both formal and informal circumstances – is a clear predictor of the team's performance. He even, of course, has a number for it: "We now know that 35% of the variation in a team's performance can be accounted for simply by the number of face-to-face exchanges among team members."[34] (You can have too much face-to-face communication, however. Beyond an ideal of "as many as dozens per working hour", Pentland notes, performance decreases.[35])

It is impossible to resist one last quote from Pentland, since this chapter began on the topic of email:

> *The most valuable form of communication is face-to-face. The next most valuable is by phone or videoconference, but with a caveat: those technologies become less effective as more people participate in the call or conference. The least valuable forms of communication are email and texting.[36]*

THE ORGANIZATIONAL UNCONSCIOUS AND THE ROLE OF EMOTION

Good communication is essential but difficult. Bad communication is commonplace and potentially disastrous. What is to be done?

Author, philosopher, and business coach Robert Rowland Smith has devised a technique he calls "Constellations", which are designed to allow individuals or organizations to explore problems which, he told us, are usually caused by "an unconscious disorder in the wider system to which we belong". The technique involves asking different members of the group to represent the aspects of the wider system that are unknown to the others – aspects of the organizational unconscious, if you like:

> *Constellations puts them into spatial relationship, because you then ask people in the room to stand up, and get into a position which corresponds with the mental picture that they have of what's going on. What happens is that once you start representing things you don't know, then you start to pick up on exactly what it feels to be that entity. It's rather spooky in way.*
>
> *What Constellations exposes is actually what people already know that is going on, but they're often too intimidated to voice, because the way people are asked to account for what is going on in their organization is often very dry, analytic – they're trying to say the right thing in front of the right people. People know that there's*

a problem with X, the other organization, or Y, which could be another different division, but they supress it because they feel they don't have a language for describing it, or it won't be accepted.

All Constellations is doing is revealing what everybody already knows is going on. It's powerful because it does that in a safe setting as opposed to sitting around the boardroom table, for example. So when I talk about the unconscious of the system it's the sort of "known unknown" – the ways in which everybody in the organization really does know what's going on, but its whether or not that truth is accepted, or has a channel that allows it to be explored, exposed, and dealt with.

The structures become a block to normal human interaction and people end up following the project plan rather than picking up the phone and saying: "Hang on, we've got a problem here." We've seen that many times over the years, where the project plan is followed slavishly and the elephant in the room is just not addressed. And I think often it's for reasons of hierarchy, and people think: "Oh, I can't say anything because I'm too junior, or I can't say anything because I'm a junior partner in the venture, or I can't say anything because they're my client, and if I say the truth here they'll sack me", or whatever it might be. And yet the truth is always welcome, because people are empowered when the truth is spoken; people find it uncomfortable but the discomfort soon goes, because people appreciate the truth being spoken.

One final thought on the problem of communicating across hierarchies: when an organization's leadership wants to communicate ideas about change to the rest of the organization, this generates anxiety, for obvious reasons. As a result, we fail to absorb the information that the leadership believes has been so successfully transmitted, because we are too absorbed in our emotional response to the news. Because what drives our behaviour is our emotions – not our rationality – our conscious mind sets out to find good reasons why the information that it has just been given, explaining why change is necessary, is in fact wrong (see Ron Emerson's comments in previous panel).

The communication challenge for modern leadership is to engage with people's feelings: don't just "dump a lot of data" on us and expect us to draw the right conclusion: explain to us what it will *feel* like when we get to the new place. Give us the new vision.

And, by the way, if the people involved don't come to believe that the new place will feel *much better* in some way than the old place, don't expect your change programme to go very well.

COMMUNICATION IS RELATIONAL

The unfortunate thing about email is that it fits the steam-engine mentality perfectly: it keeps everybody busy. Everyone is present at a workstation, glued to a screen, giving the comforting illusion of a busy production line, with everyone gainfully employed. The fact that this employment is not very gainful at all passes steam engine managers by.

Email is very two-dimensional way of communicating, and it is very badly suited for analysing multi-dimensional problems. Communication is by definition relational – it involves more than one party and, as a result, it inevitably involves relationships.

The best way to communicate is, as Alex Pentland's studies show, in a face-to-face group meeting in which the conversation flows evenly throughout the group, where there is an "equality of conversational turn taking", and the conversation is not dominated by a select group of people.

No doubt we will get better at various forms of virtual meetings; in the meantime, letting people get together for a chat and working hard to keep status out of the picture still represents the cutting edge of human communication.

TAKING THE ORGANIZATION FROM THE INDUSTRIAL ERA TO THE AGE OF IDEAS

Transforming the steam engine, one step at a time

- "Communication" has gone bonkers
  - We are linked to each other by a variety of technologies and media more than at any time in world history
  - This is improving the volume and immediacy – but not necessarily the quality – of our communications

- We ae losing the art of effective human communications
- Steam-engine organizations have got stuck with email
- Email is extremely bad at enabling genuine communication
  - Email disseminates information efficiently but makes dialogue difficult
  - Any internal email involves both hierarchies and silos; it is very hard to communicate honestly and effectively across either
- Failures of communication are always bad for the organization, and can have disastrous consequences
  - Poor communication is at the heart of most major organizational disasters
- To create good communication, it is essential to build real teams or communities
  - Real communication only happens within real communities
- The extent to which ideas can flow through any organization is a critical factor in the organization's continued success
- Successful teams sustain an evenly balanced flow of conversation, engage with each other, and continue research and dialogue outside set-piece meetings
- All interaction – including and perhaps especially "gossip" and "chat" – helps to forge successful teams
- Many communications carry emotional baggage
  - Good communicators understand and deal with this
- The answer to a difficult organizational problem is often known, but unconscious
  - There are ways to allow the unconscious to be become conscious
  - "The truth is always welcome"

CHAPTER 6

A WASTE OF SPACE
MAKING THE WORKSPACE WORK

We used to work wherever the raw materials that enabled our work happened to be. If you raised crops or tended animals, you lived on the land. If you made furniture, you worked near the woods that supplied the timber that made the chairs, tables, and cupboards. If you caught fish for a living, you lived near the water. If you owned a mill, you built your mill wherever there was water or wind to give you a source of power. If you traded in goods that came from other parts of the world, you lived and worked on a trade route.

The first Industrial Revolution, in 18th-century England, changed all of that. The new source of power – steam produced from the heat generated by coal – enabled production on a previously unimaginable scale. Small-scale cottage industries were replaced by large manufactories. Workers left the fields, woods, and coasts to be employed at these new places of work. Rapid improvements in transportation – first the canals, then the railways, and later metalled roads – began the process of globalisation that would be completed by container shipping and air transportation, and which would connect places of manufacture with the whole of the world. The disconnect between work and where people lived had begun in earnest.

For example, up until the mid-18th century – the dawn of the Industrial Revolution – Manchester, England, had been a small market town, with a long history for weaving and trading in woollen and linen textiles. It then became a centre for the industrial weaving of cotton, because it was possible to ship raw cotton to Manchester by river from the great port of Liverpool, and because the area had plenty of rivers and streams to power the first water-driven mills. So far, so traditional, though the use of water power to drive mills signalled the beginning of the end for the old home-based cottage industry of hand-weaving.

As the mills switched from water to steam power, the growing network of canals meant that it was not necessary to relocate the mill to be near a coalfield: coal could be shipped to the mills, just as raw cotton was shipped to the mills. Coal, unlike wind and water, was a transportable power source.

The growing scale of coal-powered manufacturing meant that an industrial centre was needed. The great new mills needed various supplies and services – bleachers, dyers, engineering companies to supply and service the machines – and, of course, they and all of their satellite industries needed workers. The mills stayed in Manchester, and the people came to the mills. Workers flocked to the manufactories, and great towns sprang up around them (the increasing mechanization of agricultural work played a part, as did the Potato Famine in Ireland). The population of Manchester quadrupled between 1750 and 1850, creating the world's first industrial metropolis.

The first great industrial towns were hellish places, with horrific overcrowding and no sanitation. Typhus, smallpox, TB, cholera, and scarlet fever swept through communities of workers crammed into slum houses. In 1841, the average life expectancy of a working-class person in the UK was less than 27 years – a significant and shocking reduction in life expectancy compared with that at the end of the previous century. An even more shocking figure was recorded in an 1842 report by the Poor Law Commissioners: 57% of working-class children in the UK at that time died before the age of five.

Wealthy merchants, who had once lived in near their places of work, retreated to the suburbs to avoid the filth and squalor of the inner city, and used their once grand and prestigiously located townhouses for warehousing.[37] Work was shifting from being something that you did where you lived to a place that you went to in order to work. If you were poorly paid (which, by definition, manual workers were) it was necessary to live close enough to the manufactory to be able to walk there. In the early days of the Industrial Revolution – and right up to the present day in many parts of the world – this meant living in slum housing close to the place of work. In the UK, it took the efforts of at least a generation of Victorians to clear slums, build sewage systems, create clean water supplies, provide decent housing, and set up transport infrastructure that made life in industrial cities tolerable. These efforts continue – or in some cases have yet to begin – in rapidly industrializing countries around the world.

In time, with improvements in public transport and the general transportation infrastructure, it became less necessary for people to live in such close proximity to their places of work, or for the satellite industries that supported major manufacturing industries to be located in the same, crowded urban space. It was also now feasible to locate industries away from dense centres of population.

As more and more workers became "knowledge workers" – working with their brains rather than their hands – it became clear that many of the administrative and strategic functions of a business did not need to be located at the place of production. As the number of knowledge workers needed to fill roles at corporate headquarters increased, so it became necessary to locate those headquarters wherever knowledge workers were most readily available, which was in major cities.

The corporate headquarters of a business could be located in London, while its manufacturing base would stay in the Midlands, or in Scotland, or in the Philippines. Another disconnect – that between production and administration – was almost complete. Production tended to move out of poor, inner city areas, while corporate headquarters moved into the richer and more pleasant areas of the same cities, condemning knowledge workers to the tedium of a daily commute from the affordable areas of the city to the glamorous, central location of the corporate headquarters.

With the arrival of modern communications, it became less necessary for knowledge workers to be in any particular place in order to carry out their function – but, in general, the vast majority of knowledge workers continued to travel, from many miles around, to "their" corporate headquarters, located in the middle of a city.

The corporate headquarters was on its way to becoming what it is today: a symbolic building, the real purpose of which becomes more and more mysterious. Which brings us to the central question of this chapter: what, exactly, is any modern organizational headquarters for?

THE DICTATORSHIP OF BRICKS, STEEL, AND CONCRETE

Most (but far from all) organizations still need to have a place that they can call home. That place needs to be easily accessible for the people that the organization needs in order to be able to run its business; it needs a ready source of talent within a reasonable commuting distance.

There may be good reasons why this place should be in a prestigious location, and why it should make a bold statement about the organization. We are all in favour of central locations, good architecture, and bold statements, though we would also point out that the corporate headquarters of Walmart is based in a functional building in a generic commercial area outside downtown Bentonville, the small Arkansas US town where founder Sam Walton opened his first five-and-dime store. This is a nice reflection (perhaps even a bold statement) of Walmart's corporate culture, but one that would not suit a luxury goods manufacturer or a major advertising agency.

There are many factors that affect what kind of corporate building you might need, and where it should be located. But we must fight against the dictatorship of all of this brick, steel, and concrete. We must resist the notion that, just because the organization owns a central place that stands as a symbol for why the organization exists, the people that make up that organization must be constantly present at that symbolic place: a kind of congregation, present for long hours at the organizational temple in order to justify the existence of the various priests and officials who go about their mysterious business in that place.

Very soon, by way of example, the authors of this book plan to lease a very large and prestigious building in the middle of Manhattan (or London, or Beijing, or Mumbai, or Singapore; it probably doesn't matter) in order to proclaim the significance and importance of

Powell and Gifford, Inc. We will employ large numbers of people to turn up at this high-end location on a daily basis and spend most of their waking hours doing stuff (we're not sure yet exactly what will be required, but we'll worry about that later) in order to confirm the significance of the magnificent HQ of Powell and Gifford, Inc (and indeed, of Powell and Gifford, esquires).

Or, come to think of it, we could ask our new employees what exactly it was, in their opinion, that they should best do in order to maintain an adequate flow of revenues into Powell and Gifford, Inc, and then we could tell them that they could do those various things wherever the hell they liked. At home. On the beach. In the park. In some corner of the magnificent corporate HQ. Wherever.

We don't mean to be prescriptive about this. Home working might work for your organization, or it might not. Flexi-time is (surely?) now a given: people have lives to run that may or may not fit around the archaic notion of nine-to-five office hours (or is it now seven to eleven?)

You might want to assess people's contribution on the basis of management by objectives (why can we never get away from the word "management"?) or by whatever other method rings your bell when it comes to reassuring yourself that your investment in people is reaping a sufficient reward.

We don't care.

What we are saying is that there remains more than a lurking suspicion that most steam-engine organizations view the corporate headquarters as the place to which workers are summoned on a daily basis *so that they can be supervised and controlled*. That, if people are indeed allowed to make their contribution on the beach, or at home, or even tucked away in a nice private recess somewhere in the corporate headquarters, then steam-engine managers can never be sure what they are up to.

As we will see in the next few pages, there are some very good reasons why you might want to bring people together into a central space and get them to interact with each other and with the bustling world outside the office door. Keeping paranoid steam-engine managers happy by pandering to the illusion that they are in control of everything is not one of them.

But we digress. The measurement, analysis, and control of people that goes on within the confines of the organizational headquarters is just one aspect of what is wrong with the whole steam-engine approach to bringing people together in order to achieve the organization's purpose.

The rest of this chapter will focus on what is wrong with the physical aspect and location of our workplaces – and, far more interestingly, on how these places and spaces can be changed and put to far more productive use.

THE STEAM ENGINE RULES OF ATTENDANCE

This, one might scurrilously suggest, is how the average steam-engine organization sees the relationship between the organization, the workforce, and the workplace:

- Attendance at the workplace is compulsory for the duration of every working day, with the exception of certain outside visits for precisely defined business purposes
- Attendance outside normal working hours is welcomed; absenteeism is not tolerated
- Workers have their allocated station within the workplace and will stay at their station at all times, unless their presence is required at certain internal meetings
- Socialisation within the workplace is acceptable at certain defined break times, such as coffee breaks and lunch hours, but is to be discouraged at all other times
- Private and social matters should be dealt with outside working hours; workers may be required to take work home with them, but it is not acceptable to bring the home into the workplace.

The workplace has become a part of the steam-engine organization's continuing obsession with control: it wants to assemble its workforce in one place and to supervise them at all times, to ensure that they are focussing on what management imagines to be the task at hand. Exploration, reflection, purposeful social interaction, down-time, initiative, enterprise, the development of group intelligence – none of these useful practices is encouraged by the classic steam-engine concept of the purpose and function of the modern workplace.

The workplace does fulfil a vital function for most organizations. Organizations may or may not wish to explore homeworking, virtual meetings, digital forums, and all of the other exciting and useful ways of getting together that technology is increasingly making available to us, but most organizations will still want to have a place that they can call home. A place where most of the members of the organization are gathered, most of the time, during the working week.

These places should emphatically NOT be places of supervision or places of control. They should be devoted to the vital business of encouraging and harnessing human energy in order to achieve the purpose of the organization. They should be designed and operated in ways that encourage social interaction, chance encounters, spontaneous gatherings, happy accidents, and the constant churn and flow of ideas and information. None of this happens in the battery-hen factories that most of steam-engine workplaces have become.

The next few pages will explore what a few business thinkers believe can be done to change this, for the better, using the same physical spaces that are available to all organizations.

"SEALING THEIR OWN DEATH WARRANT"

Most corporate headquarters were not designed in any meaningful sense for the purpose for which they are needed. Utility has a great deal to do with it (a drive toward cramming the maximum number of people into the minimum amount of expensive space) and the fact that most architects spend their time worrying about the outer shape of a building and assume that companies will be able to make something of the cavernous empty floors inside the supposedly attractive shell.

Once people have been crammed into cubicles on the cavernous floors, of course, mere utility is trumped by various power plays: the need for a particular department to have its own space; the need for many "executive offices", and the overwhelming need for a suite of offices that are clearly much better than the rest of the executive

NANCY HAAS, "THE HOUSE THAT BLOOMBERG BUILT",
FAST COMPANY, NOVEMBER 1995

Nothing better illustrates [Michael Bloomberg's] contempt for conventional wisdom than the 50,000-square-foot office he has had installed on floors 11 through 17 [of 499 Park Avenue] ...

Instead of streamlined silence, the former securities trader... believes in noise and cataclysm. His theory is simple: shove lots of well-paid young upstarts (2,200 employees, average age 31) together in a small space for long hours, give them the best equipment possible, and you'll get magic. "What I'm selling is information," he says. "The best way to get it faster than anyone else is to create an environment of constant creativity. You have to turn up the volume, make people a little uncomfortable." ...

To begin with, the elevators open on only one of the six floors he leases – the middle one. The idea is simple: every morning, every evening, everyone has to come through the same doors to get in and out of work. There will be interaction. Interaction will generate information sharing. Information sharing will generate new and better coverage. That's how you build an empire.

Running up the spine of the space, connecting the Bloomberg floors, is a spiral staircase. But what looks like a staircase is actually a vertical meeting room. Bloombergers, passing on the stairs, nametags clearly visible, are apt to stop and compare notes before heading off in opposite directions. More information transfer.

Then there's the food court. Set off by aquariums full of colorful tropical fish, the mini-mall offers everything from sodas to fresh fruit, cereal to candy bars. Bloomberg's design purpose? "I want people to be well-fed and satisfied. I want them to be able to grab a cup of coffee with a colleague and hash things out," he says. "But most of all I want them to stay here. I don't want them leaving."

The 2,800-square-foot newsroom holds an international news service as well as radio and TV networks. The average workspace per employee is roughly four-feet square – a purposefully tight squeeze. "I like to see people brimming over with ideas, all over the guy next to them," Bloomberg says.

Nancy Haas, 'The house that Bloomberg Built', *Fast Company*, November 1995, http://bit.ly/WG78Vp

offices: the "C Suite", so called because of all the "chiefs" that live there – the chief executive officer, the chief financial officer, and so on.

This may not be a good plan. As Tracey Camilleri, Associate Fellow of Saïd Business School, Oxford University, told us: "Increasingly, as we have less and less time, the physical pathways that you follow day in and day out, and who you run up against, becomes your network. So these executive floors with different coloured carpet are increasingly sealing their own death warrant, because they're not coming across difference and change and disruption."

We don't suppose that many senior executives are intentionally signing their own death warrants, as Camilleri suggests they may be, so some reflection on what corporate spaces are *for* and what they do – and don't do but could do – may be useful.

A number of highly successful chief executives have had some exciting and radical ideas about what they want their corporate HQ to achieve, and how they can play with the space within that place in order to achieve their goals. In 1981, Michael Bloomberg was laid off by Wall Street investment bank Salmon Brothers.

"They kicked me out on my ass," Bloomberg told *Fast Company* magazine, refreshingly, though it should be said that he was kicked out with a severance package of some $20 million. He went on to launch Bloomberg L.P., a financial services information venture that supplied financial data and software to financial houses via the eponymous Bloomberg terminal, and which grew into a media empire incorporating a wire service (Bloomberg News), a global television network (Bloomberg Television), and several magazines and websites. And then in 2001, of course, Mr Bloomberg went on to succeed Rudolph Giuliani as mayor of New York City, holding the office for three consecutive terms.

What is interesting for our purposes is what Bloomberg did – more than 20 years ago – with his then brand-new corporate headquarters, established on six floors of a skyscraper on Manhattan's prestigious Park Avenue.

You don't get much more symbolic than that, but what Bloomberg did with this expensive corporate headquarters was genuinely functional. He used the space to squash talented young people together in a pressure-cooker atmosphere, offering free food and drink to encourage them to mingle, and to keep them on the premises – thereby setting up the physical conditions that would drive the maximum number of interactions and the possibility of information exchange.

"I like to see people brimming over with ideas," he told *Fast Company*, "all over the guy next to them" (see previous panel).

ENCOURAGING SERENDIPITY

Tony Hsieh, co-founder and CEO of online shoe retailer Zappos, actively encourages a culture of "fun and a little weirdness" at the workplace. He also believes in serendipity – chance encounters that have good outcomes. The trick, he told *Inc.* magazine in 2013, is to have more chance encounters:

> *I think you can create your own luck. The key is to meet as many people as you can and really get to know them. If you're in an environment where you're always running into people, the chances of one of those collisions being meaningful is maybe 1 in 1,000. But if you do it 100 times more, your odds go up. My advice is: meet lots of different people without trying to extract value from them. You don't need to connect the dots right away. But if you think about each person as a new dot on your canvas, over time, you'll see the full picture.*

Hsieh believes this so strongly that, after a chance encounter (obviously) with the owner of a Las Vegas bar, he was persuaded not to build a new Zappos campus somewhere on the outskirts of the city (the company had previously been based in Henderson, part of the Las Vegas metropolitan area) but to move into the old Las Vegas City Hall, in the middle of the old downtown neighbourhood, and become a part of the project to revitalize the area.

Hsieh and his colleagues altered their new building in ways that would maximize the number of chance encounters between colleagues – but they also set out to maximize encounters with their new neighbours:

TONY HSIEH, CEO ZAPPOS

A HYBRID BETWEEN CORPORATION AND COMMUNITY

Wanting employees to be out and about in the community may seem counterintuitive at first. But research has shown that historically, when cities double in size, productivity and innovation per resident increases by 15%. But when companies get bigger, usually productivity per employee goes down.

Part of our goal at Zappos is to avoid that fate, by creating a hybrid between corporation and community that's never been attempted at scale before. Research has also shown that most innovation comes from something outside your industry being applied to your own, which is why we believe that collisions within a company are just as important as collisions outside of a company.

It may seem strange that although Zappos uses technology to scale, we still rely so much on face-to-face interactions. It's because our biology has evolved far, far slower than our technology.

We are a social species, designed for in-person interactions in multiple locations, not just by email and phone calls or remotely from home, and also not just in conference rooms. We are designed to be in motion, and we are designed to be creative, to share ideas, and to innovate in multiple locations throughout the day. Getting to know people in different environments and contexts leads to higher levels of trust, better communication, and can ultimately contribute to a stronger and more innovative culture.

Tony Hsieh, 'Working from home alone is the real culprit', *Forbes*, 19/03/2013, http://bit.ly/1r8gPEX

At Zappos, we do a lot to get people running into each other. At our office, for example, there are exits on all four sides of the building. We've locked them all except one. It's more inconvenient, but we prioritize collisions over convenience. The Downtown Project, our drive to revitalize downtown Las Vegas, does the same thing, but on a much bigger scale. We thought: "How can we get people in the city to run into each other more often?" So we're moving our office into the old city-hall building, and we've already *got 10 tech start-ups to set up nearby. It's all about maximizing collisions and accelerating serendipity.*[38]

"NOISOME AND DISORDERLY HOUSES"

Two of the contributors to this book – both founders of their own studios – agree with the principle of structuring lives, businesses, and buildings in ways that encourage "happy collisions".

John Willshire is the founder of the innovation studio Smithery. John, as we will see, makes it his business not to be based at any particular location: he believes in spending his time in places where he might bump into interesting new people, and be exposed to interesting new ideas.

His 'co-conspirator', as they refer to each other, is Simon Jordan the co-founder of Jump Studios, an architectural and design studio based in London's Commercial Street, once a notorious area just outside the old City of London, described in an 1838 report by a select committee of the UK's Houses of Parliament as being inhabited by "women of the lowest character, receivers of stolen goods, thieves and the most atrocious offenders".[39] The area was famous for the Spitalfields fruit and vegetable market, now relocated further to the east of the city, and for London's "rag trade" – the many small, borderline-legal sweatshop operations that typically employ immigrant workers to supply low-cost clothing to Britain's fashion retailers. The area is experiencing both a gentrification, driven by London's stratospheric housing prices, and a commercial resurgence. It is a place where people meet, ideas are exchanged, and things happen.

We met John and Simon at Shoreditch House, a members' club on Shoreditch High Street, which runs into Commercial Street from the north. Shoreditch has an even more ancient pedigree for bad behaviour, having been described in 1596 as home to a "great number of dissolute, loose, and insolent people harboured in such and the like noisome and disorderly houses, as namely poor cottages, and habitations of beggars and people without trade, stables, inns, alehouses, taverns ... dicing houses, bowling alleys, and brothel houses".[40]

Urban centres like these, located just outside the "respectable" hubs of great cities around the world, have always been the breeding ground of enterprise and creativity. Shoreditch was home to the first purpose-built playhouse in England, The Theatre, built in 1576. A young actor and playwright called William Shakespeare was drawn there from his native Warwickshire sometime around 1590; his early plays were performed at The Theatre, as they were at the nearby Curtain Theatre, also in Shoreditch. When the lease on the land that The Theatre was built on ran out in 1599, the company enterprisingly took the timbers of the old theatre to Southwark, south of the river Thames, and reassembled them to create the world-famous Globe theatre, which became home to Shakespeare's playing company.

In a nice modern echo of this idea, a "pop-up shopping mall" is sitting at the time of writing on a site on Shoreditch High Street. "Boxpark" is built entirely from old shipping containers, and will last for four years only. It offers low-rent, low-risk spaces for entrepreneurial businesses – especially the fashion businesses for which the area is famous, but also for lifestyle brand retailers, coffee shops, art galleries, performing spaces for musicians – and has become a thriving little creative community on an inner-city high street, built out of nothing at a tiny cost.

Formerly run-down and neglected urban areas like this are once again becoming the creative hubs of great cities – in exactly the way that Tony Hsieh believes that downtown Las Vegas will be revitalized to become a source of energy and income for that city. People bump into and bounce ideas off each other in these kinds of areas; new relationships are forged, business is done. Rent is lower, but billions of dollars of finance and expenditure are flowing past, just a few blocks away.

LIVING IN CORRIDORS

The Shoreditch House club where we met Simon and John occupies the top three floors and roof of a refurbished factory from the 1930s. Large open spaces have been converted to create both intimate and shared spaces. There was disappointingly little evidence of the dissolute, loose, or even insolent behaviour described in the 16th century, but a great deal of the vibrancy and energy that has always characterized these and similar inner-city areas.

The new generation of London clubs like this have come a long way from being places in town for the aristocracy, like the old clubs of Mayfair, or watering holes for journalists and media types, like the newer clubs of Soho and elsewhere. These new clubs are designed

JOHN WILLSHIRE, FOUNDER OF PRODUCT AND MARKETING INNOVATION STUDIO, SMITHERY
HELPING THE FLOW OF IDEAS
I was working with a client on some strategy stuff about their business, and a lot of their people were saying that they wanted to do more talks. They were doing some internal events and talks and so on anyway, but there was feeling that they wanted to expand this and to involve some external speakers.

So we started unpicking why we wanted to do that and what were interesting things to do, and it turned out that what they felt was that talks help you come to some resolution on any thinking you've been doing. If you've got a date in a diary when you have to stand up in a space and say things to other people, you're forced to come up with an actual view on it and an actual articulation of it. And it might not be totally formalized, it might not be finished but it helps your own method and thinking process as you go.

Having auditoriums and places to share stuff could work for formal things but also sort of informal things. If you've got an idea of something you want to talk about, you could have a digital voting system: "I might do a talk on such and such if anyone's interested." And if the "auditorium" is in a public space in the organization, then people could just be walking past the space and become interested. And so suddenly it forces pressure, rather than just sitting at email systems and doing whatever else, it becomes a physical thing. If enough people tweak that, it becomes a physical reality and suddenly it brings these ideas into the workspace.

John Willshire in conversation with the authors

to bring enterprising people from growing new industries together – to create the serendipity that Tony Hsieh of Zappos is seeking for his business by setting up shop in downtown Las Vegas.

John Willshire manages somehow to be both relaxed and intense. He has a soft Scottish brogue and a cropped, spiky hairdo. He fizzes with ideas but listens carefully to what everyone else says. His first act, after ushering us all to a couple of comfortable seats beneath factory-style windows offering a spectacular view of the City skyline, is to hand over what seems to be set of playing cards, carefully presented in a box that must be opened by pushing from the side in an unexpected way.

At first, we assume that the box we have been given is the world's most elaborate set of business cards, until we work out how to open the box. "They're called Artefact cards and they're designed to be difficult; a bit like a Chinese puzzle," John explains. The idea is to write ideas as they occur to you on one of the many bright yellow cards in the pack, and then to begin to play around with the cards/ideas in a physical way. We begin to play, scribbling ideas on the cards, scattering them on the table among the cups of coffee and glasses of water, as John continues:

> I've always been interested in the hot-spot thing, when you think of corridors. Not even well-designed spaces for interaction, just the places where you happen across people. I don't have a conventional office, I have some home office space, I have some client office space and I come to places like this, or small coffee shops, or wherever else, and I work. But I'm trying to make a much of my life corridors as possible, just because it's corridors where the stuff you don't expect to happen, happens. And organizations are bad at thinking like that. Corridors look like empty space. Instead of having space where people just walk into, they think: "Let's fill it with other people!"

"BEHAVIOUR FIRST AND FOREMOST"

John's collaborator, Simon Jordan, refers to himself as a design strategist. Simon's partner and co-founder of Jump Studios is an architect, while Simon's primary concern is with organizational behaviour: the human, cultural factors that make organizations what they are. Thoughtful, precise, articulate, and unassuming, Simon sets out to create interior spaces that facilitate what organizations are trying to achieve by enabling and encouraging the human behaviours that are most likely to lead to the desired outcome:

> My entry point to an organization, when it comes to design, is not necessarily where an architect might enter a project. They might start from the building forward, but I'm always looking at the organization, the culture and the behaviour, and the behaviours first and foremost, and then looking to see how we can design spaces that help facilitate or support those behaviours. And increasingly we do a lot of work with media and tech companies, and our clients are people like Google and Yahoo. The convention with an architect is that you will start with the building, first and foremost, you start thinking about the space, whereas we're thinking about the behaviour.

Like John, Simon and his colleagues have a thing about corridors. Corridors are spaces that people use to get from one place to another. The good news is that, in a corridor, people are not "at home". They have left their own space and are now open to encounters. Simon sees these kinds of spaces as "social condensers", or ways of "slowing people down" when they are out and about, to encourage interactions:

> We do a similar thing with circulation spaces, just trying to find a way to slow people down. Architecture should try to moderate behaviour; think about what you can do in a corridor to get people to stop, even if you just put a sofa or some chairs. We talk about corridors, but it's also about staircases, making staircases a happening point. There are a number of examples of where people have used, or even introduced a staircase to open up and connect floors in a building, so you create a much better flow, but then allow people to occupy the staircase. So it might be that

you stick a screen on a wall and suddenly the staircase becomes
an auditorium and that auditorium then effectively plays host to a
series of talks.

John elaborates on the idea of the talk – formal or informal – as
a way of helping people to articulate their ideas and to run them
past their colleagues. After all, nothing concentrates the mind like
the need to talk for 15 minutes about something that's interesting
you, but this doesn't need to be a particularly formal event. In fact,
informal gatherings in pop-up auditoriums – like Simon's staircases
– offer a way of making the exchange of ideas a natural thing;
something that the organization does all of the time, in many ways;
something that becomes the "normal" way to behave.

Offering food and drink is another trick of the trade for getting
members of the organization to engage. There has been a move
toward employing "company baristas" offering a café-style service to
employees and visitors, encouraging people to mix and chat. A new
and clever variation on this is a coffee machine – with a twist. "They
have coffee systems which can only make coffee for two or more
people," John tells us. "So you can't make just your own coffee. You
have to think: 'Who else wants a coffee?' You have to find someone
else or you'll be wasting the coffee. It's just a nice, little, subtle thing.
You can't have an individual coffee."

Simon offers a final thought on techniques for making
organizational spaces work harder to get ideas moving around. He
points out that, whereas the internet is creating greater transparency
in almost every field of activity, nearly all organizational headquarters
are resolutely opaque, sealed off deliberately from the outside world:

Another thing that I think is early – and probably an initiative
that a lot of companies find difficult to embrace but will I think,
eventually need to – is this whole idea of transparency. So if you
think about the way the internet has rendered everything much
more transparent, what does that actually mean for what have
traditionally been kind of closed, introspective spaces? We're
talking about the buildings – but actually, isn't there an opportunity

to make the building represent more than just a corporate closed private space? ... And if you talk to some corporations they're horrified by that idea, but I think there are a lot that are starting to embrace it ... imagine if they just had this big, open, co-working space for everybody with free Wi-Fi on the ground floor and then just basically pulled in everybody from the local community, into a space where people can interconnect.

THE PURPOSE OF BRINGING PEOPLE TOGETHER

Despite the increasing feasibility of virtual offices and virtual meetings, we think that organizations will continue to want a physical place that can be called home; we also think that this physical space will continue to be used to make some kind of statement about the organization, and we think that the organization will want to bring a lot of its people into this space for most of the working week.

But the organization must remind itself that the purpose of bringing people together is not to control them; it is not monitor colleagues' behaviour or to analyse and adjust it. We believe that attempts to tweak people's behaviour to make them behave in ways that are supposedly most advantageous to the organization are doomed to fail.

Physical offices for knowledge workers will always need to be situated where there are large number of knowledge workers available, which will always tend to mean large cities. There are, however, some interesting alternatives to the obvious places where corporations tend to gather: some vibrant, emerging parts of town where there may be higher levels of energy, a better mix of enterprising people and a greater flow of ideas.

The key thing to remember is that the main function of a collection of knowledge workers is not to "get stuff done". If knowledge workers are carrying out routine tasks, then these tasks can, and one day will and should be automated and given to machines.

The function of a collection of knowledge workers is to generate new and better ideas, and the way to get people to have new and better ideas is push them together in constantly shifting combinations, continually meeting new colleagues to exchange information with, and to bounce their ideas off.

There are some simple things that can be done that will encourage this. Sitting people in cubicles and encouraging them to spend as much of their time there as possible is not one these things.

TAKING THE ORGANIZATION FROM THE INDUSTRIAL ERA TO THE AGE OF IDEAS
Transforming the steam engine, one step at a time

- The Industrial Revolution introduced the model of large-scale endeavour, sucking in support services and large numbers of people to one central place of work
- In post-modern industrial societies, increasing demand for knowledge workers has drawn organizational headquarters back to the city, where knowledge workers can be found
- Modern communications make it possible to work in virtual office space, but most organizations will continue to want a central, physical place of work
- Steam-engine organizations see the central office as a place that allows them to supervise, monitor and control their workforce
  - This is not the purpose of the modern workplace
  - The core purpose of a collection of knowledge workers is not to "get stuff done", it is to have new and better ideas
- Bringing people together in a common space and actively helping them to interact is a very good way to generate and refine new ideas
  - There are many things that can to done with the design of interior corporate spaces that will encourage encounters and the flow of ideas
- Ideas need to flow into the organization from outside
  - Some city locations are more vibrant than others, and have more potential for generating useful encounters
- The corporate headquarters will endure, it just needs to reassess its purpose

CHAPTER 7

IN PRAISE OF ANARCHY
WHY CORPORATE DEMOCRACY IS NOT THE ANSWER

Many business thinkers have suggested that what organizations need is more democracy: that the solution to the screaming-out-loud problem of all the old-fashioned, steam-engine, command-and-control, scientific-management nonsense is to make the organization more democratic.

This sounds like a wonderful idea if you say it quickly and don't think about it too much. Isn't that what we all want? If you're tired of being pushed around by your numbskull of a boss – the one with the emotional intelligence of a hyena who believes that fear and micro-management are his most useful leadership tools (he sure gets around, that boss; we keep meeting him) – then, yes, you would like a bit more democracy round here. And yes, you would like to have your say about what is required of you in the place where you spend the majority of your waking hours.

It would be pointless to start splitting etymological hairs, but as a matter of observable fact, the majority of businessmen recoil when they hear the word "democracy" – and they are right to do so. We can probably all agree that organizations should be more democratic, in the wishy-washy sense that "we should try to involve everyone a bit more in the decision-making process". The trouble is that this kind of thinking leads to what the authors of this book call "steam-wash" – the merely cosmetic improvement of what are essentially steam-engine processes: a bit less control; fewer pointless metrics; a more democratic ethos in a relatively meaningless, let's-go-through-the-motions kind of way.

What is needed is something more fundamental. Something more like anarchy.

DEMOCRACY: NOT A GOOD WAY TO RUN A BUSINESS

Democracy is a very loaded word. We all have a very precise idea of what it means, and it is, of course, highly coloured by our concept of political democracy.

Democracy has come to mean, primarily, something like the election of governing bodies, based on a popular vote. The elected body then gets to do pretty much whatever it pleases for a short time, subject to the buffering forces of the media, powerful lobby groups, and the chastening knowledge that the elected body will have to face the electorate again in the not-too-distant future.

Democracy works reasonably well as a way of governing nation states. As Winston Churchill said in the House of Commons in 1947: "Democracy is the worst form of government, except for all those other forms that have been tried from time to time."

But democracy, in its commonly understood form, is not a good way to run a business. The risk that democracy becomes merely the dictatorship of the majority is very real in organizations, since organizations are not subject to the same vital buffering forces that beset and challenge a national government (the electorate, the media, lobbyists, and so on). Deciding issues democratically in business means that dissenting voices do not get aired, considered and in some way incorporated, they just get voted down by what becomes, in a very meaningful sense, "the tyranny of the majority".

To be more brutal about it, as the leader of a business, would you really want to subject your (or anybody else's) initiatives to a popular vote? How many bold new corporate visions would have seen the light of day if they had been put to the popular vote? Do we really think that democracy is the best route to cutting-edge innovation? Will democracy help us to create lean, mean, agile organizations?

We are, perhaps, being deliberately provocative here, but we would like to throw a cat or two among the pigeons. This chapter will argue that what is needed in the workplace is not more democracy but more anarchy – the primary meaning of which is "the absence of government".

The common cartoon image of the anarchist is, of course, that of a wild-eyed individual carrying a large, round bomb with a spluttering fuse – typically with the word "bomb" written on it, in case we had missed the point. But this is a travesty of what was initially a thoughtful political ideology. Many anarchists believe that people are perfectly capable of forming stable and supportive communities in the absence of central government. The early American pioneers did exactly that, and the original, non-politicized meaning of "libertarianism" was meant to reflect something a lot like this.

Let's not – really *not* – enter that particular political minefield. When this chapter argues that the organization needs to be a bit more anarchic, please try to conjure up an image of the early pioneers settling the American West, building thriving communities without the help or interference of a central government, as opposed to that wild-eyed chap with the spluttering bomb. Think about the town hall meetings of New England, held in the US since colonial days, where whole communities gathered to air opinions on an important issue. Think about any community at a time of crisis, when everyone will lend a helping hand, and natural leaders will emerge.

If you really don't like us using the word anarchy, you might prefer a more diplomatic option: "self-organization". But, please, let's get away from the word "democracy".

CONSENSUS AND SELF-ORGANIZATION

The more one looks at the small but growing band of organizations that have abandoned command and control and embraced some form of democratic process, the more it becomes evident that these exciting, new organizational processes are *not* democracy. The beating heart of these processes is generally consensus: it is self-organization, leading to decisions reached after much debate, in which every opinion is aired, but which are finally reached *consensually*.

As one worker at the GE Aviation jet engine plant at Durham, North Carolina, told *Fast Company* magazine back in 1999:

Everybody doesn't see things in the same way, but we've had training on how to reach consensus. We've had training on how to live with ideas that we might not necessarily agree with. All the things you normally fuss and moan about to yourself and your buddies – well, we have a chance to do something about them. I can't say "they" don't know what's going on, or "they" made a bad decision. I am "they".[41]

In the search for a way to describe what forward-looking organizations are doing as they experiment with new ways of working together, we would suggest that "self-organization" is the most accurate term for the most successful variants. But since what is needed to transform the steam engine into something fit for the 21st century is nothing short of a revolution, allow us at least to toy with the term anarchy – the steam-engine organization really does need a lot more anarchy.

BUILDING JET ENGINES WITHOUT MANAGERS: SELF-ORGANIZATION AT GE AVIATION

The aviation wing of the mighty General Electric Corporation (GE) has been experimenting, very successfully, with forms of self-organization at its jet engine plants in North America for over 30 years. The results, in terms of overall productivity, quality, reduced manufacturing cost, and increased turnaround time – to say nothing of employee satisfaction, flexibility, and retention – were so remarkable that, in 2010, GE Aviation decided to roll out "Teaming", as they call it, across all of its plants.

In a 2013 report, GE Aviation noted that where a "non-Teaming" site had shown a 3.9% decline in productivity, with a cycle time of 30 days and a first-time yield (products with no defects that require reworking when first completed) of 77%, one of the company's Teaming sites at Durham, North Carolina, had shown a 6.4% increase in productivity, with a 16-day cycle time and 94% first-time yield.[42] If you like a good metric, you have to admire the Durham plant's figures.

The first GE plant to embark on the Teaming route was the one in Bromont, Quebec, which embraced a "participative management" culture from the moment it first opened, way back in 1982. The plant's relatively flat management structure involved only a plant leader, a support team, and a production team. The members of the production team took on many functions that were previously the prerogative of management, typically via committees (sometimes also known as councils). The councils make decisions on issues such as multi-skilling (all engineers are required to acquire multiple skills, with at least four skills needed to reach the top pay grade), hiring, and health and safety; they can make recommendations, but not decisions, about issues to do with, for example, pay levels.

The council representatives – who are sometimes elected and, in more technical roles, are appointed by interview – make decisions on behalf of their team (a classically democratic role, we confess) and communicate the council's decisions back to the team. But the preferred method of decision-making for the councils is *consensus*: everyone gets to voice their opinion, and the final decision is embraced by all. There is no vote, and there are no winners and losers.[43]

Teams at Bromont, which range in size from 55 to 140, still have two "cell leaders", also known as coaches. In an article about Teaming at GE Aviation, *Management Innovation eXchange* describes the role of cell leaders as being to "help encourage ideas, engage their teams in the business metrics, and facilitate communication within the team when needed".[44]

In 2013, there were some 80 salaried staff at Bromont, including engineers, and 630 other staff who were paid hourly. Engineers walk the floor, talking to teams about the issues they are facing and working with them in the constant search for innovation and improvement. However, given that there are cell leaders and salaried engineers working alongside hourly-paid employees, there is still a sense of the old, scientific management split between managers and workers to the setup at the Bromont plant, progressive though it is.

GE DURHAM: MORE RADICAL, MORE ANARCHIC

If the Bromont plant represented a step forward in terms of participative management, then the Durham, North Carolina plant, launched in 1993, was far more radical – more anarchic. When *Fast Company* magazine wrote about this remarkable plant in 1999, there were 170 technicians employed; today there are over 300.

RACHEL EMMA SILVERTON, WALL STREET JOURNAL
"WHO'S THE BOSS? THERE ISN'T ONE"
For years General Electric Co. GE has run some aviation-manufacturing facilities with no foremen or shop-floor bosses. The industrial giant says it uses the system to boost productivity in low-volume factories with a relatively small number of employees, each of whom can do several tasks.

One leader, the plant manager, sets production goals and helps resolve problems but doesn't dictate daily workflow. Teams, whose members volunteer to take on various duties, meet before and after each shift to discuss the work to be done and address problems to be solved.

The first of these self-managed teams began nearly two decades ago in a Durham, N.C., plant, but in the past five years they have spread to other GE facilities. The team structure is being expanded to all of GE Aviation's 83 supply-chain sites, which employ 26,000.

Rachel Emma Silverton, Wall Street Journal, updated 19.06.2012, http://on.wsj.com/VbHgj0

And there is still just one boss — except that the boss isn't really "the boss" in the normal sense. The boss gets to make A-grade decisions all by his or herself; B-grade decision are made by the boss with input from everyone affected by the decisions; C-grade decisions, the most common type, are made by consensus between everyone affected. In 1999, the boss was Paula Sims. She told *Fast Company* that she made only about 10 A-grade decisions a year. Her main task was to keep everyone focussed on the overarching goal: to make jet engines better, faster, cheaper, safer; year after year. The teams could be relied upon to optimize their own activities; her job was to organize the plant and its output to ensure that it was competitive against other plants, and kept attracting new projects. "Each team, or group of teams, may be optimizing itself," she said, "but what's the right way to optimize the plant? If we've optimized each engine program, how do I free up resources for growth and for process improvement?"

The employees, in the meantime, go about their own business, un-managed. Like their colleagues at the Bromont plant, the Durham team members have councils that handle issues that cut across the various teams: HR issues, supplier problems, computer systems. Everything else is decided on by consensus by the individual teams (of which there were 18 in 2013[45]). As *Fast Company* reported: "At GE Durham, virtually every decision is made by a team, by consensus. Consensus is another of the founding principles of GE Durham. It is so ingrained that technicians have turned consensus into a verb: the people at the plant routinely talk about 'consensing' on something."[46]

There are two shifts at Durham, so there is a daily meeting at 2:30 pm, when the shifts overlap at the end of one team's day and the beginning of the other's. This vital meeting covers any current technical issues with the project in hand, but also forward-planning, overtime, and hiring.

The teams at Durham know everything that they need to know in order to run their businesses: information on safety, quality, delivery, and financial data is shared on a plant, team, and individual basis. Once per quarter, the team reviews its figures with the team leader.

There is a thorough and painstaking recruitment process, designed to ensure that new workers have not only the right technical skills, but also the right soft skills: teamwork, communication, mature judgment, flexibility, integrity.

One new member of the team told *Fast Company* about his first experience of working with GE Durham:

> We had to come up with a schedule. We had the chance to order tools, tool carts, and so on. We had to figure out how the assembly line to make the engine should flow. We were put on councils for every part of the business.
>
> I was never valued that much as an employee in my life. I had never been at the point where I couldn't wait to get to work. But here, I couldn't wait to get to work every day.[47]

Involved, committed, self-motivated teams of people deliver results. When the Durham plant started to produce the CFM56 engine, which had been in production at another plant for many years, the plant leader picked the first two members of the new CFM team, plus a technical-support team, and these three set about building the new team. The HR council worked out a plan to lend one member from each team to the new CFM team to tide them through the early stages, and drew up a list of volunteers who were willing to work overtime and weekends, if necessary.

Durham shipped its first CFM engine nine weeks later, at a cost 12–13% lower than the established plant.

SEMCO: DEMOCRACY OR ANARCHY?

It seems wrong to discuss democracy in the workplace without once again involving Ricardo Semler, owner of the Brazilian manufacturing company, Semco, and author of *Maverick! The Success Story Behind the World's Most Unusual Workplace* and *The Seven Day Weekend: A Better Way to Work in the 21st Century.*

Mention democracy in the workplace and people say: "Oh, have your read Semler?" And rightly so. Semler featured in chapter 1 of this book, talking about his bonfire of bureaucracies. He describes his changes as "democratic", and perhaps it is unfair to quibble with his own choice of the word. It's just that, for the reasons outlined at the start of this chapter, "democracy" really does not seem to be the best word to describe the changes that Semler put in place at Semco, the company that he inherited from his father.

Let's explore in more detail exactly what it was that Semler did at Semco, which manufactures a wide range of consumer and industrial products, including marine pumps, industrial mixers and agitators, cooling units, and food processing plants.

CATHEDRAL BUILDERS, NOT STONE CUTTERS

Semco set out to be the kind of "hero" leader that he had imagined he should be, working long and gruelling hours and jetting around the world, generating business for his company. Then, when he brought himself near to a stress-related collapse, he began to reconsider the best way to run the company. He forced himself to leave the office at 7:00 every evening, tried not to work at weekends, and "delegated furiously". But he still felt that something was missing – he felt that his workforce was alienated; that his employees were working because they had to, not because they wanted to. He felt everyone behaved like "stone cutters", whereas he wanted people who felt not only like highly skilled stone masons but, most importantly, like cathedral builders: people who felt they were making a real contribution to the great project to which they were devoting their skills and their labors.

Set out below are the most significant changes that Semler put in place[48], many of which are very similar in intent and in impact to the practices at GE Durham.

SETTING YOUR OWN PRODUCTION TARGETS

One of Semler's earliest changes was the introduction of worker councils, where his employees were invited to take decisions on matters previously reserved for management. The councils began with improvements to common areas and the plant restaurant, and swiftly moved on to more fundamental issues, such as productivity – where they began to set their own production targets and discuss product ranges, switching from line to batch production, with workers developing a wider range of skills – and finance and staffing issues.

When Semler wrote *Maverick!*, in the early 1990s, the Brazilian economy was famously erratic. During downturns, committees took decisions to lower wages or increase hours to save jobs. If layoffs were inevitable, committees took part in the selection of staff who were laid off, considering history, loyalty, the ability to find new job, and family responsibilities. The dismissal of an employee with more than three years' service, or one who was older than 50 years old, needed special approval.

"Together we tried to be socially just," Semler writes. The various processes slowed things down, but "perhaps that was an unavoidable price for corporate democracy".

THE LEADERSHIP TEAM

Semler set up weekly meetings of "all those in leadership positions". The marketing manager, for example, would present her spending plans to the other members of the leadership team to get them approved – something that had previously been the prerogative of the top management team. If the new leadership team could not agree, a vote was taken.

Agendas for the weekly leadership meetings began to get shorter as people got into the habit of making their own decisions. The new system also made leaders demonstrate exactly how they added value to the process, and since the leadership team now set budgets, management roles that were clearly ineffective risked being eliminated.

The group soon began to take real control of operational decisions. "Managers have been consulting employees for centuries," Semler writes. "It's only when bosses give up decision-making and let their employees govern themselves that the possibility exists for a business jointly managed by workers and executives."

THE ECONOMIES OF LACK OF SCALE

Semco divided its plants into smaller units. Workers in these units then chose to organize themselves into "cells": teams of workers who assembled groups of different machines and "fashion a product from beginning to end giving them accountability for the product's quality and the enormous satisfaction that comes with a complete task".

Because workers now had, in effect, a basket of jobs, the appropriate salary for this array of skills was agreed. The cells took over quality control, as well as hiring and firing.

As an interesting side issue, Semler also found that, though not being able to order in bulk was more expensive for each unit, the smaller units carried less inventory ("some of our units turn over their complete inventory seventeen times a year, as against an industry average of slightly more than three such rotations"). Products might take longer to produce, but delivery times still improved. There was no longer any need for expensive and time-consuming quality-control departments.

"In times of robust economic growth," he writes, "we have found our divided plants make more money than they did when they were larger. And we have also found that smaller plants bounce back from

ARIE DE GEUS, *THE LIVING COMPANY*
ENHANCING THE ORGANIZATION'S ABILITY TO LEARN
The arguments against distributed power are well known. They represent well-nigh irresistible temptations to many managers. It takes forever to take a decision. We do not have that sort of time. The world and the competition are moving forward; we cannot stay behind.

A wide distribution of power can be incredibly frustrating, but it means that the number of minds which are actively engaged in the decision-making process is considerably increased. There is no convincing evidence that it leads to slower action (although it certainly takes longer to come to conclusions). It may well lead to better action and it may enhance the organization's ability to learn ...

In the end, the lure of power – the need to be wanted and the need to feel in control – deters many senior executives from approving the distribution of power, thus diminishing the institutional learning capacity.

Arie de Geus, The Living Company, Nicholas Brealey, 1999 ,ch. 11

bad times or a crisis much faster than larger ones. From all of this I have come to believe that economy of scale is one of the most overrated concepts in business."

PROFIT (AND INFORMATION) SHARING

A simple formula was agreed on for the allocation of profit for each autonomous unit: 40% would go toward taxes, 25% toward dividends, and 12% to reinvestment. The remaining 23% would be shared.

There were no consolation prizes if there was no profit, and the units were free to allocate the money in whatever way they thought was most appropriate. In the event, it was decided to split the money evenly, giving the same profit share to every employee, regardless of salary. But the teams could have chosen to distribute profit by age, or seniority, or to make the money available as low-cost loans to enable team members to get onto the property ladder.

"Few ideas are as capitalist as profit-sharing, which rewards with a part of the company's earnings the people who help generate this blessed surplus," Semler writes. "What is a bonus scheme, after all, but a form of profit-sharing? ... The truth is that profit-sharing doesn't create employee involvement, it requires it."

Discussions about profit-sharing quickly led to enquiries about the salaries of top executives. Nobody was forced to reveal their salary, but "enough salaries were known to give an extremely accurate idea of pay at all levels of the company".

"The truth may not be pretty, or easily explained," Semler notes, "but it is always better to be out in the open."

APPRAISING THE BOSS

Semler allowed his workforce a say in the appraisal and appointment of senior executives. Managers were evaluated by their teams twice a year by means of anonymous multiple-choice questionnaires exploring technical ability, competence, leadership, and other aspects of the leader's performance. The questions were weighted to reflect the significance of each aspect, and the results were made public. Most managers scored around 80–85%; a score of less than 70% would create pressure for change.

New managers face a group interview with the team as part of the appointment process and were graded against the various competencies. A score of more than 70% allowed the appointment to proceed. Factions form (factory workers, engineers, administrators), but interestingly, people's instinct for compromise and fair play seems to come to the fore.

So, anarchy does not rule. Or, as we would have it, anarchy *can* rule, and is remarkably sensible and efficient.

SET YOUR OWN SALARY

Semco employees were invited to suggest their own salaries, based on what they would be able to earn outside, as well as what others with similar skills and responsibilities earned at Semco, what friends with similar backgrounds earned, and what they needed to live. Everyone came to know what everyone else was paid. It was agreed that top salaries would be no higher than 10 times entry-level pay.

Semco set its operational budget every six months, based on the clever perception that a one-year budget allows people to imagine that the second half of the year will be miraculously better than the first half. In these budget sessions, if times were hard, high salaries stood out as a target for cuts. When setting their own salaries, people began to assess their own worth quite realistically. Managers were invited to set their own goals, and then decide to what extent they had achieved them, thereby deciding the appropriate level of their own bonus.

And – that's it. That's pretty much what Semler did in terms of introducing more democracy – or more healthy anarchy – to his company.

BETTER THAN DEMOCRACY

Every change that Semler made was instigated by common agreement. There were a great many other changes that were deemed to be unsuccessful, or unwelcome, and were abandoned. Semco is now a fluid, self-organizing system – which is just what Semler wanted. Not just because he wanted to run his company "in a simpler way, a more natural way", or because he wanted to stop killing himself with overwork, but also because he thought he might make more money. "I stood to make at least as much money in partnership with a motivated workforce as I would as the sole beneficiary of the fruits of less inspired workers," he writes.

Semler, let us remind you, is still the owner. Semco is not a cooperative; it is a self-organized capitalist venture of which Semler is the majority owner. It is perfectly possible, as he has shown, to own or to run a company and make good profits (preferably for everyone) while also giving people control over their own working lives in a way that delivers deep job satisfaction and a satisfying sense of communal effort toward a shared purpose.

This is actually a more thoroughgoing form of democracy than the kind that we see in the governance of modern nation-states. In Semler's democracy (as in GE Aviation's) everyone's opinion makes a difference all of the time, not just on election day.

Technically speaking, this is not democracy in the commonly accepted sense of the term. It is something more like anarchy (in the old-fashioned sense).

A bit of anarchy can be a good thing. A degree of anarchy will destroy the steam engine and replace it with something better.

SELF-ORGANIZATION: DOING WHAT COMES NATURALLY

Left to themselves and challenged with solving a problem that significantly affects their well-being, human beings tend to get together and come up with a solution. Opinions are put forward, leaders emerge, factions form. Sometimes a show of hands is the only way of resolving an impasse, but not very often.

Once a show of hands has been required, we immediately have a dissatisfied group: the people who didn't vote for the chosen outcome. Now they are aggrieved; they feel that the wrong decision has been foisted onto them.

With self-organization, there is no such divisive moment. A solution is tried out, willingly. If it doesn't work out, we regroup. No decision in principle has been made that must now be un-made with another show of hands. We try a different route. A new set of leaders emerge. We fail or succeed. If we fail again, we try something else.

This instinctive social behaviour is how human beings got to where we are today. It comes naturally to us; we are uniquely attuned to the subtleties of group interaction. But we are currently saddled with hierarchical organizational structures that the ancient Egyptians would have felt at home with — it's as if we still believe that the best way to build a pyramid is to employ an army of slaves.

These outmoded organizational structures are stifling ingenuity and creating a generation of demotivated, disengaged, dysfunctional employees. It is time to claw our way back to modernity with new, anarchic, self-organizing systems that free up our natural human ingenuity and give us back a sense of pride and fulfilment in our work — work that we have chosen and directed ourselves.

TAKING THE ORGANIZATION FROM THE INDUSTRIAL ERA TO THE AGE OF IDEAS

Transforming the steam engine, one step at a time

- "More democratic" is good; "democracy" carries too much political baggage to be of any use as a descriptive term
  - In the modern organization, democracy, as we all understand it, will be ineffective, inefficient and, paradoxically, divisive, leading to the tyranny of the majority
- Most management functions should be handed over to the people who are doing the work
  - Teams that understand their objectives – and that have the necessary information – will organize themselves to achieve the objectives in the most effective way
- Organizations that have encouraged self-organization are reaping the rewards
  - Self-organized team are more productive, faster, safer, and produce higher-quality products at lower costs
  - They are also happier in their work, self-motivated, self-regulating, and more loyal
- Self-organized teams are more innovative
  - "The results they had witnessed convinced [GE Aviation] leaders that the best ideas for innovation and improvement often came from the plant floor and could only truly happen by giving workers the information, responsibility, and accountability to make decisions."[49]
- Changing an established team from hierarchy to self-organization is not easy
- GE Aviation established a process for the change:
  - Get ready: leadership learns teaming and develops initial strategy for teaming roll-out
  - Launch: individuals become oriented to the team and work together to determine team dynamics
  - Journey: units begin to define accountability while determining day-to-day responsibilities
  - Ownership: units begin to take ownership and accountability of their process, product and duties.
  - Growth: units are functioning as self-sustained, self-directed work teams; always looking for improvement and growth opportunities.[50]

CHAPTER 8

YOU'RE THE LEADER
NOW FIND 100 MORE LEADERS

A t several points, this book has argued that the solutions to the
destructive paradoxes faced by steam-engine organizations rely
heavily on the quality of the organization's leadership. Which, of
course, it does.

Leaders must give the organization purpose and set the moral
tone. Good leadership will empower us and set us free from petty
controls. Visionary leadership will allow us to raise our heads above
the fog of petty metrics and remind ourselves of the core purpose of
the organization. Great leadership will lead us out of the morass of
failure and onto the sunlit uplands of success.

Let's face it: it's all down to the quality of the organization's
leadership. Or is it? You will be glad to know that the answer is yes.
And no.

You will also be glad to know that we will not be reviewing all
of the different theories of leadership that have emerged since the
industrial era. Suffice it to say that we are not in favour of the old,
militaristic, command-and-control model of leadership, but we are
in favour of an emotionally intelligent leadership whose chief task is
to create an environment in which the members of the organization
are enabled to achieve the organization's overarching purpose –
preferably with as little interference from "management" as possible.
(We've got a bit of downer on management. Sorry about that. But
perhaps you do, too.)

But there is still one central paradox of leadership to address.
This book is about dragging the organization out of its 19th-century

mindset and into the 21st century. We want organizations to tear up the old scientific management handbook and enter the Age of Ideas.

Those of you who work in large (or even medium-sized) organizations will understand that this is no mean feat. Bringing about change of this magnitude in a sizeable organization is an astonishing, near-impossible task. The forces of inertia and resistance ranged against the most brilliant change leader are formidable. To achieve even minor change requires strong leadership of the highest calibre – leaders with the courage, charisma, panache, and drive to change some of the most deeply ingrained organizational habits.

But isn't strong leadership – old-fashioned, "hero" leadership – bad? Doesn't it lead us straight back to the old "jump when I say 'jump!'" school of leadership? Or, to take a more optimistic, modern view, doesn't it require the kind of "renaissance man" model of leadership that no merely human leader can actually hope to emulate: a paragon of every virtue, well-versed in every skill, compelling and charismatic, visionary yet grounded, firm yet compassionate, and with the wisdom of Solomon?

No it doesn't – thank goodness. There aren't many who fit that job description.

The paradox of leadership is real, but the solution is clear. Strong leadership is not the same as the aggressive, macho leadership of the past. All modern leaders require high levels of emotional intelligence, or they will fail to bring people with them, and they will quickly crash and burn.

The leadership qualities needed to achieve major change – such as breaking away from our outmoded "scientific management" approach – are formidable, and they must not be under-estimated, but they are not unachievable. Many people will be able to rise to this challenge. These strong, far-sighted leaders will understand that they cannot and should not attempt to single-handedly bring about change. The whole point of their leadership will be to ensure that everyone understands the purpose of the organization, and the new direction that it is taking. Large numbers of these people will then become leaders in their own right, doing things the new way: spreading the word, leading by example.

Successful modern leaders will give strong, clear direction and purpose to the organization, and then invite and enable other leaders to spring up throughout the organization to follow that direction and achieve that purpose. These new leaders must not be confined to the classic management hierarchy. Leaders can, should and will spring up at all levels of the organization. It's a simple – and as difficult – as that.

The greatest strength of this new generation of leaders will be their ability to create an organization full of leaders: people who lead in their own area, or when the occasion demands; people who are leaders in one role and who follow other leaders in a different role; un-appointed leaders; leaders who may well not head up any particular hierarchy; hundreds of leaders, passing on the message and the method, and inspiring the people around them to adopt the new ways of doing things.

In these new organizations full of leaders, old fashioned hierarchies will begin to melt away.

GOOGLE: LOOKING FOR "EMERGENT LEADERS"

There was an interesting item in the *New York Times* recently in which a journalist recalled how, in a 2013 interview, Laszlo Bock, Senior VP for People Operations at Google, had spoken about the qualities that Google looks for in new recruits:

There are five hiring attributes we have across the company. If it's a technical role, we assess your coding ability, and half the roles in the company are technical roles. For every job, though, the number one thing we look for is general cognitive ability ... It's learning ability. It's the ability to process on the fly. It's the ability to pull together disparate bits of information.

On the subject of types of leadership, Bock continued:

In particular, emergent leadership as opposed to traditional leadership. Traditional leadership is, "Were you president of the chess club?" "Were you vice president of sales?" "How quickly did you get there?" We don't care. What we care about is, when faced with a problem and you're a member of a team, do you, at the appropriate time, step in and lead? And just as critically, do you step back and stop leading, do you let someone else? Because what's critical to be an effective leader in this environment is you have to be willing to relinquish power.[51]

Emergent leadership. Pop-up leadership. Leaders at all levels with a clear grasp of what the organization is trying to achieve; who are prepared to step up and offer leadership, possibly temporarily, when the situation demands and they feel they have something to offer, or possibly on a long-term but "unofficial" basis. These are the people within any organization whom we all recognize as being de facto leaders; the people who really knows how things work, and to whom others turn for advice. These are the people to be encouraged, treasured, and honoured.

It seems to work for Google. It also certainly worked in the UK's National Health Service, as a radical and effective change programme put in place by one of our contributors demonstrated.

CREATING CHANGE IN THE UK'S NATIONAL HEALTH SERVICE

The National Health Service (NHS) is a mega-organization. It employs 1.7 million people, making it the world's fourth largest employer. (Intriguingly, the top three are the US Defence Department, the Chinese People's Liberation Army, and Walmart. McDonald's employs fewer people than Wal-Mart but more than the NHS, but it doesn't employ them directly, because of its franchise structure.)

Because the NHS is funded by taxation, it is subject to huge political interference, and has, inevitably, spawned its own monstrous bureaucracy and created its own silos. The NHS has a number of relatively flat hierarchies; it should not be assumed that general practitioners, physicians, surgeons, nurses, and hospital managers are necessarily all singing from the same hymn sheet. And even when they are, they tend to be singing different hymns – precisely because the organization is so difficult to give leadership to.

Bringing about change in the NHS is about as tough a leadership challenge as there is. One man who has created significant change in the NHS – and who has now been charged with creating more – is Dr Roland Valori.

DR ROLAND VALORI: NHS CHANGE LEADER OF THE YEAR, 2009

Doctor Roland Valori is a consultant physician specializing in the field of gastroenterology. As National Clinical Director of Endoscopy Services from 2003-2013, he was charged with raising nationwide standards in the practice of endoscopy.

Endoscopy involves looking inside the body with a miniature video camera and a light source fixed to a flexible tube. Its most common use is for investigating the gastrointestinal tract: the oesophagus and the stomach or the bowel. It is a vital diagnostic tool for a wide range of a range of illnesses, and is especially important in the early diagnosis of bowel cancer – the fourth most common form of cancer in the UK (after breast, lung and prostate cancer).

Endoscopy is a highly skilled process. If not performed successfully, it may fail to spot vital symptoms. If performed badly, it may even cause damage to patients. It is also, clearly, an invasive process, which can cause stress and anxiety in patients who are already worried about their health. There is a rigorous procedure that needs to be followed to ensure a successful outcome, and all endoscopy staff need to have received the highest calibre of training.

With the increasing use of endoscopy in large-scale screening programmes, it is essential that these highest standards and levels of training be applied to every endoscopy unit throughout the UK. Dr Valori was charged with making this happen. He achieved this, in essence, by creating a quality assurance framework. So far, so straightforward, you might think. But this quality framework was at first vehemently resisted by physicians, who saw it as an unnecessary level of bureaucracy that interfered with their independence of action.

This experience will be familiar to anyone who has tried to instigate change in an organization and come up against the disagreement or intransigence of able, talented, but unwilling colleagues. Valori eventually "sold" his quality framework to the entire endoscopy community within the NHS. He did this by a long, patient, time-consuming process of dialogue – and, in particular, he did it by creating a team of other leaders who spread the word and carried on the good work. As Valori wrote in a paper for his specialist medical journal: "Effective leadership at all levels and strong partnership between leaders were significant factors in the change to the service."

Having a great idea – grasping what the solution to a problem might be – is only the beginning of leadership. Making it happen – which remains one of the defining attributes of great leadership – is the difficult bit. Modern leaders make things happen by bringing on board an increasing number of other members at every level of the organization, who then become leaders in their own right.

"A REAL SENSE OF OWNERSHIP"

We met Dr Valori at the Royal College of Physicians. The college was created in the 16th century by a Royal Charter from King Henry VIII, and is the oldest of the UK's medical colleges. Its current headquarters is a dramatic, modernist building overlooking London's beautiful Regents Park. Built in the 1960s to replace the college's old Georgian building, which was damaged by bombing during World War II, the listed building sits comfortably but strikingly next to the white stucco facades of the nearby grand terraced houses, all built in the elegant Regency style of early 19th-century Britain and facing onto the green and leafy spaces of the park.

We waited to meet Dr Valori in the building's imposing atrium, surrounded by portraits of the college's illustrious past members, looking out over a courtyard containing part of the beautiful gardens, which are stocked entirely with plants that have a medicinal heritage.

Valori bounded up the stairs to greet us eating an apple and apologized for being perhaps three minutes late for our appointment. Our meeting took place not in a wood-panelled study decked out with leather armchairs (as we had secretly hoped) but in a nondescript meeting room somewhere deep inside the building, down long corridors and up various flights of stairs. (The functional office space has, sadly, found its way into even our most venerable institutions.)

Valori is a lot less scary than most medical consultants who, in our limited experience, tend to be rather intimidating even when they are

DR ROLAND VALORI, NHS CONSULTANT PHYSICIAN
AND STRATEGIC CONSULTANT
CREATING COLLABORATIVE CULTURES

One of the things I'm trying to do at the moment with my current work is to promote the idea of a collaborative culture at the top which would then influence the system, because it's such a complex system and there are so many flat hierarchies. It's not like an industry where it's more pyramidal.

I've talked to various senior people and one person said to me at one meeting: "Oh, well we are collaborative; we do this and this and the other," and I was thinking: "Actually, we're not really collaborative. We come up with an idea, and then we test it a bit, and then we just roll it out."

So what I'm trying to do on the accreditation acceptance front is to say: "Well, actually, this could be really effective if we all collaborate, that's the regulators, the commissioners, the providers, the professional bodies, the patients." Then we send a very strong signal to the service that that's how we want people to behave at the local level.

Dr Roland Valori in conversation with the authors

trying to be helpful. Valori, by contrast, has a straightforward, easy-going manner and friendly eyes. He talks softly and listens carefully.

One of the things I realized about previous initiatives was that their methodology was to come up with a good way of doing something and wrongly assume that, because it made sense or they could show that it worked, that everyone would adopt it. And I appreciated that you needed a full-on system to get that adoption.

We created a quality framework which the industry called a Global Rating Scale, which is a checklist of -nearly two hundred things, key requirements of service delivery and training, that need to be in place to achieve excellence, and then we created an accreditation process to ensure compliance with this checklist.

The accreditation process is carried out by peer review, and is designed to help the endoscopy units to achieve the necessary standard. Because the standards framework is demanding, the great majority of units will not pass at their first attempt. The options are "pass", "fail", or "defer", and most units will be deferred for several months while they are given help to achieve the necessary standards.

A part of the initial problem – typical of the NHS's flat hierarchies – was that while the final endoscopy procedure was typically carried out by a physician who would visit the service, perform the procedure, and leave, the service itself was run by teams of nurses

DR ROLAND VALORI, NHS CONSULTANT PHYSICIAN
AND STRATEGIC CONSULTANT
CREATING LEADERSHIP TEAMS
We created something called a strategic organizational responsibilities tool, which asked the team to indicate who was primarily responsible for this responsibility, and who was second and who was third; sometimes there wasn't a second and third, but the process of them sitting together, getting them to do that exercise, was to make them realize that they are a leadership team. And most of them wouldn't come to it in that way.

We created that leadership programme because we realized the key thing to sustainability – never mind what we did from the outside, never mind what we proposed – it was still a tick box exercise sort of approach if you didn't have the right leadership. So we tried to address this with the leadership training, and we tried to get these people to work better together.

And I think one of the legacies is that we've created a cadre across the country of very organizational-focussed clinical leaders in the service ... people with these capabilities and this focus and with this culture. And it's wonderful to meet these people sometimes; just through the conversation, you just know that they are in a different place than they were a few years ago, and they just think differently and act differently and speak differently because they have been through this process, they understand how important their role is.

Dr Roland Valori in conversation with the authors

and managers. As a result, while the physician would feel (and be) responsible for the success of the procedure, a range of other pre-existing factors could affect the success of the procedure, and would certainly affect the overall satisfaction of the patient – the customer. Now, Valori's accreditation system would give the nurses and others running any endoscopy service a real sense of ownership. It laid out the criteria that would define an excellent service, and encouraged these teams to achieve that level of excellence. And, in so doing, it created new leaders.

> To cut a long story short, this accreditation process for the service has been completely transformational. What it did, I think, was it changed the culture of the service. It empowered the nurses, in a service where the doctors particularly were coming in for half a day and weren't really responsible or didn't have any sense of responsibility for the service. It enabled the leaders of the service to exert some control ... and it completely flipped it round – it humanized the process through changing the culture and having this standards manual. Now to achieve that – I mean to get alignment across a very wide body of professionals: the screening programme, the surgeons, physicians, radiologists, nurses, managers – there was a lot of aligning people to a position, purpose, to a culture, a no-compromise position on certain things but being extremely responsive to criticism and concerns.

CREATING LEADERS

From the outset, Valori and his key associate, Debbie Johnson, recruited people who understood the aims of the programme – people who "got it" – and enabled them to become leaders in their own right. Valori's core team comprised 28 physicians, appointed to support the project for half a day each week. He calls these pioneers his "spokespersons" and his "local leaders". Then there were the all-important endoscopy training centres: 10 centres across the country, each with a lead doctor and lead nurse – another 20 leaders who also became evangelists for the programme. This core group of 48 leaders met two or three times a year, and a website enabled them to share concerns and enquiries. In an interesting demonstration of modern leadership, Valori made it clear that some issues were non-negotiable, while on others he and Debbie made substantial changes to the programme to reflect others' concerns.

Valori's programme created a team of service leaders who had not previously thought of themselves as leaders. These leaders have helped to bring about a profound and significant change to the organization, and they continue to lead, guaranteeing the longevity of the new culture:

> *I used to say that my key markers of success, and I was saying this back in 2008, was, when I stand back from this, that it goes from strength to strength; so, if I leave a legacy, it just gets better and better. I was very eager to get some key people in some key positions to hardwire what we were doing. We've just got to the place now where there's enough hardwiring in place – we're talking about the accreditation and quality assurance infrastructure here – to enable us to step back.*

Valori ascribes much of the success of the programme to the fact that it exerts a "pull" rather than attempting to "push": once teams have accepted that they must achieve new standards, most will ask for help. The hard part of Valori's work – like that of any change leader – was the long slog of spelling out the benefits his new systems would bring. Once there was a critical mass of acceptance, the leaders' roles were to help and support. "Supporting teams to achieve change is much easier than persuading them to do so," he notes.

The success of Valori's change programme was such that he has been asked to undertake similar change across the whole of the NHS, developing a Strategic Development for Accreditation to cover all clinical services.

CREATING ORGANIC CHANGE

Dr Valori's work within this most steam-engine of organizations is a perfect example of the leadership approach that will be required to bring about change to the steam engine itself. Issuing instructions from on high will not bring about change. Instructions will not cascade down the pyramid – if such a pyramid actually even exists in reality. In our experience, most organizational pyramids exist only on paper; they look nice in the organograms that sit in people's filing cabinets, but in practice the organization is a far messier, organic creature.

An idea that starts off at the top of the pyramid – think of it as a marble or a ball bearing – is highly unlikely to bounce and roll its way down neatly to the base of the pyramid and convey exactly the meaning with which it was originally invested. It is far more likely to hit an obstruction on the way down (probably sooner rather than later) or to lose its way altogether in some organizational labyrinth. Or, indeed, to make its way to the base of the pyramid, but having been miraculously transformed on its journey into an object that has entirely lost its original meaning – the ball-bearing of progress having been turned back into the ingot of stasis, the glass marble of modernism having reverted to the sand of conservatism. We are being a little fanciful here, but you will probably have had direct experience of any number of bold initiatives that died in similar ways *because the organization as a whole had not taken them to its heart.*

Successful change involves the difficult and laborious task of spreading the word right through the organization and listening to the feedback. Some aspects of the programme will be non-negotiable, while others will need to be adapted; there is no point in listening to people unless change and adaptation are possible, since people are very quick indeed to spot when feedback is invited and immediately ignored.

The key to the success of this approach is the successful recruitment of new leaders, scattered throughout the organization: people who hadn't previously perceived themselves as leaders, but who are now given ownership of areas in which they can now take personal pride; people who will spread the word about the new success story.

The leader's core ambition should be to hand over leadership: to be able, at some point, to step back and watch others take over the good work.

MARK POWELL
JAZZ LEADERSHIP
Leadership is something that has to be shared within the organization, and different people need to be taking leadership roles at different times, depending on where you are at that moment in time.

An organizational metaphor that I've worked with for a number of years is jazz – the way that a jazz ensemble makes music. This involves working with clients with a jazz ensemble in the room, which is slightly odd, but instructive!

If you look at the way a jazz group works, unlike an orchestra where there is a conductor who plays a role inside the process, there isn't actually a conductor leading a jazz ensemble. The group works together in a way where they move leadership around. At any one time in the process of creating a piece of music, the singer might be in charge; at another time the saxophone player takes the lead; another time the drummer drives what's going on.

If you look at the dynamics, what's interesting is the way the group moves people around, depending on what's needed at the time, with different people take on the leadership role.

It's a model that requires several very interesting things. The group has to have amazing trust in each other. The group has to have egos that are big enough to want to be good at what they do, but are in check, and enable them to take great pleasure and pride in the achievements of others when they are leading the group.

Mark Powell in conversation with co-author Jonathan Gifford

THE HUMAN CHALLENGES OF LEADERSHIP

The modern leader needs to strive toward the moment at which power has been successfully transferred from them to the organization.

Leadership and management consultant Jonathan Stebbings is an associate of Olivier Mythodrama. Previously a commercial lawyer, he also has a master's degree in English literature and taught literature and drama before first moving to the law and later becoming a consultant, trainer and coach.

Working with Mythodrama, Stebbings uses drama to explore aspects of power. Using Shakespeare's last play, *The Tempest*, to help groups explore core aspects of leadership, he reminds us that, at the play's end, Prospero "gives up his rough magic" – the powers which have brought him control over others – so that they can develop and change, in order to find their 'proper selves'.

He also talked to us about the way in which his work addresses the human challenges of leadership, and about the need for leaders to bring their humanity with them to the job . As Stebbings said in conversation with the authors:

PETER RAWLINS, FORMER CEO LONDON STOCK EXCHANGE; FOUNDER OF RAWLINS STRATEGY CONSULTING

I think a lot of these problems arise because people in leadership positions may be a little power-hungry; they may be inadequately secure in their own skins, and they may feel the need to hang onto a lot of reins – they're probably poor delegators and poor real empowers, and feel that they need to be tied to everything.

That's where the train crashes result, because if everything needs to be fed back to the centre to get anything done, then it's no wonder the whole foundation doesn't function. And that problem does start at the top, with people who don't know how to delegate and empower and still retain control, which is a basic tenet of large corporate leadership – I mean, if you can't do that, then you will screw things up.

Assessing people and forging teams is for me the number-one requirement of effective leaders – and then letting the team do the work and relaxing in the reflected glory of people around you who are actually a lot more competent than you are and just need to be coordinated and facilitated and empowered. That's the role of a leader – and then let everyone else do the heavy lifting. It makes for a happier life for everybody in my experience. It requires a certain ego approach on the part of the leader, that he or she doesn't need to do it all, and not all leaders are in that frame of mind, I find.

Peter Rawlins in conversation with the authors

*Our work is very much getting people to address the human
challenges of leadership, primarily through story. Organizations and
leaders live the story which they tell themselves. And to understand
the old story and imagine the new, you have to be able to think in
those terms. And so we use Shakespeare plays as myths of leadership.
We also use theatre and rehearsal process, and ideas alongside
models from organizational development ideas; psychotherapy
and all the other backgrounds of our various colleagues – put it in
a pot and stir them around. We aim to get leaders to look at their
organization as something other than a machine.*

*The "cog in a wheel" feeling for people is death to their being
able to feel motivated or to get inspired, and yet management
process and management discipline – the feeling that "I have
to manage an organization, and the organization is a thing that
exists" – is one of the myths that people mistakenly fall for …
people respond to you at a visceral level, and approaching them
and the organization like a machine isn't going to do it.*

*So, in our experience, that revelation that leaders have a duty
and they also have* permission *to bring their humanity into their
leadership, is really at the heart of all this – it's a big leap for them,
because that also gives them permission to be faulty, to have
original sin.*

*If it is my duty and my role and I have permission just to
be a human being as a leader, then I don't have to be perfect,
which means I don't have to wear this front, which means
I can then connect with people more deeply. A lot of it is shedding
the armour.*

*One of the things Prospero does is, he gives up his "rough
magic". He surrenders his power – which is his power as a
magician – because he knows that until he makes himself
powerless, other people can't change, because while he is
powerful they merely respond to his power and will continue to
do what they've already been doing. So this idea of surrender and
the servant as leader – if you're looking for a new paradigm of
leadership, then I think the new story is one of getting out of the
way and essentially making yourself redundant.*

PROSPERO GIVES UP HIS MAGIC

But this rough Magic
I here abjure; and, when I have requir'd
Some heavenly music – which even now I do –
To work mine end upon their senses that
This airy charm is for, I'll break my staff,
Bury it certain fathoms in the earth
And, deeper that did ever plummet sound,
I'll drown my book.

William Shakespeare, The Tempest, Act V, Scene I

TRAINING EMERGENT LEADERS

There is an interesting corollary to the idea of empowering others – of encouraging emergent leadership throughout the organization – which is that it strongly suggests that we are doing leadership training all wrong.

At the moment, organizations promote people into positions of leadership and then send them on a programme to learn how to be leaders. Even on the face of it, this seems more than a little odd. It would make a great deal more sense for organizations to send people on leadership programmes during the very earliest parts of their careers: to think about what leadership is; to develop their own leadership skills and to encourage them to demonstrate leadership in their own roles.

Instead of portraying leadership as something that is structured in the hierarchy – something that you only get to "do" when you get near to the top of the pyramid – we should look at leadership as a kind of behaviour that people exhibit at all levels of the organization, from the very outset, seeing leadership as being a fundamental aspect of everyone's career.

TAKING THE ORGANIZATION FROM THE INDUSTRIAL ERA TO THE AGE OF IDEAS

Transforming the steam engine, one step at a time

- Significant change needs strong leadership
  - Getting the organization out of its engrained, steam-engine habits represents major change which will require exceptionally strong leadership
  - Strong leadership does not mean old-fashioned, macho, "hero" leadership
  - Leaders need to be courageous, not merely 'strong'
  - All modern leaders need high levels of emotional intelligence
- Strong, courageous leaders set the purpose and the direction, and then find leaders throughout the organization, at every level, to lead change forward
  - This will require a huge amount of dialogue
  - Some things remain non-negotiable; other things should change in response to concerns
- Leaders are not required to be infallible
  - Leaders are required to be human
- If leaders retain control, others cannot develop and grow
  - Once the "hardwiring" is in place, other people must take the vision forward

CHAPTER 9

DON'T DO NETWORKING
BE NETWORKED

The organizational paradox of networking is very simple: most steam-engine organizations believe that they are networking, but they are not. This is because they have a fundamental misunderstanding of what a network is and of what "networking" means.

Steam-engine organizations operate, and think, in very linear terms. Raw materials come in at one end of the system, are processed into something that has greater value, and are shipped out at the other end. The organization itself operates on the basis of secrecy, control, and rigid hierarchy: it actively sets out to build high walls around itself.

There are, of course, people and other organizations outside of the walls that are essential to even the steam-engine organization, or who can have an influence on it: suppliers, contractors, services, shareholders, regulators, government. Even customers. But unreconstructed steam-engine organizations do not see this nexus of connections as a network. Suppliers and contractors are paid for the goods and services that they supply; regulators and government are lobbied; customers are persuaded to buy product. These are the limits of the relationship.

More forward-thinking steam-engine organizations would acknowledge that their enterprise is connected to the wider community by many relationships, and that this is something that requires their attention. They have, after all, read some of the huge amount of material that has been written about the importance of "stakeholders". However, these outside relationships are still seen as something that must be managed and, as far as is humanly possible, *controlled*.

MARK POWELL
LEVERAGING BOTH WORK AND SOCIAL NETWORKS
There is a very interesting issue opening around the traditional steam-engine view of the separation between work and non-work, which is heavily challenged by the evolution of real social network structures.

Individuals now do not disassociate their personal and their work networks in the same way, and organizations increasingly have to embrace the idea that part of the value that their employees bring is their own personal networks, which are both social and work networks, within which there is a great deal of trust.

A classic interview question used by senior hirers in organizations is known as the "Rolodex Question" [after the once-popular rotating filing system of cards used for storing individual contact details]. They want to know: "How many chief execs do you know? How many contacts do you have in your Rolodex that you can then go and sell stuff from our company to that you could have sold them in your previous company?" They never ask: "How big is your network, and how trusted is your network?" which is a very different question. If I was hiring an employee now, I'd be asking the question: "How can we leverage their networks, not just their contacts?"

I think this is the start of an evolution we're just beginning to see – more and more companies are beginning to look at the digital profile of their individuals, particularly with regards to their networks. What we're seeing now is, effectively, a movement from individual networking and building relationships to effectively being part of larger networks, both at an individual human level and at the level of organizations that become part of larger eco systems in order to develop products and services. The mind-set and thinking behind this, however, requires us to be able to let go of some traditional concepts around structure and trust and openness that steam-engine organizations really, really struggle with.

Mark Powell in conversation with co-author Jonathan Gifford

This is a worry for the steam-engine organization, because unlike employees, these outside entities cannot be fully controlled; they do not necessarily have to jump when the organization says "jump!". So it sets out to network. It wines, dines, sponsors, advertises, lobbies – and in some cases (so we hear) browbeats, bullies, and threatens – in an attempt to ensure that these outside factors remain under control.

There is another (related) form of networking that the steam-engine organization understands perfectly well: the sales network. The whole point of having a network of connections, in this worldview, is to sell something to them. In the world of executive recruitment, this is known as "the Rolodex question". When organizations are hiring senior executives, it is common to ask about the strength of their contacts: the people that they know and have done business with who may be useful to their new employer (see panel).

Both of these understandings – of what networks are, and of how they work – are outmoded and wrong. Networks are multi-dimensional, dynamic, organic systems. They are not linear. They can be influenced, but not controlled. You can indeed "do business" with your network, but your network is not a collection of sales leads. Any one node in a network is important and significant, but if that node were removed, the network would re-form and continue to function. A network is something that one is a member of, not the centre of.

This idea was very well expressed in a different context in a 2006 article by *Economist* correspondent Andreas Kluth about the newly emerging "participatory media", in which he notes:

With participatory media, the boundaries between audiences and creators become blurred and often invisible ... one-to-many lectures (i.e. from media companies to their audiences) are transformed into conversations among the people formerly known as the audience. This changes the tone of public discussions.

The mainstream media, says David Weinberger, a blogger, author, and fellow at Harvard University's Berkman Centre, don't get how subversive it is to take institutions and turn them into conversations. That is because institutions are closed, assume a

*hierarchy and have trouble admitting fallibility, he says, whereas
conversations are open-ended, assume equality and eagerly
concede fallibility.[52]*

Steam-engine networks are also "closed, assume a hierarchy
and have trouble admitting fallibility", while real networks are "are
open-ended, assume equality, and eagerly concede fallibility". In a
real network, any one organization is as important as the next, and
they are all tied together by weaker or stronger bonds of mutual
dependency. And, as David Weinberger is quoted as having so
perceptively said, people don't get how subversive it is to turn an
institution into a conversation.

"A MATRIX OF INTERDEPENDENCIES"

The old steam-engine, linear view of the world is changing radically.
We live in a world of dynamic systems and networks. Organizations,
large and small, will increasingly be successful – or not – based
on their ability to create, build, and make themselves part of larger
networks. The networks of all of the organization's members will
also be significant: what will come to matter is no longer the size of
a senior executive's Rolodex, but how extensive, how valuable and
how trusted are the networks that the organizations are part of – and
also the networks that their employees are part of.

Increasing numbers of small, innovative start-up organizations
are proving that it is possible to build ecosystems and networks of
relationships with individuals, customers, and suppliers (and also,
increasingly, with like-minded competitors) in a way that allows
them to compete with far larger organizations. It is no longer
essential to have the scale and resources that only large
organizations could command.

Once organizations genuinely embrace the concept of working
as part of a network, however, they must give up the traditional
concepts of control. A network is a self-controlling mechanism that
cannot be controlled by any one member.

In their book *Firms of Endearment: How World-class Companies
Profit from Purpose and Passion,* Rajandra Sisodia, David Wolfe, and

Jagdish Sheth explore the emergence of a new kind of successful, modern organizations, which they call "Firms of Endearment". These companies, they write, "seek to maximize their value to society as a whole, not just to their shareholders. They are the ultimate value creators: they create emotional value, experiential value, social value, and, of course, financial value. People who interact with such companies feel safe, secure, and pleased in their dealings. They enjoy

WOLFGANG GRULKE, FOUNDER AND CHAIRMAN EMERITUS OF FUTUREWORLD

YOU HAVE TO GIVE TRUST

Something we've advocated for ages is that the network has double the ideas — whether it's your customers, your business partners, your competitors, and so on — and that the organization has to absorb that and act on it, and that's what most organizations are absolutely incapable of.

There are very few companies that will let people comment on them about improvements they would like and so on. For those that do do it, it's a total black box; everything inside them disappears, there's no open debate, there's no blog on how the company could do better and so on. Most organizations are absolutely incapable of absorbing any kind of new ideas from the outside (or indeed from inside).

Trust is equally difficult. We do a thing called Quantum Relationships, which talks about relationships in a networked world, and makes the point that relationships in a network are fundamentally different to relationships in a hierarchy. In a hierarchy the assumption is that you can't trust anybody. In a network, it's absolutely 100% necessary that you have to trust; you have to give trust. And if somebody breaks that trust then they are immediately out of the network forever.

Organizations work on the basis that you can never trust anybody. Just look at the processes — you know, you have to get sign-off for a £1.50 parking voucher or whatever. They are incapable of giving trust.

Wolfgang Grulke in conversation with the authors

working with or for the company, buying from it, investing in it, and having it as a neighbor".[53]

In steam-engine organizations, individual stakeholders are assigned to different categories (supplier, contractor, shareholder, and so on) without the acceptance that there is an organic link between all of these groups. For such organizations, the authors of *Firms of Endearment* write:

> *Connections between stakeholders in differing categories are incidental and accidental. The picture is quite different among firms of endearment. Their leaders tend to think in unitive fashion, approaching their tasks with holistic vision in which no player in the game of commerce is a priori more important than any other player, and all are connected ... stakeholders are part of a complex network of interests that function in a matrix of interdependencies. We argue that each stakeholder tends to thrive best when all stakeholders thrive. No stakeholder group is more important than any other. To see matters otherwise is like saying the heart is more important than the lungs. Life depends on both being healthy. It is disciplined dedication to the well-being of all stakeholders that separates firms of endearment from their competition.[54]*

Real networks are like living organisms – or, perhaps more accurately, like healthy ecosystems. Everything is interdependent; everything can thrive, but not at the expense of everything else.

Modern organizations must come to understand that they play a part in a rich matrix of mutually beneficial relationships. They are not at the centre of some arbitrary and random web of relationships that they can hope to manage and control.

THE ORGANIZATION AS NETWORK

There is another, vital aspect of network thinking that has (or should have) a profound impact on how organizations structure themselves – and, as a result, on how they function – and that is that organizations should see *themselves* as a network.

This is, of course, anathema to steam-engine obsessions with control and hierarchy – with ensuring that the individual will of the many servants of the organization over time are bent to the unchanging purpose of the organization – but it is blindingly obvious to researchers who have explored ways in which organizations actually *work*.

This book argues that we are all, in effect, knowledge workers now. The term was coined by the great management thinker Peter Drucker in the late 1950s, and is taken to mean something along the lines of "someone who works primarily with information or who develops and uses knowledge in the workplace" (to quote the current Wikipedia definition).

But even if you use a spanner, or an arc welder, or a screwdriver at your place of work, you are still "developing and using knowledge". Nobody in a modern organization should be performing a routine task like a robot – or like a 19th-century mill worker. We all bring our brains to work as well as our brawn.

One of Drucker's key points about knowledge workers is that they are, by definition, highly specialized, and that they have to work as a team. As Daniel Goleman, author of *Emotional Intelligence*, writes on this subject: "Writers are not publishers; computer programmers are not software distributors." In almost every field of modern endeavour, Goleman argues, you need a team of highly specialized people in order to achieve the desired result.[55]

And in case you are thinking: "Oh yes, but that only holds true for some rarefied activities like the intellectual property publishing that Goleman is talking about," it is perfectly arguable that the same holds true even in tasks where "brawn" appears to be most in demand: ask anyone in the military about whether they need infantrymen and women to bring specialized abilities, interpersonal skills, and intelligence to the battlefield as well as muscle, guts, and firepower. The answer will be "Yes!"

Or ask the owners of any modern production-line operation if they want their workers to bring their brains to work with them. Same deal.

Think about the self-organized workers at the GE Durham plant whom we met in chapter 7. Those guys built giant jet engines with their bare hands – well, with their bare hands and some highly sophisticated tools, a load of computing power, and some heavy lifting gear. Knowledge workers? Clearly.

Working as a team of knowledge workers sounds understandable and straightforward if you think of a tug-of-war team, with everyone pulling together. But in complex organizational contexts, as we all know, it's not as simple as that. It is almost certain that no one person is able to complete a particular task on his or her own, and it also almost certain that the task is far more complex than the "all pull together" model suggested by the tug-of-war analogy.

In modern, knowledge-based organizations, teams of highly specialized experts need to make their own, highly specialized contribution to the overall effort – and then to *network* with their colleagues in order to achieve the desired goal.

And so it proves.

BELL LABORATORIES: INITIATIVE AND NETWORKING

In 1986, Robert Kelley and Janet Kaplan began a seven-year research programme that has become a classic study into the work of knowledge workers – in this case, software engineers at Bell Laboratories Switching Systems Business Unit.

These engineers wrote the code that controled the switches that enabled telephones to do an increasingly clever variety of useful things – like displaying an incoming caller's name and phone number. The work involved considerable creativity, and each task was beyond any one engineer's capability. A software application could take a team of between five and 150 engineers anything from six months to two years to complete. As Keeley and Caplan reported in their *Harvard Business Review* article in 1993, a senior engineer told them: "No one engineer can understand the entire switch or have all the knowledge needed to do his or her job."[56]

Kelley and Caplan's task was to work out what made some engineers "star performers" and others only middle performers. Every engineer at Bell Laboratories was, by definition, highly educated, intelligent, and skilled – none of the usual discriminators that might explain star performers' success actually explained the difference between them and the middle performers. It wasn't their IQ, or their problem-solving abilities, or some internal drive to succeed. As Kelley and Kaplan wrote, it was as if management at Bell assumed that star performers were "better people" in some ways. And since Kelley and Kaplan's job was to devise a training programme to encourage more engineers to become star performers, they were (rightly) sceptical that they could devise a training programme to make engineers a "better person."

As the research programme progressed, the word "networking" began to come up in conversations with the engineers themselves:

> We asked each of the expert engineers to define productivity, how they knew when they were productive, and what exactly it was that they did to be productive. For example, one expert told us that networking was crucial to getting his job done. We then asked him how he went about networking with other experts. He explained that networking was a barter system in which an engineer needed to earn his or her own way. From his perspective, that meant first becoming a technical expert in a particularly sought-after area, then letting people know of your expertise, then making yourself available to others. Once an engineer has developed his or her bargaining chips, it's possible to gain access to the rest of this knowledge network. But once in the network, you have to maintain a balance of trade to stay in.[57]

Has there ever been a more crystal clear or lucidly expressed definition of "networking"? You have to earn your right to network by demonstrating that you bring something to the party; having done this, you "make yourself available", and then you can begin to access the network – but you have to "maintain a balance of trade". It's not about control; it's about a constant *quid pro quo*.

In time, the Bell engineers identified nine work strategies that they felt made a difference:

- Taking initiative
- Networking
- Self-management

- Teamwork effectiveness
- Leadership
- Followership
- Perspective
- "Show-and-tell" (delivering a presentation about their work to colleagues and management)
- Organizational savvy.

Not surprisingly, in a creative environment, the engineers ranked initiative as the most important work strategy, though they admitted that this was "elusive". Kelley and Caplan reported one engineer as saying, rather plaintively: "I go into my supervisor's office for a performance evaluation, and she tells me that I should take more initiative. I say to myself that I'm already taking initiative, so what exactly is it that she wants me to do?"

Next on the list is networking and self-management. The significance of networking to high performance emerged clearly as the researchers dug deeper.

Discussions about networking surfaced equally revealing differences, since both stars and middle performers said networks of knowledgeable people are critical for highly productive technical work. For example, a middle performer at Bell Labs talked about being stumped by a technical problem. He painstakingly called various technical gurus and then waited, wasting valuable time while calls went unreturned and e-mail messages unanswered. Star performers, however, rarely face such situations because they do the work of building reliable networks before they actually need them. When they call someone for advice, stars almost always get a faster answer.[58]

In other words, the people with the most initiative and with the best-established networks delivered the best results. That works.

Intriguingly, middle performers tended *not* to rate initiative and networking as the most important work strategies: they chose "show and tell" and "organizational savvy". Show and tell, after all, was the one time that they got to present their work to senior management. A good presenter might indeed see his or her skills rewarded, as a result of being singled out by management for promotion or some other reward. But these good presenters were not, in fact, the best performers in terms of results.

Other middle performers thought that their work in organizing source materials, documents, and software tools in preparation for a project — organizational savvy — were highly significant. Expert engineers were, unsurprisingly, sceptical. "Organizing source materials" was seen by successful engineers as merely something every engineer has to do at the start of a project, and "writing a memo to [a] supervisor about a software bug" was seen as a waste of time; fixing the bug yourself was what showed initiative.

"MANAGERS SOMETIMES OVERLOOK IMPORTANT COMPONENTS"

As something of an aside, it is interesting how the "steam-engine" management at Bell Laboratories at the time was obsessed by the notion that some individual trait, skill or mind-set would be what set apart the star performers — not their networking ability. It is also interesting that when Kelley and Caplan asked both management and engineers to identify star performers, there was only a 50% correlation between the two lists:

> Once we started interviewing the engineers themselves, the picture grew murkier. As we discovered, managers sometimes overlook important components of star performance, like who originates an idea and who helps colleagues the most when it comes to solving critical problems. Being closer to the action, however, knowledge professionals certainly consider these skills when rating their peers.
>
> In addition, the engineers believed that the Bell Labs performance evaluation system was flawed because it turned up too many false negatives, that is, people who were outstanding performers but for reasons of work style or modesty received low ratings from managers.[59]

So, without labouring the point, what was and was not successful practice by engineers at Bell Laboratories *had little or nothing to do with the management team*. The managers were wasting their time thinking that more-successful engineer A must be a "better person" in some way than less-successful engineer B; they were duped by that impressive presentation delivered by engineer C into thinking that he or she was a star performer when, in fact, they were not; they were busy *not* seeing the potential of engineers D and E, who, in the words of Kelley and Caplan, were "outstanding performers, but for reasons of work style or modesty received low ratings from managers".

The people who really knew what mattered – the most successfully performing engineers – knew what the answer was:

☆ ☆

KATHRYN BISHOP, ASSOCIATE FELLOW, SAÏD BUSINESS SCHOOL, UNIVERSITY OF OXFORD

ENCOURAGING THE NETWORK

For many of our programmes at our Business School, a key piece of feedback from delegates is: "One of the great benefits of this programme was building a network." And they don't mean having a nice conversation over dinner, they mean: "When I go back into my territory in Malaysia and I discover I've got a problem with X, I remember talking to John in the USA who's also had that problem, and he'd solved it." So it's the creation of informal networks that are strong enough to survive the hurly-burly of a thousand emails a day; it actually brings real value to an organization.

When I first started work, my company used to take people out for regular training sessions, and it was pretty much half training and half drink. And of course, when we were young, we used to think: "Oh that's tremendous; what a laugh!" But of course it was actually a piece of serious organizational planning – there was genuinely a desire to give people something in common to talk about, and then get them to talk, because the connecting, even if it has no overt purpose right now, will pay dividends later.

There are all sorts of virtual and process ways to encourage networking; there are organizations that build into their performance appraisals some initiative and networking. It took the skills of Kelley and Caplan to reveal this to the management of Bell Laboratories.

We rest our case.

There was a very significant sting in the tail of Kelley and Caplan's article for *Harvard Business Review*.

In surveys done outside of Bell Labs, we've found that about one-third of knowledge workers don't feel tied to their company's destiny, nor do they feel that their productivity and good ideas are sufficiently rewarded. For example, teamwork is often touted by corporate headquarters as critical to both individual and company success; however, an employee's ability to work with others often

assessment of the degree to which I collaborate with others, how cooperative I am, evidence that I have shared my experience either virtually or in person; some criteria that don't replace performance criteria but add to it, so there's some sense of tangible valuing of those approaches.

RE-DRAWING THE ORGANIZATIONAL MAP

I'm very influenced by complex adaptive systems thinking, which talks about a network of nodes flexing and reacting; connecting with each other and flexing to the degree that surrounding nodes allow them to do so. A node might be an individual or it might be a team; you can draw an organizational map which shows not who reports to whom but who connects with whom at other places in the organization during their work, and are those connections healthy, are they strong, are they positive and are they focussed? And if you take that kind of node mapping approach, and thinking not about instructing but thinking about the interactions between different bits of the organization, be they people or be they teams, you get a completely different perspective of the organization – one in which we recognise that instruction is not going to work.

Kathryn Bishop in conversation with the authors

has little to do with annual performance ratings or rewards. Many
professionals know this and are right to resent it.

Yet such resentment can lead to serious drops in productivity.
A company with unproductive and actively resentful professionals,
then, may need to address additional organizational issues, such
as revising the reward system or treating its professionals as
individuals with individual needs.[60]

The whole purpose of this book is to flag up something that
– given the body of evidence on the subject – should now be
glaringly obvious: that steam-engine organizations desperately
need to address a number of what Kelley and Caplan call "additional
organizational issues" (such as, indeed, "revising the reward system
or treating its professionals as individuals with individual needs")
because if they do not, they will take their place alongside other
quaint relics of the 19th-century, such as the "silent monitor" (see
chapter 11) and the Newcomen Atmospheric Engine.

Networks work. Healthy networks are at the heart of every
successful modern organization. Modern organizations must begin
recognize and understand that they are networks, not structures, and
begin to arrange themselves and to operate in ways that recognize
and encourage this.

NEW IDEAS COME FROM THE EDGES OF NETWORKS

Lynda Gratton, professor of management practice at London
Business School, is the author of *Hot Spots*, a study of that well
known but little understood phenomenon: the hot spot. We all
recognize it when see and feel it: it's that part of the organization
where everything seems to go right; where everyone seems just
that little bit more fired up and happier in their work; where meeting
targets is a given and no problem is insurmountable (sometimes it's
even the whole organization).

Gratton's ideas about hot spots were based on a major research
survey involving 500 employees from 17 companies in the United
States, Europe, and Asia. Gratton argues that hot spots are created by
a cooperative mind-set when people network across the 'boundaries'

that exist within nearly all organizations. New ideas and innovation come from the edges of networks: from people of different backgrounds, with relatively weak personal ties.

"The truth is that new ideas and insights usually come not from strong ties but rather from the many weak ties that people have,"

LYNDA GRATTON, AUTHOR OF HOT SPOTS
"NEW IDEAS COME FROM THE MANY WEAK TIES THAT PEOPLE HAVE"
In relationships with strong ties, people talk about what they already know, and since there is much overlap among them, there is much redundancy of knowledge.

The truth is that new ideas and insights usually come not from strong ties but rather from the many weak ties that peoples have ...

Value can be created within the networks of a Hot Spot in three ways...

- Value through exploitation. Where there are many strong ties within a group ... members are particularly adept at maintaining and exploiting the tacit knowledge possessed by members of the group. They have worked together, know each other well, and see each other frequently. These are the experts – the guardians of the knowledge of the firm.
- Value through innovation. Where there are a large number of weak ties (acquaintances and associates) that cross boundaries ... information is diffused faster and is made available to a larger number of people. Here there is potential to create value through dynamic new combinations and access to novel information.
- Value through exploration. Where there are strong ties that cross boundaries ... there is potential of new ideas arising though the combination of what is known by people across the boundaries. They know each other well and can explore what each other knows, with the potential of synthesis.

What is clear from this research on innovation is that boundaries are very important to the creation of value through novel combinations. Crossing boundaries is crucial to Hot Spots.

Lynda Gratton, *Hot Spots*, Pearson Education Ltd, 2007, p 71-73 (italics as per original) writes Gratton.[61] There is a good reason for this: people with strong ties tend to talk about what they already know – they tend to fall into the same way of thinking. Strong ties are valuable, but more for exploiting and exploring ideas than for creating real innovation. Genuinely new ideas and insights tend to be generated by weak ties that cross boundaries (see panel).

THE REWARDS OF REACHING OUT

Networking, both internal and external, *is* happening in major companies. It works every time.

In 2000, A.G. Lafley took over as CEO of mighty Proctor and Gamble and turned the company around in remarkable style (see chapter 3). His key perception was that the company was too inwardly focussed. He decided, in particular, that the company should no longer assume the members of its own R&D department were the only people with bright ideas for the company.

He invited everybody – and we do mean everybody – to think about whether they had a good idea that they wanted to share with Proctor and Gamble. The company would use its immense marketing muscle and formidable distribution network to get a new product to market; what it wanted was new ideas. From anyone.

"We did all kinds of things," Lafley told an Ernst & Young Strategic Growth Forum in Palm Springs, Florida, US, in 2010.

> *We reached out to universities and research laboratories and we tried to get the word out to individual entrepreneurs. One of the things we did was we ran these big innovation fairs. We would run it for two or three days and it was sort of, you had to give if you wanted to receive. So we would show off some of our technologies that we were looking for partners on. Then we would invite people in to show off theirs. It starts out with making a couple of connections: "Gee, maybe I have an idea you might be interested in", and you talk to a third party.*

Lafley also reached out to P&G's network of current and past employees. Former 'P&Gers' were an established, meaningful community, coming together at events around the world and maintaining a vibrant, active network. Lafley tapped into this rich resource, inviting the community to contribute its ideas.

We started getting a lot of leads from former P&Ger's, colleagues of former P&Ger's, and friends of former P&Ger's,' Lafley noted.

Finally, he reached out to everyone else in the world via a new website, PGConnectDevelop.com. Anyone who felt that they had a valuable new idea for the company was invited to submit details of the basic concept via the website. The company undertook to respond within four to six weeks to let the contributor know if the idea had potential and could be taken further. If the idea eventually came to market, the originators would get their share of the rewards.[62]

Eight years after Lafley's appointment as CEO of P&G, *BusinessWeek* magazine reported that, "for the first time in the company's history, more than 50% of the new products P&G brought to market included at least one component from an external partner".[63]

NETWORK INCENTIVES

Alex Pentland, author of *Social Physics,* has evidence of another benefit of networking: network incentives are far more powerful than other incentives. If organizations want to leverage this within their own workforce, however, there's a catch.

The workforce really does have to be a real social network. Having everyone connected by email does NOT create a network. A real network cannot be "set up" – it must evolve. But when it does evolve, over time and organically, it is extremely powerful.

During the 2010 US Congressional elections, as Pentland recounts, a team of scientists from the University of California-San Diego got together with Facebook to carry out a large scale experiment. Sixty-one million Facebook users were sent various messages encouraging them to vote in the elections.

For those who received a straightforward 'get out and vote' message, results were 'disappointingly small.'

But when Facebook users were sent a message showing the faces of people in their network who had already voted, results improved dramatically.

> 'What our grandmothers would have known,' writes Pentland, 'was that nearly all the social influence occurred between close friends who had a face-to-face relationship.'

In other words, you only get a network effect when a real network already exists.

In another experiment, Pentland and his colleagues worked with a Swiss energy-utility company in a drive to encourage energy conservation in a region of the country:

In this experiment, energy users were first given a comparison between their own energy use and that of the average consumer. Even when the consumers were using more electricity than average, than his had little effect on their subsequent energy consumption.

But when they were given the same information about the energy consumption of people in their neighbourhood, they started to reduce their consumption: the behaviour of people in their own neighbourhood was something that they could relate to; something that made them consider their own behaviour more carefully.

In a final stage, the experimenters created a social network on the energy utility's website, and created an unusual reward system. Users were invited to create 'buddy groups' of their friends and acquaintances; when users reduced their own energy consumption, they were able to send gift points to their 'buddies'.

'This social network incentive caused electricity consumption to drop by 17%,' Pentland records, 'twice the best result seen in earlier energy conservation campaigns and more than four times more effective than the typical energy reduction campaign ... behaviour change was most effective when it leveraged the strength of the surrounding social ties

The powerful ability of "social ties" to influence our behaviour comes as no surprise. Pentland suggests that the reason that most organizations do not make use of the power of social incentives is because they may seem to be "fuzzy, vague, and simply 'feel good' strategies rather than reliable tools of management". He points out that the type of social incentives that companies do attempt to use – such as "employee of the month" awards – don't actually work. They "feel awkward and fake" – because they *are* awkward and fake.[64]

A real social incentive can only work when a real network is in place – when the organization has genuinely become a network – and when people willingly urge other members of the network to join in some favoured behaviour. When that does happen, the results can be remarkable.

But steam-engine organizations will never become networks. Networks are organic, dynamic, self-determining. People can only form genuine networks when they are allowed to exchange all kinds of things, freely: ideas, information, gossip, good wishes, condolences, shared moments, news, gripes, reminiscences, or pictures of their friends and children, or of their pets doing cute things.

All of this, for the steam-engine organization, is clearly a waste of the workforce's time. Which is why steam-engine organizations will never be networks.

BUILDING NETWORKS

For modern organizations, the good news is that networks can be developed. As anyone who has developed a social network will know, networks can be *built*. It is necessary to reach out and it is necessary to join in: no network will embrace a member who clearly only wants to take out, rather than to contribute. A core capability of future organizational leaders will be their ability to create and maintain networks – and, as we suggested earlier in this chapter, a key task for the organization as a whole will be to tap into, contribute to, and look for advantage from all of the networks available to it.

Looking back to the example of engineers at Bell Laboratories, successful engineers told us that it was their network of connections within the organization that enabled their success: a network of which they earned membership by demonstrating that they could make a contribution, and from which they could then draw expertise and support – provided that their "balance sheet" with the network stayed positive. Nobody in a network can take out and give nothing back.

Those networks of engineers live within the wider network that is Bell Laboratories, which is in turn connected to the outside world via its own network – and via the overlap of its own network with the external networks of its employees. Circles within circles within circles, all overlapping at various points.

This is the organic, connected networking model that can deliver a competitive edge over inward-looking, high-walled steam-engine organizations, as many modern companies are rapidly discovering. It might be time for a new organizational role. Anyone for "Chief Networking Officer"?

TAKING THE ORGANIZATION FROM THE INDUSTRIAL ERA TO THE AGE OF IDEAS
Transforming the steam engine, one step at a time
- Organizations are members of extended networks, not at the centre of their own network
  - Networks are organic and dynamic
  - Networks can be influenced but not controlled
  - Members need to earn their place in the network by making a contribution
- Work and social networks are no longer clearly separated
  - People bring their own networks with them
  - This should be acknowledged and used to benefit the organization
- Organizations are themselves networks
  - Knowledge workers must function as teams
  - We are all knowledge workers now
- Networks operate on the basis of trust and are encouraged by communication of all kinds
- There are simple things that organizations can do to encourage networking and the building of teams
  - Make networking skills and capabilities a key focus for new hires and for staff evaluation and reward
  - Invest in simple networking infrastructures

- New ideas tend to come from networking between people on the periphery of the organization
  - Because people at the centre all begin to think the same way
- New ideas can come from anywhere
  - Organizations need to open themselves up to the outside world
- Social network incentives are far more powerful than other incentives
  - The organization has to be a genuine network to be able to access this
- The rules of networking
  - Bring something to the party
  - Make yourself available
  - Access the network
  - Keep a positive balance of trade

CHAPTER 10

INCREASING THE GENE POOL
WHY DIVERSITY IS EVERYTHING AND MONOCULTURE IS NO CULTURE AT ALL

Everything that we know about life on earth (we don't know much about life anywhere else in the universe, sadly) tells us that diversity is key. Diversity is everything.

Evolution needs diversity as the raw material that spins off one billion unsuccessful variants of possible life forms – the ones that do not, in fact, have any evolutionary advantage – but also, gloriously, the one-billion-and-first variant that happens to have that magical advantage: the ability to exploit a particular environment in a slightly different way, allowing either its mere survival (which is remarkable in itself) or its possible dominance – until, that is, another new variant finds some brilliant adaption that challenges this new kid on the block. It is the process that has led to our subspecies, *Homo sapiens sapiens*, and the development of the human brain, the most complex thing in the known universe.

Here's an interesting thought. It is a slight digression, but it is worth a moment's reflection. In living systems, there is a drive toward complexity. This is paradoxical. The Second Law of Thermodynamics says that entropy (the degree of disorder of a system) always increases: things tend to get more disordered, more messy, because low-energy states are more stable than high-energy states. The kind of complexity that we see in organic life seems to run counter to this: organic life has a tendency to get more and more complex, less and less messy. Life, of course, has not broken the Second Law of

ADDY PRODD, "LIFE'S RESTLESSNESS", AEON MAGAZINE
WINNERS OF THE REPLICATIVE RACE
It rests on the mathematics of exponential growth. ... Suppose you start with a dollar. Double it every week and, in well under a year, you'll be the world's richest person (assuming no one else discovers your secret). Keep going for another five years and you'll have more dollars than there are atoms in the observable universe.

Self-replicating molecular systems can, in the right circumstances, start off on the same explosive path. But there's a twist: when they do, a new kind of chemistry emerges. Ultimately, it is this new chemistry that leads to what we term biology.

How could such a transformation come about? Why do replicating molecules give rise to replicating cells? In a word: evolution. Or, in four more: replication, variation, competition, selection.

Replicators do not always make perfect copies of themselves, and their variants have to compete with the originals for resources. Because both the originals and "bad" copies share the same tendency towards exponential growth – because neither of them will stop unless they run out of resources – the more effective replicators end up driving the less effective ones into extinction ...

Change the environmental conditions and the winner of the replicative race can change. In fact, that's exactly what makes life so capricious and the evolutionary path largely unpredictable.

Addy Pross, 'Life's restlessness', aeon magazine, http://bit.ly/1oDxa5w

Thermodynamics – it has cheated. It relies on an external source of energy – in our case, for the vast majority of life forms, energy from the sun.

This highlights another apparent paradox: life may have taken advantage of this external power source, but why is there a drive toward greater complexity? Why doesn't life increase, but stay simple?

The answer is, because more complex organic molecules – and more complex life forms – are more stable. At the most basic level, more complex organic molecules – molecules that are able to fold themselves into complex shapes, for example – can be more stable than simpler molecules, which are prone to being broken up by simple chemical reactions and even by physical forces, such as moving water. More complex organic molecules tend to survive; there is a selective evolutionary force in their favour.

Some complex organic molecules, like RNA, are even able to replicate themselves. RNA is not itself alive, but it creates the possibility of life. Intriguingly, recent research had shown that even the miraculously self-replicating single RNA molecule is not very efficient a replicator: two molecules of RNA are better than one, with each molecule catalysing the formation of the other "for the same reason that picking up an object with two fingers is a lot easier than with just one", as Addy Pross, professor of chemistry at Ben-Gurion University of the Negev, explained in *aeon* magazine. This small advantageous step in complexity was, according to Pross, "the first (conceptual) step on a thousand-mile journey – toward that stupendously effective (and inordinately complex) replicator, the bacterial cell"[65] – and on to the wonders of the rest of life on earth.

Once you have a replicating molecule, as Pross points out, all you need is "variation, competition, [and] selection' to lead you all the way to complex life forms (see panel).

Why do you need to know this? Because if it works for life on earth, it just might work for your organization. Think about it.

DIVERSITY, COMPLEXITY, AND ADAPTABILITY

Life on earth (and anywhere else it in the universe that it may have found a foothold) is driven by a simple fact: being complex has an evolutionary advantage. More importantly, before we even get to complexity, life on earth is driven by diversity – by variation. Anything that *can* replicate itself *will* replicate itself until it runs out of resources – or until some competitor arrives on the scene and competes for those resources.

This may ring a bell for your organization. Think of organizations as "replicating systems". Organizations, after all, are more like a species than an individual: they can survive, in a recognisable form, for many generations.

Your organization may have carved out a nice little niche for itself; it's doing fine, and is working hard to stay alive. Now what happens? Some upstart comes up with a new variation of what your organization does, or of the way that your organization does what it does, and it carves out a niche for itself – at your expense. Perhaps it will drive you to extinction.

What can possibly save you from extinction? The answer is "adaptation", and adaption comes from diversity. Just as life's diversity throws up new candidates for survival as conditions change, so organizations need to be adaptive; they need to have – or to be able quickly to create – other variants of the organizations that might be able to survive when conditions change.

To do this, the organization needs to contain a great deal of diversity: a large number of different types of people who may or may not be better suited to whatever entirely unpredictable set of circumstances may apply next year. Or tomorrow.

Do you get this potential diversity, adaptability, and complexity by recruiting identikit executives based on the current favoured model (which, by some strange coincidence, is usually based on the executives currently occupying the organization's most senior roles?)

You do not.

THE BIO-LOGIC OF TRULY COMPLEX SYSTEMS

In his book, *Out of Control: The New Biology of Machines, Social Systems, and the Economic World*, Kevin Kelly, co-founder and former executive editor of *Wired* magazine, explores an extremely interesting idea:

> *The world of our making has become so complex that we must turn to the world of the born to be able to understand how to manage it. That is, the more mechanical we make our fabricated environment, the more biological it will eventually have to be if it is to work at all. ... Truly complex systems such as a cell, a meadow, an economy, or a brain (natural or artificial) require a rigorous non-technological logic.*[66]

Only "bio-logic", Kelly concludes, will enable us to build – or even understand – truly complex systems. His interest is in experiments in creating living ecosystems in closed environments: tiny worlds, sealed off in glass jars, where nothing comes in and nothing goes out. The inhabitants – algae, bacteria, sometimes plants, and shrimps – must strike a balance or die; the "waste products" of all must be useful raw materials for the others; just like spaceship earth, but on a smaller scale.

A pioneer of this technique was Clair Folsome, a microbiologist at the University of Hawaii, who started to seal off collections of microbes in seawater in glass flasks. He discovered that simple microbial societies were surprisingly able to create a viable equilibrium, even when the only thing that came into the sealed system was light, and nothing was able to leave. In fact, Folsome and his co-researcher declared in 1983 that closed ecosystems "having even modest species-diversity, rarely if ever fail".

Another pioneer, marine biologist Lloyd Gomez, set out to create a living coral reef – not in a sealed environment, and one that was assisted by filtration, wave simulation, and a host of other technological support systems, but nevertheless a self-sustaining, living coral reef, in a tank at the Steinhart Aquarium in San Francisco. "After five years of constant babying," he told Kelly, "I have a full food web in my tank so I no longer need to feed them anything."

The artificial coral reef went through many changes and shifts, most of them unexpected and startling, as Gomez explained.

Organisms were dying off. I asked myself what did I do wrong? It turns out I didn't do anything wrong. That's just the community cycle. Heavy populations of microalgae need to be present at first. Then, within 10 months, they're gone. Later some initially abundant sponges disappeared, and another type popped up. Just recently a black sponge has taken up in the reef. I have no idea where it came from.

As Kelly writes, Gomez discovered that "the beginnings of complexity are rooted in chaos. But if a complex system is able to find a common balance after a period of give and take, thereafter not much will derail it".[67]

Kelly went on to investigate larger-scale experiments in creating closed ecosystems, such as the Bioshpere 2 in Arizona, which began in 1987 to explore the possibility of creating sustainable biospheres that might allow the future human colonisation of space, and to gain a better understanding of Biosphere 1: the earth.

The plan for Biosphere 2, Kelly writes, was "to stuff as many biological systems – plants, animals, insects, fish, and microorganisms – as they possibly could into a sealed glass dome, and then rely on the emergent systems own self-stabilizing tendencies to self-organize a biospheric atmosphere".

One of Biosphere 2's pioneers, Walter Adey of the Smithsonian Institute, told Kelly how he grew diversity in the mini ocean, coral reef, and lagoon that he contributed to the biosphere:

What we are doing is cramming more species in than we expect to survive. So the numbers drop. Particular the insects and lower organisms. Then, at the beginning of the next run, we overstock it again, injecting slightly different species – our second guesses. What will probably happen is that there will be a large loss again, maybe one quarter, but we re-inject again next closure. Each time the number of species will stabilize at a higher level than the first. Then complex the system, the more species it can hold. We keep doing that, building up the diversity. If you loaded up Biosphere 2 with all of the species it ends up with, it would collapse at the start.

"Life," Kelley writes, "is the business of making its environment agreeable for life. If you get a bunch of life together and then *give it enough freedom to cultivate the conditions it needed to thrive,* it would go on for ever, and no one needed to understand how it worked."[68]

There are important lessons here for the organization: that the organization should see itself as a complex ecosystem whose best chance for survival lies on bringing together as many different "species" (people) as possible. Genuinely different people.

GOING "POP"

Before we leave the notion that truly complex systems are best understood in terms of organic life forms, we need to introduce Kevin Kelly's delightful concept of "pop".

This is his charming description of the moment when ecosystems begin to work as an interconnected whole. If you have ever kept fish in an aquarium, you will recognize this as the moment when a newly-stocked aquarium becomes healthy: when the microorganisms in the gravel begin successfully to recycle the waste products of the fish, the water clears, and the fish stop gasping for oxygen at the tank's surface.

Kelly believes that all complex systems need to "pop". That large, working systems can be created by "ratcheting up complexity", and that, once the system has popped, it tends to be stable and not easily knocked backward.

"Human institutions, such as teams and companies, exhibit pop," Kelly concludes. "Some little nudge – the additional right manager, a nifty new tool – can suddenly turn 35 competent hard-working people into a creative organism in the state of runaway success."[69]

But remember – to get pop, you need diversity.

LOSING CONTROL – AGAIN

In the organic world, a certain level of complexity, combined with a certain level of diversity, is a highly successful recipe for creating a successful, new, self-sustaining system. The end result, however – the detail of this newly emergent, stable system – is utterly unpredictable.

The small changes to the ecosystem that may enable the next significant development are too subtle to forecast: a slight change in temperature; a small shift in available nutrients. We may get better at prediction – as we have with weather forecasting – but it is a fluid, organic process: exactly what will emerge from the melting pot of original components and environmental conditions could vary as a result of the most apparently insignificant change.

This should be accepted by any successful, diverse, adaptable organization. The function of this unpredictable change, after all, is to adapt to unexpected changes in the environment: it is a survival mechanism. Healthy organizations will change, in the same way, to cope with changing conditions. This does not mean that the organization changes its purpose. Coral reefs change dramatically over time; they are still coral reefs.

Unfortunately, complexity, diversity, and unexpected (though hugely exciting) outcomes are specifically NOT what industrial era, steam-engine organizations want, encourage, or even tolerate.

Steam-engine organizations want – and actively seek out – the repetition of the same task over and over again, *without variation*. Variation is bad. Variation affects quality control.

You will have heard of the "Six Sigma process". Sigma is the Greek letter used to denote a standard deviation – which, as you will be well aware, is the square root of the variance, or spread, of a set of data. Six standard deviations is the equivalent of 3.4 variations (defects) in every 1 million operations.

According to the Six Sigma handbooks:

Six Sigma at many organizations simply means a measure of quality that strives for near perfection. Six Sigma is a disciplined, data-driven approach and methodology for eliminating defects (driving toward six standard deviations between the mean and the nearest specification limit) in any process, from manufacturing to transactional and from product to service.

The statistical representation of Six Sigma describes quantitatively how a process is performing. To achieve Six Sigma, a process must not produce more than 3.4 defects per million opportunities.[70]

Six Sigma is good. Six Sigma has saved a lot of companies a lot of money, and made a lot of customers very happy, as they take delivery of products that are essentially free of defects. But as an organizational philosophy, Six Sigma is death.

All life is based on mistakes: tiny errors made as genetic material of simple organisms is replicated – some of which turn out to be very useful indeed. This is why bacteria are so quick to adapt: attack them

KAREN PHELAN, *I'M SORRY I BROKE YOUR COMPANY*
"ISN'T THE MARKETING FUNCTION MEANT TO BE CHAOTIC?"
I have a reference book for implementing Six Sigma for marketing processes, and it is full of templates for monitoring task completion and documenting stage-gate criteria. The point of these templates is to instil discipline and consistency into marketing processes.

Why would I hire smart, creative, psychologically savvy people and have them spend their time filling out document templates and monitoring progress in minute detail when they should be brainstorming new product ideas and new marketing campaigns?

Isn't the marketing function supposed to be chaotic?

Karen Phelan, *I'm Sorry I Broke Your Company,* **Berrett-Koehler Publishers Inc, 2013, Kindle file, Ch. 2**

with a bacteriocide, like penicillin, or a bacteriocidal household cleaner, and if there just happens to be even one little bacterium whose genetic material has changed, by chance, in a way that allows it to survive the bacteriocide, then it and its billions of descendants will be selected; they will survive, where their almost identical fellow bacteria do not.

Organizations may well want to produce the perfect widget – or the perfect jet engine – over and over again. But even the widget (and certainly the jet engine) must improve. People must be allowed to think: "If I just tweaked this little thing here, I'm sure it would work better." Tweaking things is the human version of the random variation that drives genetic evolution.

Six Sigma has its role, but like all management processes, it can only be set to work on a known process – a process in which we do not want variation. But, now that we are all knowledge workers, we *do* want variation. All of the time.

In an interview with *Harvard Business Review*, Netflix founder and CEO Reed Hastings explained how and why the company had created the Netflix "culture deck" in an attempt to pass on the its entrepreneurial culture to the next generation of employees:

It's our version of Letters to a Young Poet *for budding entrepreneurs. It's what we wish we had understood when we started. More than one hundred people at Netflix have made major contributions to the deck, and we have more improvements coming.*

Many of Netflix's practices go against common Human Resources practices. The company declines, for example, to carry out annual reviews of employees, instead arguing:

If you talk simply and honestly about performance on a regular basis, you can get good results – probably better ones than a company that grades everyone on a five-point scale. ...

As a society, we've had hundreds of years to work on managing industrial firms, so a lot of accepted HR practices are centred in that experience. We're just beginning to learn how to run creative firms, which is quite different. Industrial firms thrive on reducing

GARY HAMEL, *THE FUTURE OF MANAGEMENT*
INVESTING IN DIVERSITY IS NOT A LUXURY
'The risk in a fast-changing world is that a company becomes over-adapted to a particular ecological niche. In the pursuit of focus, a company can impair its ability to adapt by hiring in a single mold, narrowing the scope of its innovation efforts, relying exclusively on a single business model, or failing to experiment with new operating models.

'As change accelerates, investing in diversity is not a luxury; it's a survival strategy. There's a lot more to diversity than the shade of one's skin and the shape of one's genitals. What really matters is the sum total of one's life experiences. Despite all the rhetoric to the contrary, companies often put more effort into training the diversity out of people, through programs that indoctrinate employees in the "one best way," than they do into bringing fresh ideas into the company.'

Gary Hamel, *The Future of Management,* Harvard Business School Publishing, 2007, Kindle file, Ch. 8

variation (manufacturing errors); creative firms thrive on increasing variation (innovation).[71]

Just as we believe that we are all knowledge workers now, we also believe that there is no longer any such thing as an "industrial firm", to use Hastings's term. We believe that we are all "creative firms" now. We use our ideas to drive our businesses forward, regardless of whether we are creating metal goods or computer code.

In organizations, as in life itself, evolution and progress demand diversity, which creates the potential for adaptability. Or, as business guru Gary Hamel writes in *The Future of Management*:

> *The broader the gene pool, the better. Managers tend to marry their cousins. Not literally, of course, but they often surround themselves with people whose life experiences mirror their own. The diversity of any system determines its capacity to adapt. Greater diversity—of thought, skills, attitudes, and capabilities— equals a greater range of adaptive responses' (see panel).*

Unfortunately, the word "diversity" has been captured by human resources departments and the political correctness brigade, and has become meaningless. Organizations are now proud to boast that they employ some women, a few older people, and several people from different ethnic backgrounds – and clearly feel that they can hold their heads high, having "ticked those boxes" in the politically correct employment manual. They are now officially – *tarra!* – diverse.

Except, of course, that they are really not diverse in the only thing that matters: a true diversity of ideas, capabilities, worldviews, ways of thinking, ways of being ...

THE SILENT MONITOR

The "silent monitor" of worker productivity was introduced by the reforming 19th-century mill owner Robert Owen at his New Lanark Mills, where he strove to provide decent working and living conditions for his workforce. It was a four-sided block of wood –

each side of which was a different colour – that hung beside the station of each worker.

A superintendent (the archetypical steam-engine manager!) would turn the block each day to show the colour that represented the general performance and attitude of the worker. Black represented "bad" behaviour, blue was "indifferent", yellow was "good", and white was "excellent". Each worker's daily behaviour was recorded in a "book of character".

Steam-engine organizations still monitor their workforces with systems that are merely refinements of the silent monitor, and which

MARK POWELL

CREATING MONOCULTURES

The inability to allow diversity of types of people within the organization I think is fundamental. The diversity issue is also actively reflected in how we measure and reward people, because we have one set of measurements for everybody – which means effectively that everyone is measured in a non-diverse way.

What that tends to mean is that those who are a little bit different, who might not fit the normal concept of an organization, get nailed by the measures and the metrics. They get measured for things they're not so good at, and the things they are different and good at are largely not valued and therefore not measured.

Organizations create environments where people who are perhaps a bit different, but who might have more interesting ways of doing things, or who might have crazy ideas that just might be really important, either a) self-eject themselves from organizations or b) get ejected by the organization because they don't fit. I think this is very dangerous. Organizations are creating monocultures – a collection of individuals who all look, feel and sound the same.

I think that diversity needs to be reclaimed as a concept. We should embrace the concept of capability diversity rather than seeing diversity in very narrow race, sex, and disability lines. We need to look at it in a much broader way of human capability. I think, in the future, one of the metrics still aim to drive diversity out of the system. It is not hard, clearly, to spot members of the organization who are incapable, or lazy, or malicious – so the only other possible purpose for the book of character would seem to be to record those worrying "differences" that all human beings exhibit.

Funnily enough, Robert Owen believed that his silent monitors were enlightened and progressive. Previously, and in almost every mill other than Owen's at New Lanark, superintendents attempted to improve workers' performance by administering a stout blow with a stick or fist on yellow or blue days, or by giving them a good

☆ ☆

that I would be interested in looking at is, how do you measure human capability diversity in an organization? It's very easy to say: "Of 100 people, 40 are black, therefore we are racially diverse." I'd like to say: "Out of 100 people, we can prove that we've got 18 different types of people with different skill structures." That would be a much more interesting measure of diversity in an organization.

So, when I say "let's embrace diversity", for me, we've got to embrace a completely different type of diversity in terms of human capability and capacities. When we can learn to do this and find ways of measuring and valuing these people in organizations and enable us to maintain them, I think we can create much more powerful, much more interesting organizations that allow people with different talents and skills to put those talents and skills to use.

Ultimately, everything we do, everything we produce, and everything we sell is only a function of the people who live and or work in our organization, and we need to have a much more diverse set of people, people with genuinely diverse capabilities, if we want to maximise the ability to do interesting things – because it's the interesting things that will keep us one step ahead of the competition. Being boring is a pretty sure-fire route to finding yourself commoditised and out-innovated.

Mark Powell in conversation with Jonathan Gifford

kicking on black days. Young children, for example, were beaten if they began to flag toward the end of their 14–16 hour days.[72] Owen, however, was against corporal punishment.

Both of the authors of this book have, in fact, worked at different times with organizations that have used one or the other of these steam-engine systems of motivation – the clout 'round the ear or the good kicking, instantly applied, or the menacing, permanent record in the book of character. Both techniques have their merits – from a steam-engine perspective. But we would humbly submit that it is time for organizations to stop using either.

We take it for granted that management by fear is no longer acceptable (and can we remind steam-engine managers that verbal intimidation is still a form of intimidation?). We would suggest that the modern equivalent of the book of character persists in the guise of the appraisals system – and that it is a bizarre and unnatural practice.

"THIS IS WHAT I DON'T LIKE ABOUT YOU"

In our conversation with Karen Phelan, management consultant and author of *I'm Sorry I Broke Your Company*, she made the interesting point that there are things that we do in the process of managing people at work that we would never consider doing in any other aspect of our lives. She goes on to explain:

> In management you have to do performance reviews. You sit there with your direct report and you have a discussion about what went well and what didn't go well, and basically you're saying: "This is what I like and don't like about you."
>
> And you would never ever do that in any other part of your life, right?
>
> It's uncomfortable and awkward, and most of the time your word falls on deaf ears. Really and truly it does. And the reason why it falls on deaf ears is because most of the time you have different priorities and different value systems.
>
> I think that organizations need to ask: "Is this something I see anywhere else; does this work anywhere else? If I did this in my family

or in a church, how would people react?" And if they don't react well, why would you do this in a business setting?

For me it comes down to a very, very fundamental thing in business management. Either you trust your employees to do the right thing, or you don't trust your employees to do the right thing. And I'm not naïve enough to think that everybody is wonderful, but I think that most people want to do the right thing and want to work for a common goal because, you know, what else are they going to do?

And if you don't trust your people to do the right thing, you've really gotten yourself into a hole, because now you have to put in all sorts of monitoring systems in place, to ensure that they do the right thing. And it's like squeezing a balloon; every time you put one system in place, you force people into another outlet. If you tie people's compensation to their goals, then you ensure that they're going to meet those goals, but it doesn't matter how they meet those goals. If you tie their hands and say: "I don't trust you" – if you treat people in a manner where you say: "I don't trust you" – then they're not going to be trustworthy.[73]

FOCUSSING ON OUR WEAKNESSES

Mark Powell had a similar experience in his career: a familiar equivalent of Phelan's description of the appraisal system. In Mark's case, this appraisal was followed by the interesting (and, again, familiar) suggestion that he should focus on the areas that his organization had decided were his weakest skillsets, rather than looking for ways to get the maximum leverage out of his strengths:

To give you an example, a number of years ago when I was a partner in another firm, my evaluation process was based on 10 capabilities and they found a strange way of scoring me against all ten, and that was fine. I went in and went through the score list and they said: "Mark you're absolutely really, really, really brilliant at three of these things and you're really pretty good at four and you're a bit crap at the other three. So, that's your measurements. Now, what we want you to do is we want you to go away next year and focus on the three things you're naturally crap at."

And I sat there and I thought: "That's very interesting." Because they were focussing on the weak metrics and trying to improve them, rather than focussing on the strong metrics and try to leverage them. I think there's a very interesting question here around how the whole "appraisal" system has become a process of focussing on what you're not doing well, or what is not happening well, rather than giving much more focus on saying: "Look – you're brilliant in these three areas. What we want you to do is to find ways of getting other people to help you with the things that you're not so good at and spend more time on the three things that you're brilliant at." [74]

There are a thousand ways to tell whether someone is being productive that do not require a pseudo-psychological assessment of their strengths and weaknesses. Or, indeed, with supervising people and keeping a kind of 21st-century version of the 19th-century "book of character".

SEEKING OUT DEVIANTS

We all tend to seek out people like ourselves. We can't help it. We also begin to adjust ourselves to the norms of the group that we happen to find ourselves in. We tone down or change our normal accent to fit in with a group of people with different accents. If there is a hierarchy involved (which, in steam-engine organizations, there always is) we will begin, unconsciously, to mimic the behaviour of those above us in the pecking order.

One of the downsides of human sociability is our very tendency to form groups: to become tribal. To get diversity into our organizations takes real, conscious effort. We will need to go against our instincts and seek out things that "feel wrong" to us.

As Tracey Camilleri, Associate Fellow at Saïd Business School, University of Oxford, told us, we need to celebrate our human differences. After all, as she points out, if you were staging a version of Shakespeare's *Hamlet*, and every member of the company (or organization) decided that they wanted to be Hamlet, it wouldn't make for much of a show:

MARK POWELL

THE GENE POOL AND HIGH PERFORMANCE TEAMS

There was a study done a number of years ago, looking at high performance teams, and they took two groups of people. One group was very un-diverse. It was basically the brightest and best students and professors from a university. The other one was much more diverse. It had some professors and some students; it had some janitors and some secretaries; it had people from outside the university – a real mix of humanity of completely different education, skills and temperaments. Each group was given a series of tasks – a series of intellectual tasks; a series of practical tasks; a series of logical tasks.

In almost every single case, the diverse group won despite the fact they were competing against people who had probably a significantly higher average IQ and intelligence and experience level. The reason, when they looked at it, was quite simple, because the less diverse group had a capability effectively of 1 x 2, because most of the capability was copied in other people. So they might have had 10 people but they didn't have 10 people's worth of capability. The other group also had 10 people, but because each of the 10 people was a bit different they effectively had 10 people.

The other issue that was quite interesting when they looked at it was that the more diverse group was much more open as a group to people coming up with new and different innovative ideas and suggestions. People were much less willing in the other group to stand out or come up with anything else. There's an interesting connection here between the gene pool and high performance teams.

Now, interestingly, if you go back to industrial age organizations, that's not what they were geared up for. Individuals were basically single factors of production so having a monoculture was exactly what you wanted. You wanted people who would be quite happy sitting there on a production line, doing the same task over and over again. The last thing you needed was someone who was sitting there trying to think, rethink, how to get rid of the machine or how to do something differently because that would disrupt production -- but that's not where we are, or should be, today.

Mark Powell in conversation with Jonathan Gifford

We actually need to be human beings in this life. Isn't it fantastic that we're all different? And yet we work in these organizations where we cascade behaviours down, and we're all told what to do, and it's such a profound waste of what we are. A lot of it comes back to the ingrained heroic ideal of leadership: about people needing to be top; needing to be strongest; needing to be in control – and not being able to cope with mess or blurred edges.

You go into many meetings and every single person around that table is Hamlet. They're all at the same level. You can't put on a play where everyone is Hamlet. You need some gravediggers, you need Ophelia, you need Rosencrantz and Guildenstern to bring the thing alive.

We don't think about casting our teams like plays, but we should. What you need, you need disruption; you need someone who looks at things completely differently, you need people to question, to really be good at questioning.

And so often it's the same old grisly grey teams of people, all at the same level. We don't respect how groups function: how you make a really high-functioning group in the light of your objective; in the light of what you want.

Camilleri also echoes Mark Powell's point about the measurement (or "evaluation") of people, and the difficulty that we have in accepting – let alone embracing – difference.

It's the system that kills all these things at birth. It's the way people are evaluated and measured, it's the way people are allocated to teams, it's the way we just accept objectives without having proper beginnings, proper ends, real questionings of what these objectives are. It's the way we fail to know each other as human beings; to know our strengths and weaknesses and to be fine with that.

Ron Emerson, also Associate Fellow at Saïd Business School, spoke to the authors about the need to seek out "positive deviants" within the organization, and to make them an exemplar that the rest of the organization will naturally follow.

The real question is whether the people at the top a) recognize the need for the adaptive change, and b) seek out these positive deviants, these hot spots and publicize them and build on them, because change in organizations does not come from some big cascade from the top that goes across the whole organization.

If you don't have a hot spot, your create one, and you have somebody set up the business in the new way and you then point everyone else to this and say: "That's what we mean by the new format."

And that has a number of benefits: people can see it in operation as opposed to on a PowerPoint; they can see colleagues who've done it, so they think: "Well, if they can, then I can"; and of course, there is the compelling development that, "Well, I'm going to look pretty stupid if I can't do it and they can." So you then have a lateral movement across the organization rather than a top down cascade. You migrate this thing out across the organization.

Alex Pentland, author of *Social Physics*, talks about the need to seek out "contrarians". He had found in his research that people in intense work environments, where ideas and information were very freely exchanged, tended to fall into what he calls an "echo chamber" – a form of "groupthink". His team even recommended slowing down the flow of information in some circumstances (such as on trading floors) in order to break out of the echo chamber and allow new ideas to emerge.

We are all very prone to falling into groupthink. If you spot someone who is swimming against the tide of groupthink, Pentland argues, pay them good heed, especially if there is more than one of them: one of them might just be an oddball, but several 'contrarians' in consensus are probably onto something:

When people are behaving independently of their social learning, it is likely that they have independent information and that they believe in that information enough to fight the effects of social influence. Find as many of these "wise guys" as possible and learn from them. Such contrarians sometimes have the best ideas, but sometimes they are just oddballs. How can you know which is which? If you can find many such independent thinkers and discover that there is a consensus among a large subset of them, then a really, really good trading strategy is to follow the contrarian consensus.[73]

The existence of diversity in an organization requires a different set of relationships. If we are not all identical units of production manning our workstation, then we must be dealt with as individuals. This should not be a problem, but as you will have noticed, it is a problem for steam-engine organizations. As Kathryn Bishop, Associate Fellow at Saïd Business School, told us, organizations need to build processes for dealing with diversity. At the core of this is collaboration – real collaboration, of the kind that looks to acknowledge and complement each other's different abilities:

The key thing about diversity is not just having it, it's not just the appointing of people, but actually setting up processes whereby you can use that diversity and benefit from it. And that's really about collaboration, genuine respectful collaboration, in which, for example, I recognize that you are extremely able at this aspect, while this is really not one of my strengths, and I acknowledge how significant that is and we collaborate together. That collaborative process in organizations is one of the things I'm particularly interested in during development activity, because we're not as good at this as we need to be. People think that collaboration is handholding, you know - "I'll be nice to you and we'll have a meeting"- but it's much more than that.

OF HUMANS AND RESOURCES – AND THE IMPORTANCE OF NOT CONFUSING THE TWO

It is a sad fact that in unreconstructed steam-engine organizations, human-resources departments are a part of the problem of lack of diversity. Back in the early 20th century, the development of job descriptions was seen as a progressive move: the skills and abilities

KATHRYN BISHOP, ASSOCIATE FELLOW, SAÏD BUSINESS SCHOOL, UNIVERSITY OF OXFORD

FINDING OUTLETS FOR CREATIVE ENERGY

When I was a Human Resources director at a major financial company, somebody came to me and said: "There's a scurrilous, underground, sort of funny comic newspaper going around, here's a copy of it. I think you need to take some action."

And I looked at it and it was indeed scurrilous. But it was hilarious. It was absolutely hilarious. Witty and clever and innovative. And I just said: "No. I'm not going to do anything about it. This seems to me to be a sign of a healthy organization. ... They're clearly interested and engaged in what's going on in the organization, to the extent that they're prepared to make jokes about it. Rather than stop this, let's have a look at what other outlets there might be, possibly slightly less scurrilous, for this creative energy."

Kathryn Bishop in conversation with the authors

needed for any particular role were carefully noted and recorded, and the people whose skills and abilities were best matched with those requirements were hired to fill the roles. It was seen by both management and the workforce at the time as a safeguard against favouritism and nepotism, and as some kind of guarantee of a genuine meritocracy.

And so it was. But we have moved on.

Today, these rigidly defined roles are guaranteeing lack of diversity. If we set out to recruit exciting new talent with the mind-set that we know exactly what the ideal candidate will be like – their education, their background, their skills, abilities, social connections, politics, and every other damned facet of their lives – then we will inevitably hire clones. This, as you will know, has happened, continues to happen, and will continue to happen – unless we do something about it.

There is a remarkable consensus of opinion about this among business thinkers – yet the steam engine continues to roll.

Human Resources departments are required by organizations to examine individuals against each other: is he like other people? Is she as good as other people? They are obliged to compare people with their peers in order to evaluate their performance. This is an attempt by organizations to reassure themselves that they are "in control" by quantifying that most unquantifiable of things: a human being. It sees human beings as factors of production that need to be managed.

Here's a suggestion. There is already an ambiguity in the term "human resources". In this chapter so far, this has been taken as implying, in line with steam-engine thinking, that human beings are merely a "resource" like other, inanimate resources: raw materials, fuel, and so on.

But there is, of course, another meaning of the word "resource"; one that modern HR professionals would prefer – that the people in any organization are "our greatest resource", which carries positive connotations of that other meaning of resource, as in something one can be full of: ingenuity, quick wittedness, and so on.

In this spirit, HR departments could function as "human energy departments", applying themselves to finding ways of getting the most of out the people in the organization, rather than to classifying, appraising, and managing them. The key question then would be this: "How do we enable our diverse and exciting collection of people to be more creative, to be more innovative, to challenge conventional wisdom, to bring new ideas into the organization?"

One final thought: organizations are nothing but people – ideally "groups of people sailing in a stream of ideas". Take away the people, and all you have is some buildings and some materials: some physical "resources". What you don't have any more is an organisation.

But if you still have the people (ask any organization whose headquarters have been destroyed in some disaster) then you still have an organization: you can build everything over again from scratch.

On this analysis, people are not a resource of organizations. Organizations are groups of people.

TAKING THE ORGANIZATION FROM THE INDUSTRIAL ERA TO THE AGE OF IDEAS

Transforming the steam engine, one step at a time

- Variation drives evolution
  - The small changes that occur when molecules replicate is the basis of all organic change
- Diverse ecosystems are robust and self-sustaining
  - Systems with a sufficient diversity of species tend to be self-stabilizing and create the conditions needed for their continued survival
- Organizations, like ecosystems, need diversity, for the same reasons: to gain the ability to adapt and survive
- Complex, diverse systems are inherently unpredictable
  - Unpredictable change is a mechanism for coping with changes in the environment
  - Healthy, diverse organizations should welcome their own ability to change and adapt in order to survive
- Diversity in people must be real diversity, not politically correct diversity: a wide range of different capabilities, attitudes, approaches, and worldviews
  - We are drawn to people like ourselves; we also become more like the members of our group
  - Maintaining diversity is difficult and requires effort
  - Organisations resist diversity because it disrupts favoured systems and processes
  - It is important to seek out contrarians
- Working with diversity requires genuine collaboration
  - We need to accept our differences and use them to complement each other
- Job descriptions and competency lists tend to standardize recruitment
  - Pre-judging the skills and abilities needed for a role guarantees lack of diversity
- Steam-engine HR departments analyse, label, and process
  - We must explore ways of maximizing the human energy of the team

CHAPTER 11

GETTING EMOTIONAL
THE EMOTIONALLY HEALTHY ORGANIZATION

We have almost reached the end of our exploration of the strange persistence of 19th- and early-20th-century attitudes to management, and of the out-dated, steam-engine organizations that are the outward manifestation of these debunked management theories: steam engines clinging stubbornly to life, puffing and clanking incongruously along in the midst of the technological wonders of 21st-century life.

By way of conclusion, and as a way of looking forward, this chapter explores something that is not really a paradox, though it should be: the question of why steam-engine organizations fail to make the people who work for them happy, and how much more effective these organizations would be if they *did*, in fact, make the people who work for them happy.

This *would* be a paradox, if we could frame it in this way: "Steam-engine organizations want to make their employees happy and productive, but their processes and procedures guarantee that the members of that organization will be unhappy and stressed and, as a result, less productive, less creative, less committed and less loyal."

But we can't frame it that way, because steam-engine organizations don't consider making their workforces *happy* to be a major part of their business. Their preoccupation is with making the workforce *productive*. Every once in a while, some study or other tells them that happy workers will be more productive, and they do something really crass to promote what they think happiness means, but their hearts are not in it – unlike, for example, the online shoe retailer, Zappos, which has wholeheartedly embraced happiness as a core part of its business model (see chapter 3).

It is not necessary to argue the case too forcefully. Think about yourself; think about your circle of friends. Would they say — would *you* say? — that they (or you) are genuinely happy at their place of work? That they (or you) find great pleasure and deep personal satisfaction from the long hours spent at the workplace?

Hopefully, you and your friends are among the few who can answer "yes". But the 2012 Towers Watson *Global Workforce Study* suggests strongly that they (and perhaps you) will be in the minority.

The study covered 32,000 full-time employees in large and mid-sized corporations across a range of industries in 29 markets around the world. It explored the level of workers "sustainable engagement"

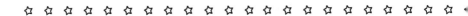

TOWERS WATSON 2012 GLOBAL WORKFORCE STUDY
Inside Sustainable Engagement

Sustainable engagement describes the intensity of employees' connection to their organization, based on three core elements:

- The extent of employees' discretionary effort committed to achieving work goals (being engaged)
- An environment that supports productivity in multiple ways (being enabled)
- A work experience that promotes well-being (feeling energized)

Traditional engagement

- Belief in company goals and objectives
- Emotional connection (pride, would recommend employer)
- Willingness to give extra effort to support success

Enablement

- Freedom from obstacles to success at work
- Availability of resources to perform well
- Ability to meet work challenges effectively

Energy

- Ability to maintain energy at work
- Supportive social environment

with their employers (see panel), and concluded that employee engagement matters. As the study notes:

> Employee engagement may have begun life as a corporate buzzword, but over the last decade, it's been widely acknowledged as a critical element in drawing out discretionary effort from workers. Studies at a number of organizations, including leading academic institutions, have shown a clear relationship between high levels of employee engagement — colloquially defined as the willingness and ability to go the extra mile — and improved financial and operational results.

In its Executive Summary, the study draws a disturbing conclusion – and one that supports the central theme of this book.

☆ ☆

- Feelings of enthusiasm/accomplishment at work

Towers Watson uses a set of nine survey questions to measure the extent to which survey respondents believe these three elements are part of their work environment. Based on a statistical analysis of their responses, we categorize respondents into four distinct segments:

HIGHLY ENGAGED: Those who score high on all three aspects of sustainable engagement **35%**

UNSUPPORTED: Those who are traditionally engaged, but lack enablement and/or energy **22%**

DETACHED: Those who feel enabled and/or energized, but lack a sense of traditional engagement **17%**

DISENGAGED: Those who score low on all three aspects of sustainable engagement **26%**

Towers Watson 2012 Global Workforce Study http://bit.ly/1pj6rfc

Our data suggest that businesses appear to be at a critical tipping point in their ability to maintain engagement over time. While most are already running their businesses very differently in today's highly interconnected global marketplace, a surprisingly large number don't appear to be keeping pace in terms of how they're managing and supporting the very people assigned to execute the work on the ground. Put starkly, they are running 21st-century businesses with 20th-century workplace practices and programs. And the cracks in the foundation are starting to show in both small and large ways.

The study's approach to the concept of "sustainable engagement" includes the following (see panel):

Whether workers felt "traditionally engaged" with the company – whether they believed in their company's goals, felt pride in it and were willing to put in extra effort to ensure its success.

Whether or not workers felt "enabled": being supported; feeling that they had the tools to do the job and were able to meet challenges successfully.

Whether or not workers felt "energized": whether they could maintain their energy levels at work, felt that they worked in a supportive social environment, were enthusiastic about their work, and were getting a sense of accomplishment from it.

The good news – in a way – is that just over a third of workers (35%) reported that they were where we would all like to be (and where our organizations would like us to be): they felt engaged, enabled, and energized. The study called these workers "highly engaged". Then again, that means that two thirds of the global workforce *doesn't* feel this way. They don't feel highly engaged. As we were saying, if you and your friends do feel highly engaged with your work, you are in the minority.

Twenty-two per cent of the workforce was described by the study as "unsupported". They felt engaged – they believed in their company's goals, were proud of their company, and were willing to put in extra effort to help it succeed – but felt that they were neither enabled nor energized. That is, 22% of the global workforce believe in their organization's goals and are committed to helping it succeed, but feel that their organization does not support them or encourage the energy that they are willing to make available. How appalling is that?

Then comes another, equally sad statistic: 17% of the global workforce feels enabled and energized, but they don't feel engaged with their organization. These workers do feel energized, and they feel that organization is giving them the tools that they need to do the job. They are raring to go, and they have no problem with the level of support the organization is giving them. These are clearly self-motivated, dynamic workers. But, sadly, they are not really too bothered if their employer sinks or swims. They couldn't really give a monkey's. Clearly, something has gone a little bit awry with the organizational leadership there.

Finally, here's a figure that is a glimpse into the abyss. Over one quarter (26%) of the global workforce is "disengaged": they don't buy into their organization in any significant way, and they don't feel enabled or energized. *One quarter of the global workforce!*

The 2012 Global Workforce Study says that the key themes to emerge from the study are that stress and anxiety about the future are common, and that security is taking precedence over almost everything (and that attracting employees, as a result, is now largely about security); and that *retaining* employees now has more to do with the quality of the work experience overall, which has to do with "the quality of employees' relationship with their managers, their trust in senior leadership, and their ability to manage stress on the job".

Finally, the study notes the workforce's "doubts about the level of interest and support coming from above. ... Just under half of the respondents agree their organization's senior leaders have a sincere interest in employee wellbeing".

This looks very much like the awful legacy of our apparent inability to shake off the outmoded habits of steam-engine management.

REASON AND EMOTION

The Industrial Revolution grew out of the 18th-century Enlightenment, with its belief in the power of reason and rationality, and its distrust of religious dogma and superstition. Rationality drove the scientific method, and science was beginning to produce the wonderful new technologies that powered the Revolution.

Reason was good. *Emotion* was bad.

This chapter is called "Getting Emotional" because steam-engine mangers are still deeply wary of emotion. "Let's not get all emotional about this," they say. "We need to keep our emotions out of this."

The trouble is that neither they, nor we, can keep our emotions out of anything. Emotions are what drive us. Emotions help us make decisions. Sometimes (especially when we feel threatened) our emotions take decisions for us. Sometimes emotions get in the way of a "rational" decision. But without emotions, we find it impossible to make decisions at all.

In a now-famous instance, a patient who had suffered damage as the result of a brain tumour to the prefrontal cortex area of his brain – the area most implicated in decision-making and cognitive behaviour – proved unable to make important life decisions successfully . In most respects, he was apparently "rational", but he was unable to see the negative or positive aspects of any of his decisions. Without these emotional "markers", the patient's decision-making was effectively useless: he had become "irrational".

Elliot (as the anonymous patient was referred to in case histories) was being treated by the neuroscientist Antonio Demasio, who wrote about Elliot's condition in his book, *Descartes' Error*. 'His ability to reach decisions was impaired,' writes Demasio, 'as was his ability to make an effective plan for the hours ahead of him, let alone to plan for the months and years of his future. These changes were in no way comparable to the slips of judgment that visit all of us from time to time. Normal and intelligent individuals of comparable education make mistakes and poor decisions, but not with such systematically dire consequences.'

Elliot, notes Demassio, had become disturbingly "dispassionate". He recounts an occasion when Elliot hit an ice patch when driving to his appointment with Demasio, and witnessed cars skidding off the road. Elliot had made the right decisions, not touching his brakes and steering in a straight line. But his account of this dramatic event lacked any emotional content – it was just something that had happened on the way to the appointment.

On the same occasion, Demasio offered Elliot the choice of two different dates, a few days apart, for his next appointment. Elliot spent almost half an hour enumerating all of the possible advantages and disadvantages of these particular dates, but showed no sign of reaching a decision. Eventually, Demasio and his colleagues suggested that Elliot should come on the second date, which he calmly accepted and noted. He had no sense of the inappropriateness of his actions; he lacked any emotional triggers that could tell him that he was wasting his own, and everybody else's time. He was not in any sense embarrassed by his failure to decide. Without any emotional content, "pure reason" might never come to a conclusion, and certainly not within an appropriate time frame.[76]

The involvement of emotion with reason is complex, and it has its advantages and disadvantages, but it is literally nonsense to say that we can make "emotionless" decisions. As Demasio writes:

'But now I had before my eyes the coolest, least emotional, intelligent human being one might imagine, and yet his practical reason was so impaired that it produced, in the wanderings of daily life, a succession of mistakes, a perpetual violation of what would be considered socially appropriate and personally advantageous. ... He had the requisite knowledge, attention, and memory; his language was flawless; he could perform calculations; he could tackle the logic of an abstract problem. There was only one significant accompaniment to his decision-making failure: a marked alteration of the ability to experience feelings. Flawed reason and impaired feelings stood out together as the consequences of a specific brain lesion, and this correlation suggested to me that feeling was an integral component of the machinery of reason.[76]

As this case so poignantly demonstrates, having no emotion involved in decision-making leads to no decision – or to very bad decisions. At this level, Demasio is talking about quite complex emotions: "somatic markers", which he describes as "both visceral and non-visceral" – gut feelings mediated by rational decision-making – which ring an automatic alarm. "Beware of danger ahead if you choose the option which leads to this outcome," as Demasio puts it [77]. This quickly narrows our range of possible choices, and leads to more effective decision-making.

For the purposes of this chapter, however, we want to consider a far less sophisticated level of decision-making and far more basic emotions.

EMOTIONS AND FEELINGS

One of our colleagues, psychologist and executive coach Dr Paul Brown, co-author of *Neuropsychology for Coaches*, make a useful distinction between the eight "basic emotions" and "feelings", which are more complex, and which he and his colleagues describe as more complex "compounds of emotions" which also involve our prefrontal cortex – our conscious minds. As Brown and his colleagues put it, feelings "are the elaboration of an extraordinarily complex and individually unique mixing of the primary emotions". [78]

Basic or primary emotions, on the other hand, are – well – basic. They are to do with survival and, in effect, sociability. Daniel Goleman, author of *Emotional Intelligence*, has suggested that there are eight primary emotions: fear, anger, disgust, shame, and sadness, which are to do with escape, avoidance, and survival; "surprise/startle", which keeps us intensely focussed until we know what the outcome of this new situation is going to be; "excitement/joy", which reinforces the things in life that we find most deeply rewarding; and "love/trust", the "attachment emotions" that link us to our fellow humans.[79]

These are the only emotions that we need to involve for the purposes of this chapter. Trust us: they are more than enough to be going along with.

Steam engine managers need not worry about us "getting emotional". We are in the grip of powerful emotional forces a long time before we get to anything as complex as "feelings".

Nothing comes into our minds without there being an emotional content attached to it. Two almond-shaped regions of the brain known as the amygdala play a pivotal role in dealing with the brain's incoming sensory stimuli, matching these against our memory of what that has happened to us before, and attaching the appropriate emotional tag.

As Dr Brown told the authors:

The amygdala seem to act a kind of guardhouse, assessing every stimulus that hits the brain – whether generated externally (perceptions) or internally (thoughts) – and assigning that stimulus to the correct emotional pathway . The amygdala assess the emotional loading of every stimulus of which the brain is aware in making "first stage" sense of everything impinging upon us.

The very first thing that the amygdala do is to assess the level of danger or threat: is this a friend or foe? When new stimuli hit us, the amygdala's task is to assign a pathway in terms of the eight basic emotions and in the light of all other prevailing data. Most of this is below the threshold of conscious perception: the amygdala will organize the body's responses within 80 milliseconds if there is threat, whereas the awareness of that doesn't get up into consciousness until about 250 milliseconds. In the presence of danger, the amygdala by-pass everything that might be to do with conscious control and mobilize all body resources within the flight/fight/freeze axes of primary survival responses.

None of us can get away from these emotions, or from the effect that they have on our behaviour. They are built into the fabric of our lives and they are present in the workplace as much as they are in the home, in our communities and on the battlefield.

The really interesting news is that our social behaviour taps directly into these basic emotions: that, just as the emotional spectrum "love/trust" is clearly to do with our relationship with other people, so, perhaps unfortunately, our more negative relations with other people draw on the same brain networks as those primary "escape, avoidance, and survival" emotions: our old friends fear, anger, disgust, shame and sadness. A manager's attitude toward us at work can trigger exactly the same emotional response as a threat to our lives.

THE EMOTIONAL FOUNDATION OF SOCIAL BEHAVIOUR

Today, thanks especially to advances in the field of neuroscience, we are able to understand exactly why stream engine management practices are doomed to produce a workforce that is not only disengaged but also stressed, anxious, unproductive, uncreative, and unhappy.

This is because steam-engine management practices are fundamentally incompatible with the social instincts that have been built into our brains by millions of years of evolution as a socially cooperative species.

We are highly conscious of social status, which has to be earned, not awarded. We are constantly trying to predict the likely immediate future in order to cope with our environment and enhance our chances of survival, and we become anxious when we experience behaviours that we do not recognize or understand, or feel that other people are concealing the real truth from us. We like to be autonomous, so that we know that can make our own choices about how we deal opportunities and threats. We are hardwired to see other people as friend or foe. We have a gut level commitment to the notion of fairness.

Steam-engine management practices might as well have been computer-designed to push the wrong buttons on every one of these most basic social behaviours – to make us feel that we are being slighted; that somebody is not telling us what is really going on around here; that we have no real degree of autonomy; that we are surrounded by hostile forces and that the social order in which we find ourselves is not even remotely "fair".

The real problem is that our brains perceive these social experiences at exactly the same level of threat as life-and-death situations. These social behaviours are driven by the instinctive drive to minimize threat and maximize reward.

David Rock, the founder and CEO of Results Coaching Systems, co-founder of the NeuroLeadership Institute and editor of

NeuroLeadership Journal, highlights some of the everyday ways in which these social behaviours are triggered in work environments, using the acronym SCARF: Status; Certainty; Autonomy; Relatedness; Fairness. Status, for example, is a major issue for us humans. Being given advice, let alone an instruction, triggers a threat to our perceived social status. "In most people," Black writes, "the question 'can I offer you some feedback?' generates a similar response to hearing fast footsteps behind you at night."[80]

This might be amusing on some level, but Black is deadly serious. These social experiences use the same brain networks that we use for our primary survival needs. A threat to these social needs is seen in the same way as a threat to our survival. Oxygen and glucose are diverted from our higher cognitive functions – the brain's prefrontal cortex. When we feel threatened at the workplace – even in a social sense – our brains hunker down into a defensive mode, exploring known routes to survival at the expense of both linear, conscious thought-processing (*"I'm struggling to get this"*) and non-linear jumps of creativity (*"I'm just not having any good ideas"*). These experiences may be very familiar to you from to last time you were faced by an angry superior at work.

Black spells out several other workplace scenarios that may well ring a bell with you. With regards to "Certainty", he says, our brains try to save time and brain energy by assuming that the future will be like the past. When we pick up a cup of coffee, to use Black's example, we draw on all of our expectations based on picking up cups of coffee on previous occasions. The brain does not "reinvent the wheel" – unless, for example, the cup is wet and slippery. Now we have the brain's full attention, using its higher functions to steer us through this unexpected situation step by step, using a lot more brainpower and energy.

Whenever organizations reduce certainty in our working environments – for example (to choose one possibility at random) by saying that "changes" are imminent but then refusing to give any details of what those changes might be or to enter into any form of discussion about them – we are thrown into a state of uncertainty and we lose a great deal of our normally available brain power.

As Black says:

Even a small amount of uncertainty generates an "error" response in the orbital frontal cortex (OFC). This takes attention away from one's goals, forcing attention to the error. If someone is not telling you the whole truth, or acting incongruously, the resulting uncertainty can fire up errors in the OFC. This is like having a flashing printer icon on your desktop when paper is jammed – the flashing cannot be ignored, and until it is resolved it is difficult to focus on other things. Larger uncertainties, like not knowing your boss's expectations or if your job is secure, can be highly debilitating.[81]

"Autonomy" is the feeling that we are in control of our environment, that we have various choices that are open to us. You may have noticed (we certainly have) that being in a high-pressure situation is stimulating, but not necessarily stressful, *provided we have a degree of control over how we deal with the situation.* Being in a high-pressure situation where you cannot influence the outcome is highly stressful.

"Relatedness" concerns whether we are "in" or "out" of a social group and whether any particular person is friend or foe. Being thrust into the presence of strangers generates an automatic "social threat" response. Small social encounters trigger the release of oxytocin, which facilitates social behaviour. This is why steam-engine organizations that frown on idle chatter and shared coffee breaks are so foolishly wrong. The brains of people who are unable to make minor social exchanges with their colleagues are behaving as if they are surrounded by a group of enemies brandishing spears. This is not conducive to a relaxed and creative frame of mind.

We are also hardwired for "Fairness". We find fair transactions to be intrinsically rewarding: studies have shown that people feel better about getting 50 cents than $10, if they are offered 50 cents as a share of $1 as opposed $10 as a share of $50. Conversely, unfair transactions are seen as a threat (and remember: the brain sees social threats in the same way that it sees physical threats).

Black offers a few workplace quotations that suggest that an "unfairness threat" may have been triggered:

"He has a different set of rules for Mike and Sally than for the rest of us."

"Management tell us that we need to lose headcount, but our sales are carrying the other division and they don't have to cut anyone."

"They do all this talk about 'values' but it's business as usual at the top."[82]

TOWARD THE EMOTIONALLY HEALTHY ORGANIZATION

The steam-engine managerial practices that lead to such stress and anxiety at work, to so much wasted energy and blunted talent, are horribly – almost laughably – familiar. Nearly all of us have witnessed and endured this kind of behaviour from a wide range of managers.

Some managers are, actually, well-meaning (no, really). They have simply become stuck in the steam-engine mentality that says that managers manage and workers work, with the unavoidable implication that it is impossible to give workers any realistic degree of autonomy; that it is essential to maintain various status differentials throughout the hierarchy to maintain respect and compliance with managerial instructions; that management must have access to more information than workers; and that it is only "fair" that senior management should be dramatically better-rewarded than anyone else in the organization (because they do all of the difficult thinking and planning, while the workers merely follow the instructions of management). The continuation of this archaic mode of management is horribly damaging: it wreaks havoc on the lives of people caught up in steam-engine organizations.

As with the 10 paradoxes that preceded this final chapter, it is fair to say that we have been aware of the problem for many years – but we still haven't found a way to do anything meaningful about it. Daniel Goleman wrote the best-selling book *Emotional Intelligence* in 1995, and argued that our non-cognitive skills – our "people skills" – were more important for success in the workplace than intelligence, as measured by IQ or other standard methods. The book was on the *New York Times* bestseller list for 18 months. Lots of people must have read it – even some steam-engine business leaders. And yet nothing seems to have changed.

Here's what Goleman has to say in his later book, *Leadership: The Power of Emotional Intelligence:*

> *Quite simply, in any human group the leader has maximal power to sway everyone's emotions. If people's emotions are pushed toward the range of enthusiasm, performance can soar; if people are driven toward rancor and anxiety, they will be thrown off stride. This indicates another important aspect of primal leadership: Its effects extend beyond ensuring that a job is well done. Followers also look to a leader for supportive emotional*

MARK POWELL

FIXING INDIVIDUALS INSTEAD OF ORGANIZATIONS

I've spent more than a decade running leadership programmes, and I've seen the damage that organizations have been doing to individuals at first-hand, and it's not insignificant. I posed myself the question for many years: "Why do organizations spend so much time and so much money putting their staff through development programmes trying to give them different skills and capabilities?" Increasingly, they're doing it because they're trying to "fix" individuals. People are sent, in many cases, on these programmes to be fixed because their approaches and behaviours are not deemed acceptable enough or good enough, or aligned enough to the requirements of the organization. It is very much a one-way contract, and as I have worked with these individuals over the years, the story they tell is very different – I've learned to appreciate just how much damage modern organizations do to individuals. They do damage to their humanity, their confidence, their loyalty, their very essence of being.

This continues to happen, despite the overwhelming evidence from psychology, from economics, and from the behavioural sciences – and *connection – for empathy. All leadership includes this primal dimension, for better or for worse. When leaders drive emotions positively ... they bring out everyone's best. We call this effect resonance. When they drive emotions negatively ... leaders spawn dissonance, undermining the emotional foundations that let people shine. Whether an organization withers or flourishes depends to a remarkable extent on the leaders' effectiveness in this primal emotional dimension.*[83]

We all know this stuff, because we experience it every day in the workplace.

Outlining a set of behaviours that could lead to an emotionally healthy organization would need another book. All that we have space to do in this book is to pay witness to the dreadful damage

increasingly now from what we know about physically how the brain works. The sort of activities and actions that inspire loyalty and creativity and innovation in humans are the very things that are destroyed by most steam engine organizations.

We live in a world where individuals are increasingly not, as has been often proved, primarily motivated by money and status. They are motivated by having value and meaning in their work world and their personal world. We live in a world where technology has enabled a complete blurring between the human life and the work life of people, not like it was in the industrial age.

The organization is at a crossroads. One of the reasons why business schools are as busy as they are with organizations sending their staff on development programmes to be fixed is because this reflects the fundamental need to fix the organization, not the individuals – but organizations are in denial about this.

Mark Powell in conversation with Jonathan Gifford

that steam-engine management is inflicting on its workforce, and to propose this is the one, best, most pressing, and most urgent reason why the steam engine must be transformed: not simply because it is time to stop damaging people in the workplace, but because a transformed workplace – and a transformed workforce – are exactly what we need to guarantee our future prosperity.

TRANSFORMING THE STEAM ENGINE

Our steam engine is broken, and it needs replacing with something completely different; something fit for the 21st century.

There is a rising tide of agreement with this proposition: it is impossible to think of any modern business thinker who has anything to say in defence of the typical, out-dated, steam-engine organization – despite the fact that so many modern institutions still fit this description and are busy blighting the lives of the people who work for them while simultaneously bemoaning their inability to leverage the immense amount of human energy at their disposal.

Steam-engine habits are deeply engrained in all of us: orthodox management thinking has failed to pull itself clear of the organizational philosophy that defined and enabled the great corporations that came into being in the early 20th century. It worked for them, they seem to argue, so why shouldn't it still work for us?

- Because times have changed
- Because we are all knowledge workers now
- Because we live in the Age of Ideas, not in the industrial era.

Changing the steam-engine organization looks like a daunting task. These are mighty behemoths. It will take brave and strong leaders to make the change. Fortunately, the world is full of brave and strong leaders, and these many leaders, working together, will bring about the necessary change.

There are many ideas, put forward by a host of business thinkers, that point to possible ways in which this momentous change might be achieved. This book has attempted to highlight some of these ideas. Our suggestion is that the new generation of leaders – you – should choose their (your) favourite ideas from these many options and experiment with them, attempting to transform the steam engine bit by bit, part by part, rather than with one almighty heave.

The joy of this approach is that the bad behaviours that make up the steam-engine mind-set are all interconnected. Making a start – beginning to change any one of the entrenched attitudes represented in our 10 paradoxes – will begin to improve all of the other organizational attitudes.

ONLY CONNECT

At the heart of the 10 paradoxes set out in this book is control – the most pernicious paradox of all. It is very hard to let go of control. Steam-engine leaders and managers feel – quite understandably – that not to be in control would, in fact, be a dereliction of their duty.

A moment's reflection will reveal that control is an illusion. No one can control a complex organization (and nor should they try to).

Here's a thought (or three):

- It is impossible to predict the future, and we do not know exactly what challenges will face the organization in the near or distant future
- Since we do not know what these challenges will be, we cannot pretend to know what the solutions will be
- If we insist that we, as leaders, are totally in control of the organization, then it will be entirely down to us, the leaders, to find a way out of each new, unpredicted situation.

When the unpredictable happens, one imagines that most leaders would feel a lot happier knowing that the organization as a whole is looking for the solution, rather than to have all eyes turn on them. And if you imagine for a moment that you are the organization, then – without meaning to be rude – you would probably prefer it if your very survival as an organization did not depend on the ideas of one person, or even those of a handful of people. You would like the organization as a whole – your corporate body – to decide what to do.

This brings us back to the realms of reason and emotion, and the fact that the human mind is inescapably involved with the human brain and body: "reason" likes to believe that it is in control, making all of the decisions, but in fact our emotions, based on the signals that they are receiving from the body as a whole, are driving many of our most basic reactions and affecting every single one of them.

The organization is, and should be, an organic, networked, living entity precisely so that it can adapt and grow in the face of an unknowable future. It has to be out of any one individual's control (and, in fact, it is, so we might as well stop pretending that it isn't).

By addressing any of the paradoxes set out in this book, we begin to dismantle the steam engine.

If we make a start on **losing control** (in the positive sense), then we will become less unhealthily obsessed with **measurement** and **efficiency**. We will begin to realize that, although the various metrics may be interesting and useful, they are not whole picture; they cannot show us what we will have to constantly assess for ourselves – the general health of the organization and its ability to fulfil its real purpose. And we will begin to worry less about "efficiencies" because, if everyone in the organization is aligned with the organization's purpose and fully signed up for the project, they can be left to decide for themselves what is the most efficient use of resources.

As we remove various controls, so the organization will begin to **communicate** better. Some simple changes to our **physical spaces** should help here. Being less obsessed about having everyone in the same physical space all of time would help, too.

With many of the old, steam-engine controls out of the way, people will be able to **self-organize**. This, at one stroke, removes most of the old problems. Starting here would be a great idea, but first you have to get used to the idea of "losing control" – it's entirely up to you.

At this point, you will probably have noticed that the whole notion of **leadership** has changed. The organization will have many leaders. A group of leaders will still be "in charge", but there will be many other leaders scattered throughout the organization, many of them arising to fill a particular need, possibly temporarily. At this point, the organization should continue to flourish even if the top leadership walks away. Other leaders would take over the top leadership functions, but the organization – clear in its purpose – would continue to function perfectly well.

By now, the organization will have become a **network** – without anyone really noticing. The trick now is merely to leverage all of the (huge) potential advantages of all of the networks that the organization is plugged into.

The one thing that may take continued effort is the guarantee of **diversity**: even healthy organizations are strongly drawn toward their own kind. "Constant vigilance!" will be the watchword, as the organization ensures that it has enough different ideas, capabilities, and attitudes to survive unpredictable changes in the environment.

And, finally, with all of this in place, the organization will be an **emotionally healthy** living thing – an interconnected network that will adapt to its environment. It will **innovate**, without even thinking about it, because innovation – variation, competition, and selection of the best ideas – will be built into the organization's fabric.

Once this change programme is embarked on, the steam engine will soon be changed beyond recognition: it will have been transformed into an entirely new kind of transportation, fit to carry people into the modern world.

One final thought: it has been one of the central arguments of this book that organizations are defined by the ideas, energy, focus and commitment of the people who make up the organisation at any particular point in time. The book has argued – hopefully persuasively – that the outmoded management techniques and philosophies that have persisted inappropriately from our early industrialisation are actively preventing modern organisations from achieving success in the Age of Ideas, by doing great damage to the creativity, cohesiveness, drive and commitment of the community of people who are the living embodiment of any organisation.

Let's suppose, just for a moment, that the cumulative effect of these inappropriate, discouraging and disheartening steam-engine managerial behaviours is reducing the human energy of modern organisations by 30 percent. The authors have no current proof that this figure is correct, but they would be very happy to enter into a debate on the subject.

Just imagine.

If removing the dead hand of steam-engine management behaviour from organisations around the world resulted in a 30 percent increase in those organisations' most important resource – their human energy – what might the impact of that be? It is easy to imagine the effect of a 30 percent increase in overall productivity, or a 30 percent reduction in total staff or energy costs, or a 30 percent increase in the number of projects in the innovation pipeline, or a 30 percent increase in top line revenue.

What could we possibly achieve if our organisations had 30 percent more human energy available to them, right now, for free?

Welcome to the Age of Ideas.

REFERENCES

1   Gary Hamel, *What Matters Now*, Jossey-Bass, 2012, p172
2   William Shakespeare, *The Tempest*, Act V, Scene 1, line 183
3   Ricardo Semler, *Maverick*, Random House Business Books, 1999, p 93
4   Douglas McGregor, *The Human Side of Enterprise*, Penguin Books, 1960, chapter 3
5   Daniel Pink, *Drive: The surprising truth about what motivates us*, Canongate Books Ltd, 2011, pp 76-77
6   Douglas McGregor, *The Human Side of Enterprise*, Penguin Books, 1960, p 49
7   Karen Phelan, I'm sorry I broke your company, Berrett-Koehler Publishers, Inc., San Francisco, 2013, Kindle file, chapter 3
8   Jim Stengel, Grow, Virgin Digital, Kindle file, ch. 1
9   See Leonard Mlodinow, *Subliminal*, Allen Lane, 2012, p 25
10 Jim Stengel, op. cit., ch 2
11 Ibid., ch. 8
12 Karen Phelan, op.cit., ch. 3
13 See ibid., ch.3
14 Michelle Conlin interview with James Sinegal, 'At Costco, good jobs and good wages', Businessweek Online Extra, 30.05.2004, http://buswk.co/1lDailg
15 'Costco's profits soar to $537 million just days after CEO supports minimum wage increase, Huffington Post, 03.12.2013 http://huff.to/TZpI9e
16 Alaina McConnell, 'Zappos' outrageous record for the longest customer service phone call ever', Business Insider, 20.12.2012, http://bit.ly/1qhPAKK
17 Kai Ryssdal, 'Zappos CEO on corporate culture and "Happiness"', Marketplace, 20.08.2010 http://www.marketplace.org/topics/business/corner-office/zappos-ceo-corporate-culture-and-happiness
18 Daniel Eisenberg, 'A Healthy Gamble', Time Magazine, September 16 2002 http://ti.me/1pc7hrm
19 'P&G CEO Quits Amid Woes', CNN Money, 08.06.2000, http://cnnmon.ie/1uAjlV4
20 Gregory Jones, 'How A.G. Lafley used innovation to increase Procter & Gamble's billion-dollar brands', Smart Business; Sep2011, Vol. 21 Issue 4, p14 http://bit.ly/Zdvnsy
21 See Noel Tichy, 'Lafley's Legacy: from Crisis to Consumer-driven', Businessweek 10.06.2009 http://buswk.co/107B99E
22 Teresa Amabile and Steven Kramer, 'How Leaders Kill Meaning at Work', McKinsey Quarterly 2012, Issue 1, p124-131 http://bit.ly/1r2BEBV
23 'Blackberry to cut 4,500 jobs amid earnings plunge', BBC News/business 20.09.2013, http://bbc.in/Vr7WwD
24 Gregory Jones, 'How A.G. Lafley used innovation to increase Procter & Gamble's billion dollar brands', Smart Business, September 2011, Vol. 21 Issue 4. http://bit.ly/Zdvnsy
25 Lockheed Martin corporate website, 'Kelly's 14 rules and practices' http://lmt.co/1qfcxyq

26 The Radicati Group Inc.,'Email Statistics Report, 2014-2018', http://bit.ly/1q5xzvY

27 Atkins, Fitzsimmons et al, Roads to Ruin, a report by Cass Business School for AIRMIC, http://www.airmic.com/jresearch/roads-ruin-analysis

28 CBS News, 'The Explosion at Texas City', 26.10 2006, http://cbsn.ws/1qtysDc

29 Alex Pentland, Social Physics, Scribe Publications Pty Ltd, 2014, Kindle Edition, Ch. 1

30 Ibid. Ch. 7

31 Ibid, Ch. 5

32 Alex Pentland, 'The New Science of Building Great Teams', Harvard Business Review, April 2012, Vol. 90, Issue 4

33 Alex Pentland, Social Physics, Ch. 5

34 Alex Pentland, 'The New Science of Building Great Teams'

35 Ibid.

36 Ibid.

37 Jane Clossick, 'Cityspace Revolution: Manchester in the Nineteenth Century, http://bit.ly/1sWQjT3

38 Tony Hsieh interviewed by Issie Lapowsky, Inc.Magazine, February 2013, http://bit.ly/1tKMfmu

39 Second Report from Select Committee on Metropolis Improvements (1838), p. 103 (Parliamentary Papers 1837-8, vol. XVI)

40 Middlesex Justices, 1596 cited in Samuel Schoenbaum, William Shakespeare: A compact documentary life, OUP, 1986, p. 126

41 Charles Fishman, 'Engines of Democracy', Fast Company, 30.09.1999 http://bit.ly/1pHa2FS

42 GE Imagination at Work, 'Teaming at GE Aviation', shown as Exhibit to Rasheedah Jones, 'Teaming at GE Aviation', Management Innovation eXchange, July 14 2013. Article http://bit.ly/1pHa2FS ; Exhibit http://bit.ly/1m5VBal

43 Rasheedah Jones, 'Teaming at GE Aviation', Management Innovation eXchange, July 14 2013. Article http://bit.ly/1pHa2FS

44 Ibid.

45 GE Imagination at Work op. cit.

46 Charles Fishman, op. cit.

47 Ibid.

48 For all references to Semco in this chapter, see Ricardo Semler, Maverick, Random House, 1999

49 Rasheedah Jones, op.cit.

50 Op.cit.

51 Thomas Friedman, 'How to get a job at Google', The New York Times, 22.02.2014, http://nyti.ms/1jyQTxG

52 Andreas Kluth 'Among the Audience', Economist Survey of New Media 22/04/2006 http://econ.st/1k2rrpY

53 Rajandra Sisodia, David Wolfe and Jagdish Sheth, Firms of Endearment: How world-class companies profit from purpose and passion, Prentice Hall 2007, Kindle file, Ch. 1

54 Ibid., Prologue

55 See Daniel Goleman, Leadership: The power of emotional intelligence, More Than Sound LLC, 2001, Ch. 5 'The Group Intelligence'

[56] Robert Kelley and Janet Caplan, 'How Bell Labs creates star performers', Harvard Business Review,, Jul/Aug1993, Vol. 71, Issue 4, http://bit.ly/1xtHNsv

[57] Ibid.

[58] Ibid.

[59] Ibid.

[60] Ibid.

[61] Lynda Gratton, Hot Spots, Pearson Education Ltd, 2007, p 72

[62] John Gregory, 'How A.G. Lafley used innovation to increase Procter & Gamble's billion-dollar brands', Smart Business magazine, Sept 2011, Vol. 21 Issue 4, http://bit.ly/Zdvnsy

[63] Noel Tichy, 'Lafley's Legacy: from Crisis to Consumer-driven', Businessweek 10.06.2009 http://buswk.co/107B99E

[64] Alex Pentland, Social Physics, Scribe Publications, 2014, Kindle file, Ch. 4

[65] Addy Pross, 'Life's restlessness', aeon magazine, http://bit.ly/1oDxa5w

[66] Kevin Kelly, Out of Control, Addison-Wesley Publishing Company, 1995, p2

[67] Ibid, pp 129-131

[68] Ibid. p. 139-146

[69] Ibid. p161

[70] iSixSigma http://bit.ly/1u4fkJJ

[71] Patty McCord, 'How Netflix Reinvented HR', Harvard Business Review, Jan/Feb2014, Vol. 92, Issue ½, http://bit.ly/1sBmp4m

[72] Doug Peacock, 'Cotton Times: Understanding the Industrial revolution', http://bit.ly/1tNkycA

[73] Karen Phelan in conversation with the authors

[74] Mark Powell in conversation with co-author, Jonathan Gifford

[75] Alex Pentland, Social Physics, Scribe Publications Pty Ltd, 2014, Kindle Edition, Ch. 2

[76] Antonio Demasio, Descartes' Error, Vintage, 2006, Kindle file, Ch. 3

[77] Ibid., chapter 8

[78] Dr. Paul Brown, Dr. Tara Stewart, Jane Meyler, 'Emotional Intelligence and the Amygdala', NeuroLeadership Journal, Issue 2 2009, http://bit.ly/1kTIH1m

[79] Ibid.

[80] David Rock, 'SCARF: a brain-based model for collaborating with and influencing others', NeuroLeadership Journal, Issue 1, 2008, http://bit.ly/1vr3m1f

[81] Ibid.

[82] Ibid.

[83] Daniel Goleman, Leadership: The Power of Emotional Intelligence, More than Sound LLC, 2011, Kindle file, Ch. 6

"I enjoyed this book, was stimulated, amused and provoked by it. Considering most other business books are not only badly written, but set themselves up as second rate Bibles, I applaud this work. It is a Bible for the flawed but willing. And a record of how these vices can be turned into virtues to the benefit of millions of people."

Tim Smit KBE, Co-founder and CEO, Eden Project.

ORGANIZATIONS THAT DISTURB THE STATUS QUO

Challenger organizations are those that are disrupting their market, challenging their own habits and taking on dominant competitors.
They are typically innovative and radical but what of those that lead them?

This book analyzes the practices and disciplines that underpin the successful Challenger organization. In particular it looks at how Challenger leadership and culture can be developed in large, complex, established businesses.

ISBN: 978-1-907794-64-3